Also available at all good book stores

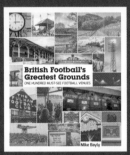

9781785316470

9781785313929

9781785315466

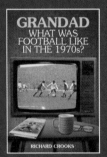

9781785312632

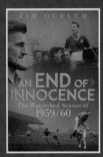

9781785317583

9781785317576

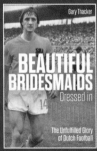

9781785318467

9781785318399

9781785315534

`71/
`72

'71/ '72

Football's Greatest Season?

Daniel Abrahams

First published by Pitch Publishing, 2021

Pitch Publishing
A2 Yeoman Gate
Yeoman Way
Worthing
Sussex
BN13 3QZ
www.pitchpublishing.co.uk
info@pitchpublishing.co.uk

A CIP catalogue record is available for this book
from the British Library.

ISBN 978 1 78531 870 2

Typesetting and origination by Pitch Publishing
Printed and bound in India by Replika Press Pvt. Ltd.

CONTENTS

DEDICATIONS

To the memories of the always-missed Bob Abrahams and Johnny Corne, whose love, knowledge and unending enthusiasm for the game spilled over into me. To my cousin, Greg, for riding shotgun on this. And thanks must go to John Motson, for providing some of the soundtrack to the 1971/72 season and the decades that followed.

FOREWORD

by John Motson

THE 1971/72 season for me was nothing short of a fairy tale. It will always hold a special place in my heart. It had so many amazing twists, turns and stories that I often think back on it, and wonder how it has not been the topic of further conversation or a book, such as the one you now hold in your hands.

In 1971 I was working at BBC Radio 2, as it was then. I had come from the *Sheffield Telegraph*, a morning paper, and the *Barnet Press* before that. I joined Radio 2 in 1968, reading racing results and so on. My first commentary match was in 1969, Everton versus Derby. Amazingly, I celebrated 50 years as a commentator at Aston Villa versus Southampton in 2019. But it all began with this amazing season.

I had not been in radio very long and *Match of the Day* gave me a test commentary at Leeds, on 9 October 1971. Off the back of that I was given a contract for *MoTD*, *Sportsnight*, *Grandstand* and all the attendant things that went with the BBC TV channel. For most people, the Hereford vs Newcastle match – with Ronnie Radford and that incredible goal – was the first I covered, but it wasn't. That was a goalless draw at Anfield, between Liverpool and Chelsea.

For me, those early matches were very difficult, I was struggling, and I remember coming up against Malcolm Allison and getting a rollicking for my commentary of a Man City game. I wasn't sure if I was cut out for this commentary lark. Then the FA Cup came around and my first match was the third-round tie between Blackpool and Chelsea at Bloomfield Road. The result was 1-0 to the visitors. The game between Hereford and Newcastle in the same round had been postponed. I covered the subsequent 2-2 draw, but the replay at Hereford was postponed so many times (you could do that in those days) that the Newcastle team were down there for about a fortnight. The replay was eventually played on fourth-round day. So, Barry Davis and David Coleman did the big fourth-round games and I was sent to Hereford to mop it up. 'It'll probably be 2-0 to Newcastle,' they said. Well lo and behold we now know it wasn't, and it is fair to say that Ronnie Radford's goal changed my life. In some ways, his strike epitomised that incredible season, which has been captured in this book.

As the book discusses, the world of football was a totally different place to today's game. There was a charm to things back then. For the Hereford clash I had travelled down in the same car as Ricky George, who was and still is a close personal friend of mine. Ricky came on as a substitute for the hosts and scored the winner in extra time. Afterwards we went back to the late Billy Meadows' house, with Ricky and their wives, to celebrate. I remember 'American Pie' by Don McClean, the big hit at the time, being played into the early hours. Hereford's fairy tale continued until they were beaten by West Ham in the next round, following a replay. They subsequently got into the Football League at the end of the season. For me, the fairy tale never ended; it went on for another 47 seasons at *MoTD*.

There were so many tales in these pages that stirred up such great memories, and plenty that I had forgotten about, and what a delight it has been to dust them off and relive them again. To cap it all off, of course, Derby County won the league. With their season over, manager Brian Clough had taken his family away to the Scilly Isles on holiday. I clearly recall Bob Wilson made a call on *Sportsnight* and Cloughie was at his most compelling: 'Very nice of you to ring me, Bob' and all that stuff. It was just unbelievable.

If Leeds had beaten Wolves when they played them after the FA Cup Final, where they beat Arsenal, they would have won the Double. The stories, as you will read here, just never seemed to end that season, and for me, following the Hereford game, the BBC thought I might have more potential than they had first thought. From there I started getting better games – Home Internationals and so on – and then my first World Cup in 1974. So, to be completely truthful, my career emanated from here.

I always look back on it, because it was such a memorable one both football-wise and personally. It really does have such an important place in my heart. Reading through these pages rekindled so many more memories for me, as I am sure it will for any reader.

Glorious.

John Motson, September 2020

INTRODUCTION

THE IDEA for this book came about in the summer of 2016 as I enjoyed some Mediterranean sun on holiday. Britain had just voted to leave the EU, which was going to be the biggest change for the country in living memory. As political pundits and economists tried to assess the potential pros and cons of Brexit, my first thoughts were, as usual, about football. Would it mean we couldn't sign foreign players anymore? Would we have to give them back? Would England still receive four Champions League places?

Then came the Paul Pogba transfer. Four years after he had left Manchester United on a free transfer, they were signing him back for nearly £90m. The agent pocketed the thick end of £25m, while his client would be paid £250,000 per week. That was the point at which I realised that the modern game had finally gone insane.

Pogba is a good athlete, but he didn't look a player to quicken the pulse, unlike their other summer signing, Zlatan Ibrahimović. Ibrahimović was signed on a free transfer and, as such, United felt obliged to pay him £367,640 per week.

Two of my childhood heroes, Johan Cruyff and David Bowie, had recently died and the game I loved was becoming unrecognisable. It was 50 years since England had won the World Cup and, to tie in with the anniversary, a film about Bobby Moore had been released. While I was too young to remember 1966, the majority of the players were still playing when I first started watching football. Worryingly, many were still the backbone of the England team. Now that I was firmly into middle age, I found myself reminiscing more and more about 70s football, watching old matches and reading countless articles from the era.

After a while, I began to zero in on the 1971/72 season. As well as being the first season I remember in depth, it coincided with us getting our first colour television, just in time to watch the England versus West Germany game at Wembley. Anyone who has grown up with a wall-mounted flatscreen 3D HD smart television will never appreciate the wonder of first seeing any TV programme in colour, let alone a football match. Coincidentally, 1971/72 was also the season when Britain started gearing up to join the EU – or the Common Market, as it was known then.

The country was polarised by the narrow Brexit vote, so it was interesting to discover that on the day Britain joined the EU, a Mori poll found that 38 per cent were happy, 39 per cent were unhappy and 23 per cent undecided. Opinions hadn't really changed in 40-odd years of membership.

While researching the season I was surprised by how much happened during 1971 and 1972. The first email was sent, the first eBook was written, and we also saw the first widely available microprocessor and video game. Fantasy football debuted in England and London got Europe's first artificial pitch, something that was confidently tipped to be the playing surface of the future.

Football-wise, the championship race was the closest in history. When I say the championship, I don't mean Division Two. I mean Division One. No, not the Third Division. The top division. The one that nowadays only the four teams who have lots of money can win. Back then, leagues were divisions and they followed the rules of mathematics, not marketing. The Second Division was second rate, not fourth rate.

By 1971, the fame of managers had begun to outstrip that of the players, and our season would be when four of the most famous characters in English football history – Bill Shankly, Malcolm Allison, Don Revie and Brian Clough – battled it out for the title. It would be the last season where any team from half the league could conceivably win it. The season would crown the seventh different title winner in seven seasons, but it also marked the start of the rise of Liverpool, and the beginning of a few clubs dominating the many.

The centenary of the FA Cup would see the tenth different winner in ten seasons, at a time when winning the cup was surprisingly more important than finishing fourth in the league. For some, it was more important than winning the title. The FA Cup that year gave us a seemingly never-ending tie and the most famous giant-killing of all time, which introduced us to John Motson as football began to embrace television. Throw in some record-breaking scoring against the world's unluckiest goalkeeper and it would be quite a competition.

When I say television started to embrace football, live football only amounted to three or four live games a season, but 20 million people watched the weekend's highlights during a period when TV enhanced football, rather than ruled it.

The League Cup came of age, giving us the greatest ever cup tie and a final in which the man who did so much to improve footballers' lives scored the winning goal. The competition also gave us a song which outsold Michael Jackson's debut single.

Just a decade after the end of the maximum wage, the superstars of the game could earn up to £15,000 per year as clubs' wage bills nudged £200,000 per annum. Although footballers were now rich, several still supplemented their income by playing cricket in the summer. The high-profile players were also making their way on to the front pages, their lifestyles appalling managers whose own playing careers had been truncated by the Second World War.

As players sported flares and shoulder-length hair, our national manager, Sir Alf Ramsey, looked increasingly like a man out of his time. We would discover not only that England no longer ruled the world at football, but that we were struggling to keep a seat at the top table. We witnessed the beginning of the decline of our national skipper, Bobby Moore, and the emergence of future captain, Kevin Keegan. Moore had a particularly busy season. He saved a penalty for his club, but his decline was cruelly exposed by West Germany. Off the field, he embarked on a disastrous business venture, but would demonstrate his defensive talent against the taxman.

Our other World Cup winners also kept themselves busy. Gordon Banks eventually thwarted Geoff Hurst in a penalty duel. One Charlton would witness the disintegration of his United side, while his brother would see the peak of his. Alan Ball, when not trying to launch *Fantasy Football*, *Championship Manager* or coloured football boots 20 years early, would be the subject of a record transfer which effectively destroyed two great sides.

Fees were still measured in low six figures in a transfer market that would also see the convoluted transfer of Ian Storey-Moore and Rodney Marsh, a transfer which, together with management strife, finished Manchester City as a top club for 40 years.

Match-fixing reared its ugly head in West Germany and our season ended with rumours of corruption as players from the scandal of 1964 were finally pardoned. We saw the last flickering of the genius of George Best and the quiet dignity of his namesake, Clyde, as he inspired future generations of black players at a time when Enoch Powell was the most popular politician in the land.

Franz Beckenbauer and Johan Cruyff visited our shores to introduce us to Total Football, and Pelé and Eusébio popped over to play friendly matches. Football would hear the first of Diego Maradona and the last of Garrincha.

In the three European club trophies, Total Football destroyed Catenaccio in one final, and in another, a team lifted the trophy after losing an earlier penalty shoot-out. The other final was decided in the exotic locations of North London and Wolverhampton.

Historically, we were in the strongest ever domestic era for goalkeepers. We would see Gordon Banks, Pat Jennings, Peter Bonetti, Ray Clemence and Peter Shilton elevate a trade that included Chic Brodie, David Icke, James Herriot and, briefly, Dave Webb.

Although English clubs continued to be thwarted when they tried to recruit from abroad, a Scottish club did manage to import three foreign players in exchange for some washing machines. Every team had a British manager and we even had enough talent to export some.

Women's Lib was in the news and would herald the first official women's international match, and in the same season we had an unofficial and quite sexist women's World Cup.

Peterborough would be the darlings of the 15 million pools punters, at a time when the National Lottery was just a twinkle in the nation's eye.

Jimmy Savile and Rolf Harris were top showbusiness personalities, while Stuart Hall kept himself busy hosting *Quizball* and *It's a Knockout*.[1]

It was the era of the maverick. Muhammad Ali, Ilie Nastase and David Bedford captured the lion's share of the headlines in their sports, snooker was transformed by colour television and Alex Higgins, and even chess had Bobby Fischer.[2] And for every footballing maverick there was a hatchet man; Peter Osgood and Alan Hudson lined up alongside Chopper Harris to face Charlie George and Peter Storey ...

As the game tried to eliminate violence on the pitch, it could do little to prevent its rise in the stands of the crumbling grounds. The Wheatley Report on the Ibrox disaster was published, its recommendations all but ignored as the game continued its slow march to the Bradford and Hillsborough disasters. Jock Stein turned down the Manchester United job and stayed to replace the Lisbon Lions with the Quality Street Gang, as Celtic continued to dominate Scottish football.

Scotland, together with Wales and Ireland, finally got the release of their players for international matches which, together with the new parentage rule, helped the Scottish national team regain its pride. Against the background of The Troubles, Northern Ireland were forced to play their matches away, in locations such as Hull, before finishing the season by celebrating one of their greatest triumphs without their greatest player …

Teams were still numbered one to 11, we had linesmen instead of referee's assistants, and no technical areas for managers to shout at them from. Confusing goal average was still part of the game and suspensions were measured in weeks rather than games. We had midweek kick-offs in the afternoon and Scotland still had football on Christmas Day.

You'll also dive into Batty's World XIs, a pensioner employed by a football club to row across the River Severn; Manchester United being cheered from the Anfield Kop; Wembley Toni revolutionising the NFL; and Aldo Poy scoring the most celebrated goal of all time – all happening while the scorer of Luton's greatest ever goal missed the season for shooting someone.

If you remember the season, I hope I will jog some pleasant memories. If you are too young to remember, and believe football began in 1992 – like the journalist who wrote that Derby County's eighth-place Premier League finish in 1998/99 was the club's 'best-ever finish in the top flight' – then you will hopefully discover that football really began in 1971.

PRE-SEASON

' ... I was born in this team, and in
this team I will die.'

Georgi Asparuhov

BY THE summer of 1971, England were no longer world champions, having lost to West Germany in the quarter-final of the previous year's World Cup. A few months later The British Empire was no more, bar a handful of scattered possessions such as Hong Kong, Gibraltar and the Falkland Islands, which few in Britain at the time could point out on a map. In place of the Empire came a Commonwealth, holding its first conference in Singapore the following January.

The Brutalist concrete architecture of the 60s was already falling apart, while violent crime had risen 62 per cent since 1967, signalling the start of inner-city estates becoming the crime-ridden hellholes they remain.

America was mired in Vietnam. The South Tower of the World Trade Centre was topped out at 1,362ft, becoming the second tallest building in the world, just six feet shorter than the North Tower. Education Secretary, Margaret Thatcher, became the most unpopular politician in Britain with her proposals to end free school milk for children aged over seven years old. She added to her popularity amongst children the following February, when she raised the school leaving age from 15 to 16.

The summer had seen the last showdown between the old moral pillars of the British Establishment and the new wave unleashed in the 60s, with the obscenity trial of the editors of *Oz* magazine. The title had featured children's cartoon character, Rupert Bear, having sex with a naked granny, and the courts sentenced its editors to prison. The public response to the harsh sentences served to further discredit the old censorious laws.

With pre-season preparations and the football season fast approaching, a strong case could be made for eight or nine sides winning the title, coupled with at least a dozen who could challenge for the domestic cups. Among the favourites were the previous season's Double winners, Arsenal. Charlie George apart, they had been fortunate with injuries the previous term, with nine of the team playing in at least 36 league games. The veteran of the side, Frank McLintock, 32 in December, was at his peak and would be good for a couple of years yet.[1] The next oldest outfield player, Bob McNab, had just turned 28, with goalkeeper, Bob Wilson, on the right side of 30. On the eve of the season, their coach Don Howe left to manage West Bromwich Albion, replacing Alan Ashman, who learnt of his dismissal from a waiter while holidaying in Greece.

Howe's appointment started a sequence of Don, John, Ron, John, Ron, Ron, Ron, John, Ron and Ron, as Messrs Howe, Giles, Allen, Wile, Atkinson, Allen (again), Wylie, Giles (again), Saunders and Atkinson (again) took turns holding the West Brom reins. Brian Whitehouse (two months) and Nobby Stiles (four months) would be the only interludes in 17 years of Don, Rons and Johns.

The 1969 champions, Leeds United, runners-up for the last two years, having only lost two away games the previous season, would have to play their first four home games away from Elland Road. Strong and experienced in every position, all were the right side of 30, bar Jack Charlton and Johnny Giles. Leeds would be considered as favourites for every competition, but fixture congestion had cost them before.

Spurs would be a strong contenders for any cup and, if new signing Ralph Coates settled and Steve Perryman continued to mature, many thought they could be worth a bet for the title, due mainly to having Martin Chivers, the best centre-forward in the country.

Wolves' fourth-place finish had brought top-level European football back to Molineux for the first time in a decade, making them another good cup bet.

Fifth in the previous two seasons, Liverpool hoped the rebuilding of their side was over. Shankly had been slow to break up the 60s side before their cup defeat at Watford in February 1970 forced his hand and saw the last start of Ian St John, who left to become a football coach in South Africa during the summer of 1970.[2] Ray Clemence immediately replaced Tommy Lawrence in goal, utility man Geoff Strong was quickly moved on to Coventry, and Larry Lloyd took over from Ron Yeats at centre-half. Steve Heighway, one of the discoveries of the previous season, was likely to keep Peter Thompson on the periphery, and although he was struggling for goals, Liverpool hoped that John Toshack could recapture his Cardiff form and that teenager Alun Evans would start justifying his £100,000 fee.

Chelsea had been in the top six for the last four seasons, without seriously challenging, but the Cup Winners' Cup winners could beat any team on their day. While Alan Hudson had recovered from his broken ankle, he was no longer the mercurial presence he had been previously, and Peter Osgood had also been below par, scoring just five goals in the league. Keith Weller, their acquisition from Millwall, had been Chelsea's top scorer in his first season, while goalkeeper, Peter Bonetti, had missed a third of the previous season with illness and injury.

Jock Stein had verbally agreed in the summer to take over at Manchester United, but changed his mind. Having signed just three players in seven years, United looked stale. New manager Frank O'Farrell would have to inspire his current crop of players or hope that the club would allow him to break out the cheque book.

Across town, City, title winners in 1968, had settled into being a mid-table cup team. After eight games the previous season they looked to be the side to beat, but Glyn Pardoe's broken leg against United had all but stopped their momentum. As well as losing Pardoe, they were without Mike Doyle, Tommy Booth, Keith Oakes, Neil Young, Colin Bell and Mike Summerbee for significant parts of the season. They finished 11th after taking just 14 points in the second half of the season. There were also problems off the pitch, with boardroom strife and tension between the management team of Joe Mercer and Malcolm Allison. They hoped new signing, Wyn Davis, could recreate his Bolton partnership with Francis Lee, and a reduction in injuries might see them challenging for the title.

After finishing fourth in 1970, ninth place in 1971 was a disappointment for Derby[3]. Having lost the talismanic Dave Mackay[4], they looked to Colin Todd to prove himself an adequate replacement. They had a decent enough first team, but their squad was painfully thin.

Many blamed the conditions in Mexico which had seemed to affect their England players, most notably Alan Ball, for Everton's woeful defence of their 1970 title. They also missed the injured Brian Labone for long periods. New signing Henry Newton didn't settle into the team and, with the league beyond them, they suffered a dreadful week in March when they were knocked out of the FA Cup and European Cup by Liverpool and Panathinaikos respectively. Given that they had the same squad as in 70, plus Newton, many felt they must surely improve and challenge for the title.

Newly promoted Leicester and Sheffield United looked strong enough to avoid a quick return to the Second Division.

In the Second Division, relegated Burnley were tipped to challenge, although Coates would be missed. Of the other contenders, Hull would lose Chris Chilton to Coventry early in the season, and Luton would miss Malcolm Macdonald and the 'resting' Graham French. Cardiff might have achieved promotion in the previous season had they held on to Toshack. Bob Latchford and Trevor Francis looked capable of firing Birmingham into a promotion slot, while Ron Saunders' rebuild of Norwich looked complete.

After the previous season's sixth place, many tipped Luton for promotion. The sale of Malcolm Macdonald, however, coupled with the absence of Graham French, might be too much to overcome. In an era of mavericks, Graham French reigned supreme. This is a bold statement about a player most haven't heard of, but one I can best justify by explaining his absence from the Luton side. It wasn't through injury, suspension, lack of form or even a bust-up with the manager. No, French was unavailable due to being in the middle of a jail sentence for shooting someone. He spent his childhood in care, only attending school long enough to impress at football. A Shrewsbury Town scout spotted him, and at 18 he was a key figure in the England team which won the European Under-18 Championship in 1963.

Swindon signed him for £15,000, but French's love of partying and gambling meant Swindon moved him on after just seven games.

His next stop was Watford, where he played just four games after ignoring Bill McGarry's insistence that he shed some of his 14 stone. He moved to non-league Wellington Town, where his performances persuaded Luton to sign him for £5,000 in 1965. Luton had earmarked French to replace the precociously talented David Pleat, who had broken his leg in training. That injury all but finished any chance the former England Schoolboy and Youth international had of living up to his early promise. Still only 26, Pleat had recently joined Nuneaton Borough as player-manager, but he would rejoin Luton the following year as a coach.

French seized the opportunity and would play more than 200 games for the Hatters. His goal for Luton against Mansfield Town in September 1968 is regarded as Luton Town's greatest. Legend has it that French placed a bet at 15-1 that he could dribble past every opposition player in a single run before scoring. He made two unsuccessful attempts in the first half of the game, beating seven men on one occasion and then five during the second attempt. In the second half, he collected the ball on the edge of his own penalty area and worked his way from one side of the pitch to the other and back again, outwitting opponents with sleight of foot and fast surging swerves, on a mazy run through the Mansfield team. Allegedly, he beat a couple of players twice as they doubled back to try to stop him. French ended his run by drawing the goalkeeper off his line, rounding him and slotting the ball into the net.

In the summer of 1970, while absent from training due to a contract dispute, French entered Caesar's Palace nightclub in Luton with some friends, looking to exact revenge on a local character known as the King Joker. French was in possession of a revolver which went off, lodging a bullet in his victim's shoulder.

On 7 December, with Luton lying second in the table, French's case was heard in court. Although the attempted murder charge had been reduced to GBH and possession of a firearm, French was still sentenced to three years' imprisonment. Needless to say, Luton's promotion bid faltered after his sentencing.

After being released on parole in September 1972, French made his comeback appearance three months later, scoring against Millwall. Despite the goal it was obvious that prison had finished off what little fitness French's much-abused body still had. He would make just seven more appearances before going to Reading on loan in November 1973. However, French couldn't settle. Reading, needing a calmer, steadier character, signed Robin Friday from Hayes a month later to replace him. It was like The Who replacing Keith Moon with Ozzy Osborne

French left for America but played just three games for the Boston Minutemen before returning to England and drifting out of the game for two years. In March 1976, the now renamed Graham Lafite played a couple of games for Southport before disappearing from the game.

In the Third Division, it was hard to look beyond Halifax and Aston Villa, although Notts County and Bournemouth, freshly promoted from the Fourth, might make an impact.

In the Fourth, Oldham, Colchester and Northampton had their supporters, while Scunthorpe, Lincoln, Southend and Grimsby all struggled in the previous season and needed to improve.

Another new manager joining Frank O'Farrell and Don Howe in the First Division was Jimmy Bloomfield at Leicester. As was the fashion of the day, they could all expect a decent length of time to build a side.

Ted Bates, Tony Waddington, Bill Nicholson, Bill Shankly, John Harris, Ron Greenwood, Harry Catterick and Don Revie had been at the helm of their clubs for over ten years.[5], some admittedly surviving past their sell-by date. Greenwood was only the fourth manager in West Ham's 70-year history.[6] While he'd had some previous success at Upton Park, the 1970/71 season was their sixth without silverware, and most of that time had seen them at the wrong end of the table. Nowadays, Chelsea regularly sack managers even if they've won the Premier League or Champions League the previous season. Leicester sacked their manager in the February after winning their first-ever Premier League title as 5,000-1 outsiders.

The big news of the summer, at least from a ten-year-old's immediate world perspective, was the amalgamation of *Scorcher* and *Score* magazines at the start of July. For us insatiable football nuts, the new title gave us the greatest hits of the game in comic strips for the generous price of 3½p. Despite the loss of some favourites, you still had an abundance of riches as you flicked through the pages, including the 'Billy's Boots' strip, which had started in *Tiger* ten years earlier. It chronicled the adventures of Billy Dane who, when cleaning out his Gran's attic, had found a pair of old football boots that once belonged to Charles "Dead Shot" Keen. When Billy wore the boots, it gave him the ability to play football like the old England star, but when he didn't, he went back to being useless. For 20 years the story comprehensively depicted every conceivable way in which a young boy (he remained around 12 years old throughout the storyline) could lose a pair of football boots. It was 'Billy's Boots' that supplied the big story of the new combined issue, as Billy finally met the cobbler who claimed to have made Dead Shot Keen's boots. Pierre Callet, operating out of a little shop on a cobbled backstreet in France, made Billy a second pair so that he'd never again be bothered by having the boots stolen or accidentally dropped in a dustbin. Obviously, the new boots didn't work otherwise that would have killed the story.

Scorcher and *Score* ran until 5 October 1974 when it amalgamated with *Tiger* to share space with the daddy of all football comic strips, Roy Race, who had starred in the 'Roy of the Rovers' strip since 1954. Roy was busy himself during the summer of 1971, meeting the secretary to Melchester Rovers manager Ben Galloway, Penny Laine. During the subsequent season, as their romance blossomed, his 17 goals fired Rovers to their first league and cup double. Despite worrying about how his mother would feel about him leaving the family nest at, by my calculations, just 37 years of age, Roy married Penny in 1976. The same year he earned his own spin-off comic named, appropriately enough, *Roy of The Rovers*, taking with him 'Billy's Boots', 'Hot Shot Hamish' and 'The Football Family Robinson', among others. In March 1993, Roy Race's playing career ended prematurely at the age of 54 when his left foot had to be amputated following a helicopter crash. A further tragedy shattered the Race family two years later, when Penny died in a car crash, the true circumstances of which remain a mystery.

NOTES FROM ABROAD

Football's second biggest story of the summer was in Germany, where the revelation of a match-fixing scandal would lead to 50 German players and coaches being suspended for corruption. The man who blew the whistle was the chairman of Kickers Offenbach, Horst-Gregorio Canellas.

Canellas initially contacted the DFB (the German FA) after receiving a call from the Cologne goalkeeper, Manfred Manglitz, demanding 25,000 Deutschmarks (around £3,000) to beat Essen. The DFB advised Canellas that there was nothing in the rules which forbade such a third-party 'win bonus'.

Manglitz was left out of the Cologne side for the vital final match of the season versus Offenbach. Kickers were level and mathematically safe from relegation with 12 minutes remaining, but lost 4-2. Together with other results – Oberhausen's draw away at Braunschweig, and Bielefeld's incredible 1-0 win at Hertha Berlin – the loss proved enough to relegate Offenbach by a solitary goal on goal difference.

Canellas believed the relegation of his side, who were cup holders and had been promoted to the top division just 12 months earlier, would be temporary. Once he produced the information that he had gathered, the DFB would have no choice but to demote Bielefeld instead.

On 6 June 1971, the day after the final game of the eighth Bundesliga campaign, Canellas celebrated his 50th birthday with a garden party. Among his guests were national coach Helmut Schön, DFB general secretary, Wilfried Straub, and a selection of handpicked journalists. The guests were played a taped phone conversation between Canellas and two Hertha Berlin players discussing a 140,000 Deutschmark bribe from Canellas to guarantee a win over Arminia Bielefeld. Another conversation revealed national goalkeeper Manglitz demanding 100,000 Deutschmarks from Canellas to ensure Cologne lost to Offenbach. The calls were just the tip of the iceberg in what was the biggest scandal to hit German football. By the end of the investigations, it was discovered that 18 games directly affecting relegation in the 1970/71 season had been fixed, and that 1m Deutschmarks had changed hands in the process. Canellas subsequently received a lifetime ban from German football as a result of his part in the affair. It was never clear whether he was playing along with the cheats to collect evidence or was playing it safe, so that if another club bid more money than he did, he could blow the whistle and still appear honest. Outraged at his ban, he dug some more and came up with enough dirt to keep the DFB and the courts busy for months, in some cases years ... By the time the whole story was revealed, more than 50 players from seven clubs – together with two coaches and six officials – were found guilty. All were fined and suspended, in many cases for life, although most were pardoned as early as 1974. Arminia Bielefeld were demoted to the Regionalliga by the DFB in 1972.

The DFB admitted that the maximum wage system had caused more problems than it had solved, and so from 1972 onwards players were allowed to earn whatever clubs were willing to pay them. Kickers have never returned to the Bundesliga, currently residing in the fourth tier of the German game.

As for Canellas, in 1977, the year after his ban was repealed, he and his daughter were caught up in the hijacking of Lufthansa flight 181 by four Palestinian terrorists. The German counter-terrorism unit liberated 90 of the 91 captives on the runway in Mogadishu, Somalia, after a five-day ordeal.

With Barcelona's new manager, Rinus Michels, eyeing Johan Cruyff, Ajax were keen to tie up the player's future. Cruyff signed a seven-year contract extension in July. He would receive a basic wage of 95,000 Dutch guilders (£11,000) per year, and an early pension from Ajax's main sponsor of 60,000 Dutch guilders annually until he turned 65 and received his state pension. So, Cruyff stayed and scored 33 goals to inspire Ajax to the most successful season in their history. They won their first treble and added the Intercontinental Cup in September 1972, as well as the European Super Cup in January 1973. With Cruyff preparing to take on the mantle of the world's greatest player, 138,000 watched Pelé's last international for Brazil against Yugoslavia at the Maracanã on 18 July.

The summer saw the retirements of two giants of the game, Gento and Lev Yashin. Yashin's testimonial match was held on 27 May 1971 at the Lenin Stadium in Moscow, with 100,000 fans attending. A Moscow XI played a World XI captained by Bobby Charlton. Despite being personally invited to play by Yashin, Georgi Asparuhov was denied permission to attend by the Bulgarian Government over fears he would defect.

When most people think of Bulgarian football, they think of Hristo Stoichkov, as few remember Asparuhov, despite him being chosen as Bulgaria's best footballer of the 20th century. Asparuhov was courted by AC Milan, who offered him $500,000, a safe escape from Bulgaria and a wage equal to that of Gianni Rivera. Asparuhov refused, informing the representatives from AC Milan: 'There is a country called Bulgaria and there's a Bulgarian team called Levski. You may not have heard of it, but I was born in this team, and in this team I will die.'

A month after Yashin's testimonial, Asparuhov agreed to appear in an exhibition match in the mountain town of Vratsa. He never arrived, dying aged just 28 in a car accident at the Vitinya Pass, along with his close friend and fellow Bulgarian great, Nikola 'The Cat' Kotkov. More than half a million people attended his funeral to bid farewell to one of football's greatest players

AUGUST

'United played a home match at Anfield?
Give over.'

Alan Gowling

THE MONTH started with the Watney Cup, English football's first sponsored competition. The Watney Mann Invitation Cup, to give it its full name, had joined the fixture list the previous season. It was competed for by two teams from each of the four divisions, who in the previous season had been the top scorers in their division but not been promoted or won a place in a European competition. Watney paid each participating side £4,000 and the Football League and Football Association shared £50,000.

The tournament was used as an opportunity to experiment with the laws of the game. The previous season's semi-final between Hull and Manchester United saw the first-ever penalty shoot-out, which had only been ratified a month earlier by the International Football Association. George Best took and converted the first kick. Denis Law earned the dubious distinction of being the first to miss when Hull keeper Ian McKechnie saved his kick. The day turned sour for McKechnie when his own missed kick sent Manchester United through to the final.

This year's innovation was to restrict offside to the penalty area. It proved to be a success, with fewer stoppages and less

29

defensive play, but it was never subsequently introduced. The season would see a rule change in Scotland whereby goal difference replaced the confusing goal average as the deciding factor when teams were level on points. Goal average was calculated by dividing the goals scored by the goals conceded. It took until the 1976/77 season for England to embrace the change.

Arsenal were the main promoters of the amendment, having unsuccessfully proposed the change seven years earlier. Ironically, had goal difference been implemented then, it might have cost Arsenal the 1971 title. In their final match of the season, Arsenal needed to win at Tottenham to take the title by a point. A goalless draw would give them the title on a goal average of 2.413, as opposed to Leeds' goal average of 2.4. A score draw, however, would have reduced Arsenal's goal average to 2.366 and handed the title to Leeds. Under the simpler goal difference, any draw would have handed the title to Leeds. Fortunately for Arsenal, and those who struggle with long division, Ray Kennedy headed home the only goal at White Hart Lane. Arsenal got the benefit of the rule change in 1989 when the title came down to goal difference and subsequently goals scored. Under the old rules, despite Arsenal winning 2-0 at Anfield, Liverpool would still have taken the title by a goal average of 2.32 to 2.03.

The teams for the 1971 Watney Cup were Manchester United and West Bromwich Albion from the First Division, Carlisle United and Luton Town from the Second, Halifax Town and Wrexham from the Third, and Colchester United and Crewe Alexandra from the Fourth.

Manchester United faced a Halifax team experimenting with their shirt numbers on both the back and the front of their shirts. The *Match of the Day* cameras saw Bill Atkins nod Halifax in front after three minutes, and then recorded his side doubling their advantage after 26 minutes with a Bob Wallace penalty, barely a minute after keeper Alex Smith had saved Willie Morgan's spot-kick at the other end. George Best converted a penalty to pull a goal back for United with eight minutes to go, but Halifax survived late pressure to claim the club's most famous victory in front of a record crowd of 19,965.[1]

The previous season's cup heroics probably cost Fourth Division Colchester promotion. Ray Crawford had been lured from non-League Kettering and scored 35 goals, including two in their famous Cup win over Leeds.[2] The 34-year-old Crawford had been top scorer for Alf Ramsey's title-winning Ipswich side in 1962. The tournament saw Crawford play his last game for Colchester in the 1-0 victory over Luton, after which he left for South Africa to join Johnny Haynes at Durban City.

Colchester defeated Carlisle in the semi-final, before meeting West Brom in the final. After a thrilling match that ended 4-4, Colchester overcame the First Division side 4-3 on penalties. Lifting the cup for Colchester was captain, Bobby Cram[3], who had played in both of West Brom's losing League Cup Final appearances in the 60s. The Watney Cup would continue for another two years before being abandoned.

While the semi-finals of the Watney Cup were being played, Arsenal played the second leg of their pre-season friendly tie against Benfica. Trailing 2-0 from the first leg in Lisbon, the Gunners soon turned around the deficit and were leading 3-0 at half-time. Although Eusébio was taken off at half-time, Benfica pulled two goals back before the incident that turned the game into a near riot. Frank McLintock took a free kick and George Graham turned the ball home from a suspiciously offside position. The entire Benfica side swarmed around referee, Norman Burtenshaw, pushing him to the touchline. The Arsenal players did their best to protect the referee, which no doubt amused those who remembered their badgering of the same official at Leeds the previous season. After the Graham goal was allowed to stand, Benfica gave up the ghost and Arsenal ran out 6-2 winners.

The Benfica friendlies were behind Arsenal's decision not to play in the Charity Shield. The fixture had been the traditional opener to the season since 1908. After trying a few formats, such as Professionals versus Amateurs and First Division champions versus Second Division champions, Division One champions against the FA Cup winners became the chosen match from 1930 onwards.

The 1961 Tottenham Double win threw a spanner in the works, but this was solved when they played against an FA select XI. Without last season's Double winners, up stepped the Second Division champions, Leicester, and FA Cup runners-up, Liverpool. Home-side Leicester won the match with a goal from 19-year-old full-back Steve Whitworth.

As the beginning of the league season approached, Leeds were installed as favourites despite their four-game home-match ban as a result of events from the previous season.

To recap those events, Leeds and Arsenal had been battling it out for the title when an out-of-form West Bromwich Albion travelled to Yorkshire. Leeds were two points clear at the top of the table, although the London side had two games in hand. One of those games was to be at Elland Road.

Despite early pressure from the home side, Albion took a 19th-minute lead when Tony Brown slid the ball past Gary Sprake. Leeds now abandoned all pretence of defence and virtually camped in the Albion half. In the 69th minute came the incident that cost Leeds the title. Norman Hunter's square pass was intercepted by Brown, who raced forward. The linesman instantly raised his flag for offside against Colin Suggett, the only man in the Leeds half apart from Sprake. Brown pulled up, but referee Ray Tinkler waved play on. Brown ran on and passed the ball to Jeff Astle, who tapped in. Leeds believed that Astle was also offside, but he appeared to come from behind the ball according to our one-camera coverage.

The match was screened that evening on *Match of the Day*. The commentary by Barry Davies sets the scene: 'Pass intercepted, but Suggett is offside. The referee's waving him on. Brown is going straight through ... taking on Sprake, and the goal by Astle,' says Davies, his voice rising several octaves. 'And Leeds will go mad, and they've every right to go mad because everybody stopped with the linesman's flag. Leeds have every justification for going mad, although one must add that they played to the linesman and not the whistle.' Tinkler consulted with his linesman, but only to confirm his original decision that the goal was good. 'Don Revie is on the pitch, the linesman is going to talk to the referee,' cried Davies, adding, as Revie trudged off the pitch shaking his head, 'Don Revie, a sickened man. Look at him looking at the heavens in disgust.'

That signalled an invasion of supporters furiously trying to get at the referee. A missile thrown from the crowd hit one of the linesmen, knocking him to the ground. When the game eventually restarted, Allan Clarke pulled a goal back, but the equaliser would not come. The result all but handed the title to Arsenal and, following the match, hundreds of Leeds supporters went on the rampage in the city.

In June, a Football Association disciplinary committee reached a verdict on the events. Leeds chairman, Percy Woodward, and manager, Don Revie, were severely reprimanded for bringing the game into disrepute, and Elland Road would be closed from 14 August to 4 September. This meant that the club's first four home games would have to be staged on neutral grounds at least 12 miles away. In addition, if attendances fell below the previous season's average, United would have to compensate visiting clubs. Don Revie complained that: 'We are starting the season under a severe handicap … I can't think of any side which has won the championship after playing four more away games than their rivals.'

To this day, Leeds supporters believe that the Elland Road closure cost them the title in 1972, and they blame Tinkler for losing them two titles. Had Tinkler not waved play on that day, and all other results stayed the same, Leeds would have ended with the same points as Arsenal and won the title on goal average.

Bearing that in mind, let's have another look at Astle's goal. It's true that one of the West Bromwich players, Suggett, was standing in an offside position, and the linesman did raise his flag straight away. Nevertheless, Tinkler waved play on and the ball never went anywhere near Suggett. The problem was that the linesman kept his flag up and several Leeds players wrongly assumed that play had stopped. Even the supportive Barry Davies pointed out that 'they played to the linesman, and not the whistle'.

Many believe to this day that the 'interfering with play' interpretation was not in force back in 1971, but it had in fact been introduced in 1903. 'It is not a breach of Law for a player simply to be in an offside position, but only when in that position, he causes the play to be affected.' That interpretation was reinforced in 1920 and further clarified in 1924. Although the rules were clear enough, it is fair to say that not many referees interpreted them correctly. Tinkler, however, was known for playing advantage, and it would be a surprise if that wasn't covered in Revie's detailed dossiers, which included the idiosyncrasies of the match officials.

On August 14, the league season opened for all teams in all divisions, as was the fashion of the day. Leeds got off to a great start at Maine Road when Peter Lorimer lifted Allan Clark's flick over Joe Corrigan to seal the points. Full of confidence, they headed to Bramall Lane for a midweek match against the newly promoted Sheffield United and promptly lost 3-0. The win wasn't quite as emphatic as the score indicates, two of the goals coming in the final three minutes. Don Revie complained bitterly that United were denied three blatant penalties.

After starting off with two away games, Leeds finally got to play a 'home' game at Huddersfield's Leeds Road. The goalless draw with Wolves was followed by another 'home' game at Hull against Tottenham. Billy Bremner equalised a first-half Alan Gilzean goal to earn Leeds another point. Given that these were two of only four games during the season where they dropped any home points, their supporters insist to this day that those lost points away from Elland Road cost Leeds the title.

The claim seems logical enough until you study it in a little more depth. The two other drawn home games were played at Elland Road against West Ham and Ipswich. It is important to point out that Wolves and Tottenham were far stronger sides than West Ham and Ipswich at the time. Tottenham had won at Elland Road the previous season. So the 1-1 draw was, if anything, an improvement for Leeds. In their corresponding fixture the following season, Wolves would hold Leeds to another draw, this time at Elland Road.

Returning to the 71/72 season, Leeds finished the month with a routine 2-0 win at Ipswich.

Before the opening game at Highbury, Arsenal and Chelsea paraded their silverware. The FA Cup and League Championship Trophy for Arsenal, the European Cup Winners' Cup for Chelsea. Arsenal's captain, Frank McLintock, turned in John Radford's long throw to give Arsenal a deserved half-time lead. Man of the match, Ray Kennedy, scored Arsenal's second from the edge of the box before Radford helped himself to the third, ten minutes from time. Kennedy netted again in the 1-0 win at Huddersfield before the defending champions lost their next three games: a 3-1 reverse against Manchester United and two single-goal defeats at home to Sheffield United and Stoke.

Facing Wolves on the opening day, Tottenham's Mike England returned from long-term injury to play his first game of 1971. He would be given a torrid afternoon by Derek Dougan at Molineux. Wolves' 38th-minute opener came from Dougan racing on to a Bernard Shaw centre. In the confusion England crashed into Pat Jennings who spilt the ball, allowing Bobby Gould to score. In the 71st minute Dougan cut the ball back to Kenny Hibbitt, whose shot was handled for a penalty. Jim McCalliog converted from the spot. Spurs managed to snatch a draw in the last ten minutes through Martin Chivers and Alan

Gilzean, assisted by a couple of errors from the Wolves keeper, Phil Parkes. Tottenham then played out a home draw with Newcastle before beating Huddersfield 4-1. Gilzean's fourth goal in four games earned them a point at Leeds before Spurs finished the month by getting hammered 4-0 at Maine Road in front of the *Match of the Day* cameras.

Wolves were disappointed to draw after leading Tottenham by two goals, but the game marked an improvement on last season's 3-0 loss in the corresponding fixture – one of three defeats in their opening three games. After such a poor start it had been a considerable achievement to finish fourth, and it marked the start of a four-year period when they were one of the leading clubs in the country. They ultimately fell short of challenging for the title and will always wonder if Peter Knowles would have made a difference. Knowles' former team-mate and friend, Frank Munro, believed that Wolves would have won the title with Knowles.

In *The Glory Game*, Hunter Davis writes of the visit of Spurs full-back Cyril Knowles' brother Peter to the Spurs dressing room before the opening game of the season: 'There was a knock at the door. It opened and Cyril's brother came in, looking very scrubbed and neat in a short white raincoat. He stood hesitantly in a corner, looking around. Peter Knowles used to be one of the stars of Wolves, and still lives in the area. He gave it all up a few years ago to become a Jehovah's Witness, something you would never expect Cyril to do. "That your brother then, Cyril?" asked someone when Peter had gone. "Yeah," said Cyril, "still got a lot of skill."

'"Must have," said Alan Gilzean, "Takes a lot of skill to read the Bible."'

Peter Knowles had played with an arrogant belief in his ability. His image off the field reflected this, driving around as he did in a gold-sprayed MGB sports car with his name painted down the side. Knowles made his debut in the 1963/64 season and would score 64 goals in 191 appearances for Wolves. In the summer of 1969, instead of an expected call-up to join the England tour, he instead went on tour as part of the Wolves team competing in the NASL under the banner of Kansas City Spurs. While he was in the Midwest, his life changed direction following a conversation with two Jehovah's Witnesses. The talk struck a chord and set off a chain reaction in Knowles. The footballer began to read the Bible and question not only his lifestyle, but also 'the level of aggression I used to take out on to the pitch'.

The adulation he was receiving began to concern him. He felt that his life need not be so shallow, and that God had chosen a different path for him. He informed everyone: 'I shall continue playing football for the time being, but I have lost my ambition. Though I shall still do my best on the field I need more time to learn about the Bible and may give up football.' Bill Shankly had tried to sign him for Liverpool during the 1968/69 season but, by the summer of 1969, Knowles didn't want to move to Liverpool or stay in football.

After helping Wolves win their opening four games, he announced he would be retiring within six weeks. Although Knowles was open about his new-found beliefs and his intention to walk away from football, the club and his team-mates didn't fully believe it. Knowles took to the field for the last time as a professional player on 6 September 1969 against Nottingham Forest. Wolves' boss Bill McGarry wrote in his programme notes that Peter's training kit would be laid out again on Monday and he fully expected him to be there. Nevertheless, Knowles kept to his word and turned his back on the game three weeks short of his 24th birthday. As the days turned to weeks and the weeks turned to months, the reality sunk in. Wolves held on to his registration, each year sending him a new contract only to receive it back unsigned. Finally, on 5 June 1982, with Knowles now 36, Wolves finally accepted that the player would not be returning and he was allowed to officially leave Molineux. Knowles has never professed regret about leaving football and continues to knock on doors for the Jehovah's Witnesses.

Before the opening game against Nottingham Forest, Liverpool supporters heard the voice of George Sephton, the new stadium announcer, who would become the voice of Anfield for the next 49 years and counting.[4] Also making his debut at Anfield was the little-known Kevin Keegan. Bought from Scunthorpe, Keegan had been signed to eventually replace the ageing Ian Callaghan, who had missed a large part of the previous season through injury.[5] Having failed to make the line-up for the Charity Shield, Keegan looked to be starting the season in the reserves, but Shankly surprisingly picked him to play up front on the opening day. After 12 minutes, Keegan scored Liverpool's first goal of the season, his scuffed shot from Peter Thompson's pullback creeping into the corner of the net. That sort of fortune complemented Keegan's workrate throughout his career. He had a hardworking ethos and never gave up on a lost cause or let defenders relax for a single second. Keegan would never play in a single reserve fixture and would prove to be nothing less than a sensation during his six years on Merseyside. In a season which would see George Best go off the rails, Keegan had taken his first steps to becoming the poster boy of English football. Liverpool followed the win over Forest by defeating Wolves 3-2 before travelling to St James' Park.

Newcastle had played two games in the capital against Crystal Palace and Spurs, picking up a point but no goals. A near 40,000 crowd rolled up at St James' Park to see Malcolm Macdonald and Terry Hibbitt make their home debuts. Macdonald and Hibbitt were key signings by Newcastle manager Joe Harvey, who continued to break up his 1969 Fairs Cup-winning side. In February 1971, Harvey sold Pop Robson to West Ham for £120,000, replacing him with Sheffield United's John Tudor.

Having only just got used to the loss of Robson, Magpies fans heard that Wyn Davies had been sold to Manchester

City for £60,000 over the summer. Harvey was keen to steer his side away from the long-ball game that Davies' presence inevitably engendered. Using the money from the Robson and Davies deals, he paid £180,000 to Luton Town for Malcolm Macdonald. Macdonald had started his professional career as a full-back at Southern League Tonbridge, before being bought by Fulham for £1,000 on the recommendation of his old manager at Tonbridge, Harry Haslam, now the chief scout under Bobby Robson at Craven Cottage. After a number of injuries at the club, Macdonald was put up front and started scoring freely, but was dropped back to the reserves after Fulham sacked Robson. Haslam, now at Luton, persuaded Alec Stock to buy Macdonald for £18,500. His 27 goals in his first season in Division Three fired Luton to promotion, and he followed with another 30 in Division Two. In his last game for Luton, he signed off with a hat-trick.

Harvey declared: 'I just know this feller can be another Jackie Milburn to the supporters.' Macdonald turned up for his first Tyneside press call in a white Rolls-Royce and announced that he would score 30 goals in his first season. Newcastle's other signing, Terry Hibbitt, had been a Leeds United reserve. Over the next four seasons the pair would form an almost telepathic understanding.

Emlyn Hughes opened the scoring for Liverpool before Macdonald grabbed a hat-trick and Keegan a late consolation for Liverpool. Another star had been born. The player previously dubbed 'Super Mouth' by the press was now quickly to become 'Supermac'. His hat-trick against Liverpool was heralded with the headline 'Mac Cracks In Super Three' in the *Newcastle Evening Chronicle Pink*. After Macdonald hit his promised goal target, Sir Alf Ramsey selected him for the Home Internationals, making him Newcastle's first England international since 1954.

The Macdonald cover would be chosen to adorn a special 'Farewell to The Pink' pull-out on Saturday, 17 December

2005, when after 110 years the last edition of *The Pink* rolled off the presses. Although London had lost its Saturday sports paper when *The Evening News* stopped printing on Saturdays in June 1979, up and down the country the results papers on a Saturday continued to be printed until the start of the 21st century. To distinguish them from the weekday white papers, they were printed on a pink, green, blue or buff background and were nicknamed accordingly.

On 9 December 2017, the final Saturday sports paper, *The Southern Daily Echo's Sports Pink*, closed. And so ended the tradition of crowds queuing outside newsagents at tea time, waiting for the vans to arrive with the pink and green 'uns. Ironically, it was a newspaperman, Rupert Murdoch, who did more than the internet to drain the colour from that particular newspaper tradition. It is due to his Sky television that fewer and fewer matches kick-off at 3pm on a Saturday. 'Newcastle United had just ten three o'clock kick-offs in 21 games up to Christmas,' Paul Robertson, editor of the city's *Evening Chronicle*, complained as he took the decision to close the title. Although interest in football has never been higher, fans now check results on the internet or their mobile phones. I can't help but feel they are somehow missing out.

Liverpool saw out the month with a workmanlike 1-0 win over Crystal Palace, before taking revenge on Leicester for the Charity Shield defeat with a thrilling 3-2 win.

Manchester City recovered from the home defeat against Leeds with a powerful performance to defeat Crystal Palace 4-0. It was an inconsistent opening month from City, despite the form of new signing Wyn Davies and his burgeoning partnership with Francis Lee. Lee scored six goals in four games, half of them penalties. City welcomed Colin Bell back for their last game of the month and duly hammered Tottenham 4-0, with goals from Bell, Mike Summerbee, Davies and Lee. City were a different side with Bell in it. Of the eight games he'd missed the previous season, City lost five and drew three.

In a mouth-watering opening-day fixture, Derby fought back from 2-0 down against Manchester United to share the points. In Derby's next game, against West Ham, their second-minute opener came off the top of Bobby Moore's head. The game was settled five minutes later, when Frank Wignall headed home the second. Derby then won at Leicester, but drew the next three to finish the month unbeaten in fifth.

West Bromwich Albion started the season strongly under new manager Don Howe. The First Division's top scorer from the previous season, Tony Brown, scored in all of their opening matches, with wins over West Ham and Everton, followed by a 1-1 draw with Coventry City. Although Brown scored his fourth goal in four games against Manchester United, Best replied with two goals and Alan Gowling with one to win 3-1 at their temporary home at Stoke City's Victoria Ground. Albion rounded off a good opening month by earning a draw at Sheffield United, the surprise early league leaders.

The Blades had fought off the challenge of Cardiff, Carlisle and Hull to clinch promotion behind champions Leicester City. The turning point of their season had come after they sold John Tudor to Newcastle United at the end of January, with manager John Harris using £40,000 of the fee to buy Birmingham City captain, Trevor Hockey. The Blades only lost two of their final 17 matches as Hockey provided extra protection to the solid back four of Len Badger, Ted Hemsley, Eddie Colquhoun and John Flynn.

Goalkeeper John Hope's move to Second Division Sheffield United, as part of the John Tudor transfer, meant that in five seasons and just seven appearances, he had played in all four divisions of the Football League. On the opening Saturday, Sheffield United beat Southampton 3-1 at Bramall Lane. And next, a 3-0 win over Leeds might have flattered them, but the Blades stunned the First Division title favourites by playing with intelligence and style. On the second weekend of the season, Alan Woodward fired a second-half winner at Everton, to send them top. Three days later, they sprang another huge shock by winning at champions Arsenal. In three games United had defeated the three previous champions. Next up were West Brom, who visited Bramall Lane without Jeff Astle, ruled out with a stomach strain. The absence of Astle forced West Brom to defend in depth and the goalless draw was the first point dropped by the Yorkshire club. On the last day of the month, Huddersfield were dispatched 3-1 to lift the Blades three points clear of the chasing pack of Leeds, Derby and Manchester United, extending their unbeaten league run to 17 games.

The undeniable star of the Blades side, 21-year-old Tony Currie, had been rejected by QPR and Chelsea as a centre-half. Amazingly, neither club thought of trying him in a different position.[6] The disappointed Currie started working as a labourer and playing Sunday League football for Hendon Boys, where he caught the eye of Frank Grimes, the youth coach at Third Division Watford. After breaking into the first team as a forward, Currie had scored nine goals in 18 games when he was sold to Sheffield United for £26,500. The then manager, Ken Furphy, objected to the sale of the 18-year-old, but Watford needed the money to extend the lease on their ground. Currie had been bought to replace Alan Birchenall[7], whose transfer, together with the sale of Mick Jones, was blamed by many supporters for the club's slide towards relegation after 50 years in the top flight. Blades manager, John Harris, saw more talent than just scoring goals and moved Currie into midfield at the start of the 1970/71 season. He would go on to be the conductor as United won promotion back to the First Division. He would be labelled one of the '70s mavericks, mainly due to the hair and extravagant skills, but he was a shy man off the field and didn't drink, gamble or chase women.

At the end of the season, Currie would be capped by England against Northern Ireland, but would only add 16 further caps under Ramsey, Revie and Greenwood as successive England managers found it impossible to accommodate individuals like

Currie within the national team. In 1976, just a season after Sheffield United came within a few points of winning the First Division, Currie moved to Leeds for £250,000 to ease United's financial problems. Unfortunately, his arrival at Elland Road coincided with the decline of the great Leeds team. In August 1979, after 124 games, 16 goals and three losing domestic cup semi-finals, Currie moved to QPR for £400,000, primarily to try to save his marriage. The move back to London and the Second Division ended an England career which had never really got started, while his marriage still ended in divorce a year later. He had his best moment in club football at QPR when he captained them in the 1982 FA Cup Final replay against Tottenham, in place of the suspended Glenn Roeder.[8] A crippling knee injury followed, and he dropped down the divisions with Southend and Torquay before finishing his career at Tranmere. After playing in non-league football, he spent the next five years out of football before Sheffield United came to the rescue by making him their community officer, a post he filled for 20 years. In 2014, to celebrate Sheffield United's 125th anniversary, Currie was voted the club's greatest ever player. Today he is a club ambassador and escorts supporters to the Tony Currie Suite.

Frank O'Farrell's first act at Manchester United was to raise George Best's wages above the level of Bobby Charlton, Denis Law and Willie Morgan, to £225 per week, making him the highest paid player at the club.

O'Farrell had to play the first game at Derby without the suspended midfielder Pat Crerand, who had been sent off in United's penultimate match of the previous season and made what would be his last appearance for Manchester United in the Watney Cup against Halifax. Although he had been given a year's contract in the summer of 1971, he never regained his place in the team and was given the responsibility of looking after the kids at Old Trafford when he retired in December.

To compensate for the loss of Crerand, O'Farrell moved both Willie Morgan from the wing and Alan Gowling from attack, into midfield. Gowling was a graduate from Manchester University and gained England caps at amateur, schoolboy and Under-23 level. He had represented the British Olympic side during the qualifying rounds for the 1968 Olympics. His season got off to a good start when he added a second to Law's opener against Derby. In the second half – to the accompaniment of thunder, lightning and rain – Derby bombarded the United goal. Frank Wignall began to terrorise the centre-back partnership of David Sadler and Steve James, although he did appear to foul goalkeeper Alex Stepney for Kevin Hector's 49th-minute goal. Wignall himself got a deserved equaliser on the hour.

In a five-goal thriller at Stamford Bridge, George Best grabbed the headlines for all the wrong reasons. Best, who was already upset by United having a goal disallowed, reached boiling point in the 40th minute when Peter Osgood fouled Dave Sadler in the build-up to Tommy Baldwin's opening goal. All the United players protested, but none so angrily as Best, who called the referee 'a f***ing disgrace'. Norman Burtenshaw immediately sent him off and United coach Malcolm Musgrove led the crying Best off the pitch. At 1-0 down at half-time with ten men, United rallied to win the game 3-2, the winner coming from a Bobby Charlton 25-yard rocket. The following Monday, Best approached Willie Morgan to ask him if he would testify that it was him that Best had sworn at. As Best was already on a six-week suspended ban, Morgan reluctantly agreed. In mid-September, they went to the FA headquarters in London where Morgan, with the aid of a Subbuteo table, managed to convince them that it was him who Best was abusing, and they won the appeal. Maybe the commission believed it was plausible given the two players' antipathy dating back to Morgan's Burnley days.

There does seem to be evidence that Morgan was more than a little jealous of Best, and the comparisons between the two did shape and undermine Morgan's career at United. Whether or not Morgan actually said he was a better player than Best is a matter for conjecture, but his autobiography illustrates that he was not known for false modesty, stating that in 1968, 'I was one of the two biggest stars in football.' To remind you, this was the era of Pelé, Beckenbauer, Eusébio and a young Johan Cruyff. Even in Britain there was Bobby Moore, Jimmy Greaves and Jimmy Johnstone – and if Morgan had looked across the United dressing room he would have seen Best, Charlton and Law.

Two days later Manchester United tried to confuse new announcer George Sephton by playing their first 'home' game of the season at Anfield. 'It was a very strange occasion, Manchester United versus Arsenal at Anfield in the First Division, as it was then,' Sephton recalled.

Near Arsenal's home ground at Highbury, the day had started with a police raid on a flat in Stoke Newington. The flat was the headquarters of The Angry Brigade, England's only urban terrorist group. In a campaign which had begun the previous August, the left-wing adventurers had bombed banks, embassies and the homes of Conservative politicians, as well as Government and corporate offices. The group used small bombs in order to maximise media exposure to their demands, while keeping collateral damage to a minimum. The police arrested six people after finding more than 60 rounds of ammunition, a Browning revolver, a Beretta pistol, a Sten gun, 33 sticks of gelignite and detonators. A series of round-ups and raids in the months that followed led to the arrest of dozens of Angry Brigade suspects. In the subsequent trial, from May to December 1972, five people received sentences of ten years.

The Manchester United versus Arsenal (Anfield) match was played on a Friday night to avoid clashing with Everton's home fixture the following day. United had been ordered to play their first two home games away from Old Trafford after their ground had witnessed numerous violent incidents during the previous season, climaxing in the February clash with

Newcastle when the home supporters threw various missiles, including a knife.

Anfield was an interesting choice for a United home game. While the rivalry between the clubs was not as poisonous as it would later become, they weren't exactly what you could call firm friends. In fact, the game may well have laid some of the groundwork for future clashes between rival supporters. Outside the ground, United fans found themselves confronted by a mob of 500 Liverpool supporters, who had to be dispersed by police dogs. Inside, before the match, United supporters charged across the pitch from the Kop end in an attempt to reach Arsenal supporters. The following day, newspapers focused their coverage on the crowd disturbances. Throughout this and following seasons, inflammatory front-page headlines stoked the fires and provoked hostilities between fans, as the hooligan groups sought to outdo each other.

As for the game, a lethargic first-half performance by United found them trailing to a fourth-minute Frank McLintock bicycle kick. After the break, United enjoyed a stirring comeback, inspired by Best, leading to an equaliser lifted over Bob Wilson by Gowling. You would think a United goal at Anfield, celebrated by the home fans, must be quite a memory for Gowling, but years later he had no memory of the game: 'United played a home match at Anfield? Give over.'

Bobby Charlton scored his team's second goal by curling a free kick around the wall before Brian Kidd wrapped things up with a goal in the dying minutes.

United would suffer a further financial punishment as Liverpool were given 15 per cent of the gate receipts from the 27,649 fans who attended the game, and United were instructed by the FA to pay Arsenal compensation because the gate was below the 48,000 who attended the fixture at Old Trafford the previous year.[9] United played their second 'home' game at Stoke's Victoria Ground, comfortably seeing off West Brom with a brace from Best and Gowling's third of the season. Best got the equaliser at Wolves to give United a share of the points, before a disappointing loss to Everton. After six games in 17 days, United were still waiting to play at Old Trafford.

In Division Two, Bristol City gathered seven points from their first four games to lead the table. Chris Garland scored in the first three games to earn a £100,000 transfer to Chelsea at the end of the month. He returned to Ashton Gate five years later, via Leicester, his departure hastened by breaking Jeff Blockley's cheekbone with a punch during training. By that time Bristol City were in the First Division, but would slump from a 13th-place finish in the top tier to the Fourth Division in consecutive seasons.

Together with the club's on-field troubles came a litany of financial mismanagement incidents in which key players had been signed on lucrative ten-year deals. Garland and seven team-mates were given an ultimatum: tear up their contracts or the club would die. The 'Ashton Eight' had until the morning of 3 February 1982 to decide – or the club would cease trading at midday. At the time the players were portrayed as rich and greedy, which was far from the case. After much soul-searching the players ripped up their contracts.[10]

Hot on Bristol City's heels were Blackpool, who opened their season with a 4-1 win over Swindon. Alan Ainscow, replacing Tommy Hutchison, grabbed a goal, as did Tony Green to add to converted forward Glyn James' brace. Manager Bob Stokoe's move of veteran Welsh defender James to the forward line paid immediate dividends, with James scoring four in their opening two games.

In the Third, Bournemouth topped the table closely followed by a Brighton side boosted by Kit Napier's five goals. Notts County eased into third, inspired by Don Masson's craft and veteran Tony Hateley's goals. Aston Villa were fifth.

In the Fourth Division, Matt Tees, in his second spell at Grimsby, hit a hat-trick on the opening day of the season against Scunthorpe to give Lawrie McMenemy a flying start to his reign. Tees kept in the goals as Grimsby took five points from their next three games. Scunthorpe, adjusting to life after Kevin Keegan, recovered well from their opening-day mauling to beat Lincoln, Crewe and Southend, finishing the month in sixth after a tough run of fixtures.

SEPTEMBER

*'The trouble with referees is that they know the
rules but don't know the game.'*

Bill Shankly

IN THE Middle East an era began in which Qatar declared independence from Britain. Any thought that within 40 years the 2022 World Cup would be awarded to a desert nation with a small, predominantly migrant, population would have seemed ludicrous.[1] Brian Glanville would describe Qatar as a 'wretched little anonymity of a football country'. Its size, the heat, the lack of football pedigree, were all factors that for most observers should have precluded it from even being a contender. Before the vote in 2010, there were several trade deals between Qatar and the home nations of the executive committee members. The *Sunday Times* alleged that Qatar paid $1.5m in bribes to members of that committee. We will take another look at FIFA in the post-season chapter, when we look at the rise of Sepp Blatter's mentor, João Havelange.

In the UK, an era ended on the first day of the month when the pre-decimal penny and threepence ceased to be legal tender. Some of my decimal birthday money was used to purchase the Chelsea and West Ham kits from Palitoy's Famous Football Clubs range to get my Action Man involved in the season. The Spurs kit would sadly not be available until 1973. Only having one Action Man, albeit one with more clothes than me, gave me the same logistical problems for a London derby as my Second World War battles between my British Infantryman and German Stormtrooper. Namely, the quick wardrobe changes hindered the flow of a match as much as a battle. Peter Osgood would be through on goal, only to have his kit quickly removed and a West Ham kit quickly fitted on John McDowell to make a tackle. On the occasions when Osgood got past McDowell, the white jumper from the Action Man Adventurer uniform would be seamlessly put over McDowell's head to transform him into the West Ham keeper, Bobby Ferguson. While white wasn't an ideal colour choice for a goalkeeper – and would only start to be showcased by Peter Shilton in 1973 – it did look a little more authentic than the khaki infantryman tunic, my only green option.

On 4 September, the centenary FA Cup competition began. In all, 426 teams would take part, and the final on 6 May would be the 530th match. After the preliminary round, the 22 successful clubs were joined by 266 others for the first qualifying round. One hundred years previously, just 15 teams had entered the inaugural tournament. Five teams would subsequently withdraw, allowing The Wanderers to lift the first FA Cup after winning just two games.

In the First Division, Sheffield United's three wins and a draw kept them three points clear at the top of the table.

Manchester United recovered from their loss at Everton with three straight wins to keep on Sheffield United's tail. United had been lucky to come away with the points after Ipswich's new signing, Bryan Hamilton, twice put the ball over the bar from five yards. Frank Clarke and Jimmy Robertson also missed from close range. United's 43rd-minute winner did have an element of fortune when Best scored directly from a corner kick. United then travelled to Selhurst Park, where Brian Kidd opened the scoring and Denis Law added a brace to see off Crystal Palace.

Luckily, the Granada TV cameras were at Old Trafford for the visit of West Ham to capture a George Best masterclass.

He opened the scoring with a header before West Ham's own Best, Clyde, equalised. A couple of minutes before half-time, Charlton's corner dropped to Best who pivoted on his right leg before dispatching the ball home with a left-footed, waist-high volley. Trevor Brooking levelled the scores with his first goal of the season before Bobby Charlton re-established United's lead after a Harry Redknapp mistake. Best sealed the win with the goal of the game. From a short corner, he turned John McDowell inside out and eased past Moore before hammering home a right-foot shot for his hat-trick. In their next game, United showed their resilience to get a draw after being 2-0 down at Liverpool.

By the end of the month, Derby County remained the division's only unbeaten team. They began the month with wins over Everton and Stoke, and ended it by drawing against Chelsea and a West Brom side that earned their first point in five games by putting eight and sometimes nine players behind the ball. Derby added to their small squad by signing 20-year-old centre-forward Roger Davies from Southern League Worcester City for a non-league record of £14,000.

Manchester City started to find some form after an inconsistent start to the season. A second-half Ian Mellor goal gave them the points at home to Liverpool. A goalless draw at Leicester was followed by a 2-1 home win over Newcastle. They shared four second-half goals and the points with Nottingham Forest before a 3-0 win over Southampton took them to fourth. To add to Southampton's troubles, Ron Davies limped off after only five minutes.

Leeds finished their Elland Road exile with wins over Newcastle and Crystal Palace. Their chairman, Percy Woodward, estimated that the Elland Road closure had cost Leeds £50,000 in lost gate receipts and having to pay compensation to visiting clubs for the lower attendances.

Another 50 players were booked, bringing the total for the season to 292. The Professional Footballers' Association demanded an 'immediate and urgent' meeting with the football authorities. Their main complaint was that this refereeing initiative (more on which later) started without any warning, and they threatened to strike if the League did not listen to their concerns. Despite the clean-up, attendances were already 250,000 down on the previous season.

Leeds, without Gary Sprake, Terry Cooper, Mick Jones and Eddie Gray, were soundly beaten at Highbury by Arsenal's most impressive performance of the season. Liverpool represented a stern test for Leeds' first game of the season at Elland Road, but a Lorimer goal was enough to give the Yorkshire club the points. Leeds slipped up as Huddersfield lifted themselves clear of the relegation places with their third win of the month. Leeds were disappointing on what should have felt like familiar territory given that two of their 'home' fixtures had been played there earlier in the season.

Arsenal's win over Leeds was one of three as they recovered from their poor start to the season ... A rare John Roberts goal finally managed to break down a West Brom defence that had been well drilled by ex-coach Don Howe. Jeff Astle briefly returned after missing Albion's previous two matches with a strained stomach muscle, but would go into hospital the following Tuesday for an appendix operation. As Astle was expected to be out for eight weeks, Howe signed Bobby Gould to add a much-needed forward threat. Apart from a goal by John Wile against Everton back in mid-August, no one other than Tony Brown had scored during the season so far. Another Arsenal victory was in a drab game against Leicester, in which John Radford got two goals to complete his century of goals for Arsenal and Pat Rice scored the first of his career. Charlie George came on as substitute, just 50 days after a cartilage operation, to enliven proceedings with some typical flourishes.

There was quite a lot of transfer activity in the month as clubs looked to get in reinforcements after poor starts. Transfers during the season were always the bane of football card collectors. My feeling back then was that the transfer deadline should end at least a month before the production run of the A&BC football cards. It appeared that sometime in June was production time. Ralph Coates' June transfer from Burnley saw him featured in his new Spurs kit, whereas Allan Clarke's transfer from Leicester City to Leeds United in June 1969 had seen him remain in the Leicester cards. A&BC did later produce a second version of the Clarke card, with the text 'Transferred to Leeds United' on the front. It wasn't perfect, but it was a more elegant solution than their attempts at airbrushing. It was in the days before Photoshop, so 'crudely painting' would be a more accurate description.

Player transfers were generally ignored by A&BC or handled in a fairly ham-fisted way. A&BC somehow missed the news that Ronnie Rees transferred to Nottingham Forest in February 1969 and kept him at West Brom for the 1969/70 season. By the start of the following season, they finally transferred Rees to Forest. Rather than dispatching a photographer to take a new picture, however, they continued to use the same picture, slightly zoomed in, with his West Brom shirt clumsily filled in with red. The transfer of Frank McLintock to QPR in June 1973 would be half caught by A&BC. He featured among the QPR cards, but no matter how much they cropped the picture it was obvious that he was still wearing his Arsenal shirt.

It had been back in 1871 that American company, Allen and Ginter, began inserting pieces of card to protect their cigarettes from being damaged. Before long, tobacco companies started printing advertisements on the cards, and by 1876 they began producing cards that smokers could collect. By 1896 the collectable cards included sports cards.

Simon Anysz, Rudolph Braun, Douglas Coakley and his brother, Tony Coakley, formed A&BC in 1949. They produced chewing gum with a new artificial sweetener which enabled them to circumvent the post-war rationing of sugar. To promote the gum, they produced their first card collection in 1953, and in 1958 they produced their first set of 92 football cards. Card number three was Bobby Charlton, sporting a full head of hair in a widow's peak style ... I highly recommend the website, Nigel's Webspace – *Galleries of English and Scottish Football Cards 1965/66 to 1979/80*, which lovingly details the history of football cards and much more. You can peruse the galleries and track Bobby Charlton's diminishing hairline through the years.

Straight after school, Jimmy Greaves liked to visit his mother who worked at the A&BC factory. From 1959 he would start to appear on the cards himself. The same year, A&BC struck a deal with its American equivalent, Topps, to enable both companies to sell in each other's market. Because of their agreement, A&BC started putting Topps' Bazooka Joe bubble gum in its packets.

Douglas Coakley designed the cards himself, employing an agent to travel to each club to sign up the players for £10 each. The £10 fee for appearing on the cards never increased and took no account of the profile or marketability of the player. Generally, the players – whether they needed the £10 or not – were honoured to be featured in the A&BC collections, although Tommy Smith, the Liverpool captain, once refused to sign up, believing the amount too small. Once Douglas Coakley explained to Smith that it was an across-the-board payment, which was a decent amount of money for younger players just starting out and players in the lower divisions who did not earn much, Smith was happy to sign. The players seemed to be allowed two poses; full face shot or crouched down on one knee. I think it's fair to say that the photographer didn't have a creative talent for the medium.

In the early 70s Topps and A&BC fell out when Topps wanted to replace their nominated director, Douglas Coakley, with their international marketing executive. The Coakleys refused. Topps petitioned for a winding-up order on just and equitable grounds because the Coakleys were not willing to accept the wording of their agreement. The Coakley brothers lost the case in June 1974 and, as per the licence agreement, their business was wound up after 25 years. The 1974/75 red-backed football collection would be the last to be produced by A&BC. From 1958–74, they had produced 30 football collections for the English market, and 13 for the Scottish market, among their 94 collections.

For the 1971/72 season we had 290 purple-backed cards printed over three series, representing the 22 First Division teams and Cardiff City. I assume that when they started gearing up for production, A&BC still fancied Cardiff to pip Sheffield United to the last promotion spot. As there wasn't an album, you were effectively collecting the cards 'blind' until you or another kid obtained the three checklist cards.

Series one had 109 cards, series two had 110, and series three had 71. As a bonus, series two also included a club badge – again all the First Division clubs plus Cardiff – which could be stuck in an album costing an outrageous 8p. Bear in mind, a pack of five cards and a stick of gum cost 2p. Series three gave you the bonus of a superstar sticker to put alongside the club badge in your 8p album. Manchester City's superstar was Tony Book, and Chelsea showcased Ron Harris, so it was an eclectic choice. Personally, I traded the club badges and superstars, my pocket money not running to 8p for the album.

It's difficult to describe the joy of ripping open the yellow wax packet of cards and smelling the bubble gum. Often you would get a light dusting of powder from the gum on one of the cards to add to the sensory overload. It was a brave lad who actually ate the gum, which had the consistency of a ceramic razor blade. Health-wise, it might have been better if they had gone back to including cigarettes.

After the initial exhilaration of opening the packet, I usually came crashing down to earth with the realisation that I had yet another John Aston. Throughout 1971, Aston's face haunted me every time I opened a fresh packet of cards. Although half the fun was having a thick wad of swaps in your blazer pocket for school break times, 27 John Astons had little currency in the playground beyond blocking a clacker attack to your ribs from the school bully. I suspected distribution of the cards might be a regional thing and wondered, if I went to Manchester, might I be the subject of adulation as I bought my collection of rare John Astons to the area. Might they have their own mountain of Charlie George swaps?

I have nothing against John Aston. He had been man of the match in the 1968 European Cup final, but by 1971 he wasn't even a first-team regular, generally only playing if George Best didn't show up. Sometimes I would open a packet and the bubble gum would be missing, but it was rare if John Aston was.

When you finally got the checklists, you realised that George Best had indeed not shown up and you could call off the quest for his card. At the end of the 1960s, Best's agent refused the standard £10 fee and asked for £1,000 to reflect Best's growing fame. A&BC refused, so Best's appearance in the 1968/69 set would be his last.

Tragically, my many collections were thrown out by my mother after I left home. Nowadays you could get around £400 for a complete collection of the 1971 purple backs, and individual cards go for between £2 and £5. If there are any men in their late 50s who have spent the last 49 years hunting down that elusive John Aston card, there are 27 of you who can now blame my mother.

Nowadays, of course, you can send away and buy any missing stickers from the manufacturer, but to me this is blatant cheating, indicative of the want-it-now, entitled generation we have spawned. I am all for progress, but doing playground swaps was a great grounding in life. Hearing on the grapevine that a kid you barely knew, or despised, possessed a Martin Chivers swap was excellent training in social skills. You had to research what they might be missing (hopefully John Aston), start a conversation and negotiate for that coveted Chivers card.

Getting back to the transfer business, Leicester were in freefall and, in a bid to stop the rot, bought Alan Birchenall from fellow strugglers Crystal Palace for £100,000. Palace gave Leicester back £50,000 for Bobby Kellard, and bought John Craven from Blackpool with the change. The following day, Palace sold Steve Kember to Chelsea for £170,000, and also bought Sammy Goodwin from Aidrieonians for £40,000. Goodwin had been making a living as a car salesman while playing part-time.

To make room for Kember, Chelsea sold Keith Weller to Leicester for £100,000. Weller, following Jon Sammels and Birchenall, was Leicester's third six-figure purchase of the season. They were also trying to agree a fee with Orient for Dennis Rofe, who would cost in the region of £90,000.[2] Quite a spending spree for a club that had made a loss of £168,000 the previous season.

Chelsea had sold Weller to recoup some of the £270,000 spent on Chris Garland and Steve Kember. Dave Sexton would call selling Weller 'the biggest mistake I ever made'. David Webb believed the sale: '... was the beginning of the end; that made me stop believing in Chelsea as a force that was going onwards and upwards.' Weller would win four England caps while becoming a legend at Leicester, so you can but wonder what he might have achieved at Chelsea.

Steve Kember's last appearance for Crystal Palace was in their 3-0 defeat at White Hart Lane, which was featured on *The Big Match*. As the home side, Spurs wore their normal white shirts and blue shorts, so Palace helpfully decided to wear a change kit of yellow shirts and blue shorts. Brian Moore advised the majority of viewers still watching in black and white to look for the dark band around the Palace players' socks to help differentiate the two teams.

Tottenham, still a model of inconsistency, would start the month with a fine 2-0 win over Liverpool[3] and finish it by losing at Coventry, where they faced former Liverpool striker, Ian St John. St John was back in the First Division after an

18-month absence playing in South Africa, helping Hellenic to the title.

West Ham's Clyde Best outperformed his namesake, George, to become the First Division's player of the month. West Ham had grabbed their first away point of the season with a 2-2 draw at Newcastle before Best scored both their goals in the win over Chelsea. He grabbed another goal in the loss to Manchester United before scoring his seventh goal in seven games to open the scoring against Stoke. John Ritchie took advantage of confusion in the West Ham defence to equalise, but Bobby Moore scored the winner when his hopeful shot from 25 yards hit Denis Smith's foot to loop over Gordon Banks.

Ron Greenwood said of Best after the Chelsea game: 'If Clyde maintains this form he could become as big in the game as other coloured players like Pelé and Eusébio.' Before readers jump on Greenwood, calling black people coloured was common back then. Don't forget the NAACP in America stands for the National Association for the Advancement of Colored People, an organisation even the most sensitive liberal would struggle to call racist. As well as being one of the first club managers to select black players, Greenwood was the first England manager to cap a black player at senior level. Whatever criticisms can be levelled at Greenwood, racism isn't one of them.

Clyde Best had helped the Somerset Trojans to the 1966 Bermudian championship when just 15. After playing for Bermuda at the 1968 Pan American Games, he was invited for a trial at West Ham. He made his debut against Arsenal on 25 August 1969 and scored his first goal against Halifax in the League Cup a week later. The retirement of Jimmy Greaves in the summer of 1971 gave Best a regular starting place and he grabbed it with both hands, scoring 23 goals in all competitions. Geoff Hurst's unselfish running off the ball was a major contribution to Clyde's success so, after Hurst left for Stoke City in the summer of 1972, Best had a much harder time finding the net.

Had Hurst remained, Best might have developed into a superstar, but without him he found the net just ten times the following season. By the 1974/75 season, Best found opportunities limited and was heartbroken not to make at least the bench for the 1975 FA Cup Final. Best left for America shortly afterwards and, in his first season with Tampa Bay Rowdies, scored the decisive second goal against Portland Timbers as they won the Soccer Bowl. In 1977 he returned to Europe to sign for Dutch club, Feyenoord, but scored just three times in 23 league matches. Best returned to the NASL to play for the Portland Timbers and then Toronto Blizzard with great success until his retirement in 1982.

He returned to Bermuda to become technical director to the national side in 1997, but results were poor and his contract was not renewed. Since then he has worked in a transitional centre for prison inmates and run his foundation helping youngsters develop their soccer skills. In 2006, he was awarded an MBE for services to Bermudian football and the community, emulating his father who had received an MBE for his work in the prison service. The increased profile of televised football made Clyde a role model for many black youngsters and his influence on the generations that followed is incalculable. We will revisit the subject in April's chapter.

After being turned down by Falkirk's Willie Cunningham, the Scottish Football Association appointed Hull's assistant manager Tommy Docherty to replace Bobby Brown as Scotland manager on a temporary basis. Hull boss Terry Neill had been appointed player-manager of Northern Ireland a fortnight earlier, leaving the Second Division side in the unique position of being managed by two international managers. Coincidentally, Docherty and Neill had been half-backs at Arsenal back in 1959, together with the Wales manager, Dave Bowen.

After starting the month with a draw, their third from their opening four games, Norwich's five wins on the trot overhauled Bristol City and gave the Canaries a three-point lead at the top of the Second Division. They finished the month as one of only five unbeaten teams in the league.

Birmingham, another of the favourites for promotion, had a faltering start to the season. After four games they had only managed a narrow win over Carlisle. When visitors Charlton went in at half-time 1-0 up, the St Andrews crowd showed their frustration by booing Bob Latchford. Suitably fired up, he returned after the break and scored his first professional hat-trick to add to Trevor Francis's equaliser. Latchford got a second hat-trick at the end of the month in the win over Watford to extend Birmingham's unbeaten home run to 18 months.

Watford's consolation goal in the 4-1 defeat was only their fifth in their opening nine games. In an attempt to recruit some firepower, manager George Kirby unsuccessfully attempted to lure Jimmy Greaves out of retirement. Kirby felt Greaves had retired too early and could thrive now that referees were taking a tougher line on tackling.

Burnley moved into third after the latest winger from their production line made his first appearance of the season. Leighton James scored both goals at home to Fulham in only his fourth senior game. James would become one of the biggest talents in the British game as he starred in the young Burnley side that was tipped to be the team of the 70s.

In 1986, after spells at Derby, QPR, a return to Burnley, Swansea, Sunderland, Bury and Newport County, James returned to Turf Moor for a third time. Burnley had just spent their first season in the Fourth Division, and although James was 33 and past his best, his ten goals were enough to help Burnley maintain their league status, 27 years after winning the First Division title. He was released at the end of the season but within weeks he was back as youth team coach. After Ray Deakin was injured, James returned to the first team to play in a defensive role. His final season saw him play at Wembley in the Sherpa Van Trophy Final. His 400 appearances over four spells guarantee him a place in most Burnley supporters' greatest ever XIs.

Notts County's 2-1 win over Walsall fired them to the top of the Third Division, Tony Hateley's two goals giving him six in five games. Hateley had started his career at Notts County as an apprentice, where he thrived under the tutelage of Tommy Lawton. Like fellow apprentice Jeff Astle, Hateley became a magnificent header of the ball. His form in County's promotion season of 1961 earned him a move to First Division Aston Villa, where his goals played a significant part in saving the club from relegation. In October 1966, Chelsea manager Tommy Docherty signed him for £100,000 to replace broken-leg victim Peter Osgood.

While Hateley's aerial ability was as good as any, he struggled to adapt to Chelsea's quick passing style. Nevertheless, his nine goals in 33 appearances were enough to convince Liverpool's Bill Shankly to ask how much Docherty wanted for Hateley. Upon hearing '100,000 wouldn't buy him', Shankly replied: 'I know, I'm one of them. I just want to know how much.' He signed him for £96,000, but soon discovered that Hateley's aerial ability encouraged his teams to play a long-ball game, which Shankly hated. The manager transferred him to Coventry for £80,000, but after a disappointing season there, Hateley moved to Birmingham City. The centre-forward would refer to his time at Coventry and Birmingham as two years in the wilderness.

Hateley returned to Notts County for £20,000 in November 1970. He doubled the previous home attendance to more than 20,000 on his debut, and his 22 goals helped Jimmy Sirrel's men to the Fourth Division championship.

An injury in March 1972 would end Hateley's season – and with it, County's hopes of promotion. He would join Oldham Athletic in the summer but, having not fully recovered from a knee operation, figured only briefly as the Latics lifted the Third Division title. Thereafter Hateley served the Boston Minutemen in the US before dropping into non-league football.

At the time of his retirement in 1974, his combined transfer fees of nearly £400,000 were a British record. He would be remembered as one of the greatest headers of a football the English game had seen. Sadly, he died in February 2014. Like his old team-mate, Jeff Astle, his later years were blighted by Alzheimer's disease.

Honours were even when County met Bournemouth. Ted MacDougall got the opener for Bournemouth two minutes before half-time, but straight after the restart Don Masson was brought down. He dispatched the penalty himself for his fourth goal of the season.

In the Fourth Division, no clear leaders were emerging. Southend inflicted Grimsby's first defeat of the season with their first win in six games. Billy Best scored a hat-trick the night before his namesake, George, scored his own treble against West Ham. A John O'Mara hat-trick in the 6-0 win over Hartlepool gave Brentford their biggest win for eight years at the start of the month, before a 2-0 win over Stockport in front of their biggest crowd of the season saw the Bees finish the month top.

At 40 years old Brian Phillips successfully applied to the Football Association to have his life ban from football lifted. His was the first application after the recent decision to allow suspended players to apply for reinstatement after seven years. Phillips had, together with Kenneth Thomson and Esmond Million, been a team-mate of Brian Clough at Middlesbrough. Although they were never charged in connection with their time at Middlesbrough, Phillips, Thomson and Million were later found guilty of corruption.

While Thomson's confession to the *Sunday People* – that he received £200 to help Hartlepool lose to Exeter – was the first firm indicator of corruption, it was Esmond Million that originally set off alarm bells. In 1962, goalkeeper Million moved to a new home after signing for Bristol Rovers and put his bungalow up for sale. As the weeks passed there were no buyers, forcing him to take out a bridging loan. By April 1963, his money problems had begun to stack up and he was approached by former team-mate, Brian Phillips. Phillips, now at Mansfield Town, offered him £300 to throw an away game at Bradford Park Avenue. Million accepted and approached team-mate Keith Williams and others.

During the Third Division game, on 20 April, Hugh Ryden and Bobby Jones gave Rovers an early 2-0 lead, with Bradford Park levelling before half-time. Bradford's first goal came from 18-year-old Kevin Hector after Million dropped a cross, before a farcical own goal from a gentle Ray Mabbutt back pass. As Ray[4] later explained, 'I turned to run upfield and heard the roar of the crowd. Somehow our keeper had let it go through his hands, it was extraordinary.' Keith Williams reportedly groaned, 'Oh, bloody hell, Es!' to his co-conspirator. Full-back Gwyn Jones, who had been approached by Million before the game, asking him if he wanted to earn £100, reported his concerns to Rovers captain Geoff Bradford at half-time. The second half of the game passed without incident or further goals. Rumours of the attempt at match-fixing spread and, though Rovers were struggling against relegation, manager Bert Tann sacked Million and Williams.

With the story now out in the open, *The People* led with it the following weekend, leading Mansfield to suspend Phillips. In July 1963, Million, Williams and Phillips were charged under the Prevention of Corruption Act. Million was fined £100 and the others were fined £50 at Doncaster Magistrates Court. The following month, the Football Association banned them for life. The story escalated into what *The People* called 'the biggest soccer scandal of the century'. 24 hours after the final match of the 1963/64 season, five Mansfield players were named as having provided money to fix a win at Hartlepool the previous season. Mansfield's skipper, Sammy Chapman, was suspended by the club, while the Football League suspended ex-player Jimmy Gauld for life the following month.

Gauld, who had played for Everton, Swindon and Plymouth Argyle, was the mastermind behind the fraud. After being forced to retire after breaking his leg, he pursued a career in match-fixing with a ring of up to 30 corrupt players. On 26 January 1965, Phillips was found guilty of conspiracy to defraud and jailed for 15 months. Six other footballers were jailed, including Peter Swan, Tony Kay and David Layne of Sheffield Wednesday. There is further analysis on their part in the scandal in the February chapter.

The big clubs joined the League Cup for the second round. It was the first time that entry to the competition was compulsory, so we had a full complement of clubs. Sheffield United saw off Second Division strugglers Fulham with ease. In their tie against Manchester United, Ipswich – who had scored only once in their previous seven games – led through Jimmy Robertson and were much the better side until Willie Morgan levelled from the penalty spot. A minute later Ipswich had a chance to retake the lead when Frank Clarke headed against the top of the bar, before George Best stepped up with two goals in five minutes. Ipswich supporters spent the last ten minutes chanting for manager Bobby Robson to be sacked. Transfer-listed Tommy Carroll added to Robson's troubles by walking out for the second time in six weeks.

In a bid to strengthen his struggling side, Robson signed Blackburn's Allan Hunter for £60,000 plus Bobby Bell. Northern Ireland international Hunter would become one of the cornerstones of the great Ipswich side of the 1970s.

Southampton overcame Everton 2-1. The Toffees nearly snatched an undeserved draw, but Brian Labone's header was disallowed for an apparent foul on the goalkeeper. It would have been a nice way for Labone to mark what would prove to be his final game for the Blues. Shortly after the game, he broke down with the same Achilles problem that had plagued him since the 1970 title run-in. After 534 senior appearances, stretching across three decades, he would call it a day at the end of the season.

The Harris brothers faced off at Stamford Bridge as Plymouth, captained by Alan, lost to Ron's Chelsea. Norwich put their promotion chase on hold to overcome Third Division challengers Brighton. West Brom lost to Spurs when Jimmy Pearce got the winner in his first appearance of the season. In the tie of the round, Derby outplayed Leeds but had to settle for a goalless draw. A thrilling game at Maine Road saw Manchester City pull back a two-goal deficit to overcome Wolves 4-3.

In Iceland, Spurs started the British clubs' assault on the European trophies with a 6-1 win on Keflavik's lava-dust surface. Gilzean scored a hat-trick, the first by a Tottenham player in the away leg of European competition. Graeme Souness replaced Alan Mullery for the last 15 minutes in what would be his only appearance for Spurs.

Tottenham had signed the coveted Edinburgh-born Souness as an apprentice in April 1969. The following year he was part of Tottenham's FA Youth Cup-winning side when they beat Coventry City over four matches. Souness netted in the first and fourth games, while being sent off in the third for punching Dennis Mortimer. Souness formed a formidable midfield partnership with Steve Perryman, who had already broken into the first team at 17, and made no secret of the fact that he felt his own debut was long overdue. 'I have never known such an ambitious and impatient young man,' an exasperated Bill Nicholson complained.

Souness signed professional forms in May 1970, but four months later went home to Edinburgh, claiming he was homesick. Spurs suspended him for two weeks without pay and threatened to extend the suspension at fortnightly intervals until he returned. Scottish MP, Tam Dalyell, raised questions in Parliament about what right a football club had to deal with a homesick minor in such a way. As the story crossed from the back to the front pages, Souness became the best-known teenage footballer in the land. He eventually returned and frequently told Bill Nicholson that he was the best player at the club as he pushed for first-team football.

When Nicholson selected John Pratt to replace the injured Mullery at the end of October, Souness grew even more exasperated. After Mullery was sold and Pratt started the next season in his place, Souness asked for a transfer. Nicholson decided, reluctantly, that he had no option but to let him go, selling him to Middlesbrough for £27,000.

Souness played a prominent part in Middlesbrough winning the Second Division championship in 1973/74 and establishing themselves in the First Division. In 1978 Liverpool signed him for a record £352,000, and over the next seven seasons Souness won five League championships, three European Cups and four League Cups. He also became a Scotland regular. During the 1982 World Cup, he played against a New Zealand side that contained his old Spurs Youth Cup-winning team-mate Bobby Almond in central defence.

In the home leg against Keflavik, the Icelanders were only saved the embarrassment of a double-figure scoreline by Spurs squandering a succession of chances. The eventual aggregate of 15 goals was just one short of the British record in Europe set by Leeds.

Leeds felt they had comfortably put themselves into the second round of the UEFA cup after an impressive 2-0 win in Lierse. Revie had used the opportunity to give a run-out to some of his squad players, and he again called up more of his reserves for the home leg. Paul Reaney, Terry Cooper and Peter Lorimer were the only first-teamers playing in their accustomed positions, although Revie did name Gary Sprake and Norman Hunter among the substitutes. Lierse manager Frank De Munck's sole ambition was to avoid disgrace. 'We will do our very best, but I think we will have to be satisfied if we can avoid a very heavy defeat.'

Although 17-year-old goalkeeper John Shaw's handling was understandably jittery early on, Leeds began the game looking assured, clearly expecting to win easily. They had a shock in the 32nd minute when Lierse centre-forward Frans Janssens found the net via a deflection off Reaney. Four minutes later Leeds stopped in anticipation of being awarded a free kick for an obstruction on Paul Madeley. The whistle never came and Janssens passed for Peter Ressel to level on aggregate. Lierse were on the attack from the restart and Shaw allowed Ressel's centre to go through his hands for Janssens to score. It was no surprise when Sprake replaced Shaw and Hunter came on for Jimmy Mann at the interval.

After half-time, Lorimer hit the crossbar and Cooper and Madeley went close as Leeds battled to save the tie. Lierse weathered the pressure and, with ten minutes of the game remaining, grabbed another goal to complete an amazing rout. With Leeds overcommitted in attack, they were caught on the break as Ressel snatched his second goal to confirm Leeds were out of the UEFA Cup.

Wolves celebrated the return of first-class European competition to Molineux after an 11-year absence by beating Portuguese amateurs, Academica de Coimbra, with goals from John McAlle, John Richards and Derek Dougan. They finished the job off in Portugal with a 4-1 win, although Danny Hegan stupidly got himself sent off with Wolves cruising. Dougan got his second hat-trick in a week and John McAlle scored the other for his third goal of the month. McAlle had netted in the League Cup defeat at Manchester City at the start of the month and his goal was his second in this tie.[5]

Ronnie Allen brought his Athletic Bilbao side to one of their spiritual homes, Southampton. It had been expatriate steel and shipyard workers from Southampton and Sunderland who introduced football to Bilbao in the late 19th century. In 1898, students formed the Athletic Club and, five years later, Basque students formed Athletic Club Madrid, which later evolved into Atlético Madrid. Athletic's strip was blue-and-white halves until 1909, when Bilbao student Juan Elorduy picked up 50 shirts in Southampton before catching the ship home. The club started using its now-familiar colours, sending the surplus shirts from Elorduy's haul to Atlético Madrid. Keeping the English connection, six of Bilbao's first eight managers were English, although Allen was their first English manager for 20 years.

Bilbao took the lead just after the interval, but were pegged back within six minutes when Tom Jenkins got Southampton's equaliser after latching on to a long ball from Denis Hollywood. Although Mick Channon converted Southampton's second penalty of the night to give the home side a narrow win, they would rue Jimmy Gabriel's earlier penalty miss.

In Bilbao, Southampton managed to hold on to their first-leg lead until the 68th minute, when substitute Jose Ortuondo snatched a goal for the Spaniards. Needing a goal to save the tie, Southampton threw caution to the wind and Bilbao hit their second with a minute to go.

Ronnie Allen's connection with Bilbao actually stretched back to 1958, when he had scored there for West Brom in a testimonial match for the long-serving Augustin Gainza. Allen ended a magnificent playing career at Crystal Palace. When he scored for Palace during the 1964/65 season, he became the only player to score a league goal in the first 20 seasons of post-war football.

After being sacked by Wolves, he took up the reins at Athletic Bilbao in March 1969, leading them to the Copa del Rey later that season and a second-place finish in La Liga in 1970. During the season, they thrashed Real Madrid 6-0 and only lost the title on goal average. They had qualified for this year's UEFA Cup by finishing fifth in the previous season. Allen would be sacked two months after the Southampton win, just eight games into the season.

In the Cup Winners' Cup, holders Chelsea put Jeunesse Hautcharage to the sword, while Liverpool and Rangers squeezed into the next round. Luxembourg Third Division side Jeunesse Hautcharage are undoubtedly the smallest club to have ever appeared on the European stage, after surprisingly lifting their domestic cup. Their village only had a population of a few hundred, and just a few dozen would watch the side play in the local park. Looking at their squad for the Chelsea game, the omens weren't good. The four Welscher brothers formed the core of a team which had a bespectacled midfielder, two players over the age of 40 and a 15-year-old on the bench. If that wasn't enough, their striker, Guy Thill, had been born with only one arm.

By half-time Peter Osgood had scored a hat-trick to help Chelsea to a 6-0 lead. The *Daily Mirror's* Nigel Clarke reported: 'It was only the enthusiasm of the amateurs, inspired at times by a splendid brass band, that kept them running.' Tommy Baldwin and David Webb added two more for Chelsea in the second half. Sadly, the occasion was spoilt for the village amateurs by the behaviour of some Chelsea fans.

Back at Stamford Bridge, the slaughter continued. Osgood scored a brace in the first five minutes, and Alan Hudson, John Hollins, Ron Harris and Webb made it 6-0 by half-time. Osgood bagged a second-half hat-trick to become the fourth Chelsea player to score five goals in a match. Chelsea's 13-0 win remains their largest victory and the only time they have reached double figures. The 21-0 aggregate scoreline remains a European record.

Distillery hosted Barcelona in Belfast for the first leg of their Cup Winners' Cup tie. In the 77th minute, with the hosts 2-0 down, 19-year-old Martin O'Neill tried a one-two with Martin Donnelly, but the return was played behind him. O'Neill managed to stretch back, drag the ball forward and strike it in one movement. The ball cannoned into the net off the post with the keeper Miguel Reina[6] well beaten. Distillery lost 3-1, but the highlight of the game was O'Neill's wonder goal. Barcelona finished the tie off with a 4-0 win at the Nou Camp, although O'Neill again impressed, making several electrifying runs, including one in which he calmly waltzed past five opponents.

In the European Cup, Celtic suffered an embarrassing 2-1 defeat to Danish part-timers BK 1903 of Copenhagen, but were far more professional with a 3-0 win in the home leg.

Peter Marinello, Arsenal's forgotten £100,000 signing, was Arsenal's man of the match away to Strømsgodset. After only two minutes, his cross was nodded down by Ray Kennedy for Peter Simpson to rifle home from 20 yards. In the 20th minute he scored the goal of the night, chipping the keeper after a solo run. The hosts pulled a goal back in the 57th minute, but Eddie Kelly's thundering shot from 20 yards in the last five minutes restored the two-goal cushion. Charlie George played his first full game of the season in the return leg as Arsenal ran out 4-0 winners.

European Cup-holders Ajax overcame Dynamo Dresden 2-0 on aggregate, while their Dutch rivals, Feyenoord, thrashed Olympiakos Nicosia, managed by Englishman Rod Bradley, 17-0 over two legs.

In International news, Northern Ireland lost their must-win European Championship tie against the Soviet Union to a first-half Vladimir Muntyan penalty. Although Ireland had George Best on duty, they were missing their other world-class player, Pat Jennings. Newcastle's Ian McFaul replaced him for only his fourth cap.

UEFA staged a play-off to decide who would retain the European Fairs Cup in perpetuity following its replacement by the UEFA Cup. Given their respective records in the Fairs Cup, UEFA decided that Barcelona and Leeds would be the teams to face each other.

The teams met at Barcelona's Nou Camp on a winner-takes-all basis. The match was one of ten September fixtures for Leeds, coming between the two legs of their tie against Lierse. Their 30 per cent of the gate receipts was useful income for Leeds, still suffering from the cost of the Elland Road closure.

Both sides took the game seriously, and several times the referee had to call the players and captains together after heated exchanges. Five minutes after the restart the home side took the lead through Teófilo Dueñas, but Leeds equalised within two minutes. Goalkeeper Salvador Sadurní fumbled Lorimer's 25-yard free kick and 19-year-old Joe Jordan, making his first start for United, moved in quickly to dispatch the loose ball. Barça took control and looked the better side, getting their reward in the 83rd minute when Dueñas collected a defence-splitting pass and hammered the ball past Gary Sprake for the winner.

NOTES FROM ABROAD

Despite Nîmes gaining their first-ever European win in the UEFA Cup with a Jean-Pierre Adams winner in the last minute, they lost to Victoria Setubal on the away goals rule. Adams had been superb in the previous season, helping Nîmes to the runners-up spot behind Olympique de Marseille to qualify for this year's tournament. He would make his debut for France at the end of the season in the Independence Cup and go on to win 22 caps, forming a centre-back partnership with Marius Tresor that Franz Beckenbauer called: 'One of the best centre-back pairings in all of Europe.'

Following his retirement in 1981, Adams was admitted to a Lyon hospital for a knee operation. The anaesthetic he was given should have knocked him out for a few hours. 39 years later, he has yet to wake. There had been a problem with Adams' supply of anaesthetic, starving his brain of oxygen and sending him into a coma. He is looked after by his wife, Bernadette, in their house, which she named the House of the Beautiful Sleeping Athlete. She still holds out hope that he might wake one day. Jean-Pierre has been introduced to all of his grandchildren and his birthday is still celebrated in the household.

It was in 1921 that the English FA had banned women from playing on any of its associated pitches. Many other European organisations followed suit and implemented their own bans.

After relegating female competition to local and regional events for nearly 50 years, several national associations began to lift their bans on women's soccer in the late 1960s. The FA dropped its restriction in 1969, an action which stemmed more from their fear of losing control of the increasingly popular female game, than any promotion of equality.

Women's Lib was a burning topic of the day as women were becoming more strident in their bid for equality around the world. On 5 September, with Germaine Greer's book *The Female Eunuch* riding high in the bestseller lists, a crowd of 111,000 watched Denmark beat hosts Mexico 3-0 to win the Women's World Championship with a hat-trick from 15-year-old Susanne Augustesen.

For this, the second Women's World Championship, the head of the organising committee, Jaime De Hargo, explained that they were 'really going to stress the feminine angle'. He wanted to capitalise upon 'the two passions of most men around the world – soccer and women'.

To that end, stadium goalposts were adorned with painted pink hoops, and tournament staff were kitted out in distinctive pink outfits. At the end of a match, players went into the beauty salons situated inside the changing rooms to prepare themselves for interviews and public ceremonies.

The 14-strong English squad, only two of whom were over the age of 20, lost their three games: 4-1 to Argentina, 4-0 to Mexico, and 3-2 to France. The tournament was a financial success, with all of Mexico's games drawing more than 50,000 spectators, and generally matches drew an average gate of 15,000.

In a chapter giving us 'a wretched little anonymity of a football country' in Qatar, and Luxembourg minnows, Jeunesse Hautcharage, it would be remiss not to mention the football tournament held at the 1971 South Pacific Games in Tahiti. The average of 9.36 goals per game is the highest of any tournament in history. The whipping boys were the

Cook Islands, defeated 30-0 by Tahiti and 16-1 by Papua New Guinea to concede the lion's share of the 103 goals scored during the 11 games played.

On 28 September, Diego Maradona was mentioned in the Argentinian national press for the first time as he entertained the crowd by performing tricks during the half-time break of the Argentinos vs Independiente game. Although Maradona went on to become, for many, the greatest player of all time, he never managed to impress *World Soccer's* long-term editor, Eric Batty.

Every September, Batty published his yearly World XI. The World XIs published between 1960 and 1992 sometimes defied common sense or were ... well, just batty. Batty was a football purist who loved to go against the general acceptance of a player's world-class credentials. His 1971 side was no exception. Gordon Banks was in goal and the defence was made up of Carlos Alberto, Berti Vogts, Bobby Moore and Franz Beckenbauer. We had a midfield of Sandro Mazzola, Gérson and Roberto Rivelino, and up front were Jairzinho, Gerd Müller and Luigi Riva.

The inclusion of the four Brazilians leads me to think that the side was heavily influenced by the 1970 World Cup. Given that there wasn't a World XI published for 1970, we can assume the team covers 1970 and 1971. No Pelé? Maybe Eric felt he was a little past his best. The last time Pelé featured was in his 1966 side, which didn't feature any of the England World Cup winners. No Tostão, the 1971 South American Footballer of the Year? I suppose if you are going to omit the European Footballer of the Year, Johan Cruyff, you might as well complete the set. Cruyff would only appear in Batty's 1972 and 1977 sides. He didn't get in the 1973 side despite captaining Ajax to their third straight European Cup, or the 1974 side after inspiring Barcelona to their first title for 14 years and starring in the Dutch World Cup side. Batty would scold Cruyff for his World Cup Final performance: 'He let down his colleagues atrociously.' The following year, he wrote off Cruyff's season as 'pathetic'.

As the book dissects the 1971 and 1972 calendar years, let's look at Batty's team for 1972. Banks in goal, Karol Dobiaš, Hans-Georg Schwarzenbeck, Moore and Paul Breitner in defence, with Beckenbauer and Günter Netzer in midfield. Jairzinho and Włodzimierz Lubański were on the wings, with Cruyff and Müller as the forwards. Ajax had retained the European Cup in an era in which they won everything they entered, but this still wasn't enough for Eric to forget his apparent distaste for Dutch players. Teófilo Cubillas, the South American footballer of the year, also missed out, although Jairzinho (who came third) was selected. Bobby Moore can count himself as fortunate to get in the side, although Batty would select him again in 1973 when even Moore's biggest fans would have to admit he was no longer world class.

By 1973, Cruyff was out of favour again. As was Europe's top scorer, Eusébio. They had 'performed way below their potential when I've seen them in the last 12 months.' Eusébio had won the Golden Boot by scoring 45 goals in 35 games, so Eric was unlucky to catch him on a bad day. Eusébio hadn't been picked in 1962, when he scored two goals in the European Cup Final, or in 1966, when he was the top scorer at the World Cup. The only time he made Batty's side was in 1965, while European Footballer of the Year. Not that being European Footballer of the Year was an automatic route to a place in Eric's side. The 1968 winner, George Best, didn't feature in that year or any other.

Batty's main fire was usually saved for Cruyff in the 70s and Diego Maradona the following decade. They were selected for just two World XIs each and, when omitted, would be criticised for drifting out of games. Almost single-handedly winning the World Cup for Argentina wasn't enough for Maradona to make the 1986 World XI. Batty explained: 'In my book too many stars today take little breaks, or in Maradona's case long breaks; hiding among the masses in midfield, once their team is winning.'

In 1978, the World Cup's top scorer Mario Kempes found the centre-forward slot taken by Gerd Müller. Nor could a place be found for the Argentinian captain, Daniel Passarella, with Dave Watson and Luis Pereira making up the central-defence places. Passarella would be selected along with Ossie Ardiles in 1982, because 'they both played as well as in 1978'. They hadn't, but let's not split hairs.

In April 1980, Batty stated that as well as Greenwood's West Ham his other favourite sides were Borussia Mönchengladbach, when Netzer was in the side, and Ajax, who 'played my kind of football in the early years of Johan Cruyff and Rinus Michels'.

Let's have a closer look at that love of Ajax. In ten seasons from 1966 – when Ajax announced themselves on the European scene by thrashing Liverpool 5-1 – until 1975, Batty only selected two Ajax players – Cruyff in 1972 and Barry Hulshoff in 1973. He dismissed any thought that Holland missed Cruyff in Argentina for the 1978 World Cup by saying that would only be true if it had been the peak Cruyff of seven years before. Batty seemed to forget that in 1971, when admittedly Cruyff was at his peak, he omitted him, stating that he was a better player before he was famous, when he still left him out.

In October 1983, Batty treated us to his all-time World XI. Cruyff and Eusébio were obviously omitted. The pair, 'although wearing shirts, went out on the pitch and did nothing. Cruyff especially is great at telling others what to do, but like Eusébio, he only really did it himself before he became a household name.'

He expanded on Cruyff when omitting Maradona in 1986. 'I never chose Cruyff in the years after he became a star, and for just the same reason I leave out the world's own pin-up boy, Diego Maradona. Maradona plays the way he wants to play. Stars such as he, Cruyff (at his peak) and Eusébio (for most of his career) lived on their reputations.'

With the exception of his beloved Ron Greenwood, Batty was scathing about the standard of coaching in the British game. In April 1982, Batty tipped Greenwood to take England to third in the upcoming World Cup and criticised those who wanted to replace him. 'Of course, I know, just as the fans know, that Brian Clough or Lawrie McMenemy could take an English team further in the FA Cup. But they play that in English football with the final at Wembley, and Greenwood's ideas were always on a different plane.'

He had the idea that Greenwood somehow had the advantage over Clough because of West Ham's Cup Winners' Cup win 17 years earlier, seemingly ignoring the fact that Clough's Forest side were a month away from retaining the European Cup.

Sadly, Eric Batty passed away in 1994, so the current generation are spared the joys of perusing his World XIs to see Lionel Messi and Cristiano Ronaldo omitted for an obscure player from one of European football's minnows, with Neymar shoehorned in at right-back.

OCTOBER

*'I didn't want to clamber over Joe. I wanted
recognition of my work with the team. I
wanted to be the team manager.'*

Malcolm Allison

THE THIRD round of the League Cup featured four all-
First Division ties. Steve Heighway's 50th-minute goal for
Liverpool saw off Southampton in a dull game, while Chelsea
needed a replay to overcome Nottingham Forest. Arsenal's
John Radford celebrated his recall to the England squad with
two goals against Newcastle. Ray Kennedy, with a tremendous
first-time shot, and a George Graham header completed the
scoring.

West Ham were unlucky not to beat Leeds at Upton Park
after having three goals disallowed. Despite appearing to have
missed their opportunity, they would give one of their great
performances in the replay at Elland Road. A superb Bobby
Moore marshalled his defence and the always-dangerous Clyde
Best headed home the winner six minutes into extra time.

At Torquay, holders Tottenham needed an early goal from
the home side to wake them up. A Chivers brace, Peters' penalty
and a goal by substitute Jimmy Pearce eventually put them into
the fourth round.

Last year's runners-up, Aston Villa, fought back from a two-
goal deficit at Crystal Palace to take the tie to a replay, where

goals from Andy Lochhead and Ray Graydon were enough to put them into the next round. League leaders Manchester United trailed to a Leighton James goal against Burnley, before a Bobby Charlton volley earned them a replay in which Charlton fired home the only goal.

In the shock of the round, United's neighbours, City, fell to 20-year-old Gary Jones's hat-trick at Bolton. The loss triggered a management reshuffle at Maine Road by the new board. Since the European Cup Winners' Cup success of 1970, the Mercer–Allison partnership had been strained. This was due, in the main, to the younger man's ambition and Joe Mercer's broken promises to stand down. Allison had emerged from the summer of 1970 with a high national profile as a result of his television appearances during the World Cup, so he was even less inclined to remain as a number two. He felt he deserved the position of team manager, believing that right at the start of their partnership Mercer had promised to stand aside by August 1968. Mercer had twice reneged on that commitment and, by the time of the Cup Winners' Cup victory against Gornik Zabrze, Allison believed he should have been in charge. 'I thought my time had come. I had slogged for five years and now I was ready to receive real status. I didn't want to clamber over Joe. I wanted recognition of my work with the team. I wanted to be the team manager.'

Their relationship was further strained by being on opposite sides of a boardroom takeover. Mercer remained loyal to Albert Alexander, whereas Allison favoured the ultimately successful consortium that included future chairman, Peter Swales. City's season began with the North Stand finally open to the public, and with a new signing in the form of Wyn Davies. Allison was convinced that Lee and Davies recreating their Bolton partnership would help City challenge for the title. Mercer put up little resistance to the signing of Davies, but had blocked the signing of QPR's Rodney Marsh. He didn't like the potential fee or the player.

Two days after the Bolton defeat, club secretary Walter Griffiths announced: 'The board is pleased to announce the appointment of Malcolm Allison to the position of team manager with full responsibilities to the board for all team management. Mr Joe Mercer will continue as manager of the club.' Although Mercer officially had the title of club manager, he soon found himself marginalised by Allison.

Allison's first game in charge saw City overcome Everton in a scrappy 1-0 home win. When asked after the game what sort of manager he would make, Allison typically answered: 'Probably the best ever.'

Within weeks, further changes were announced. Albert Alexander retired, and his son, Eric, became the youngest chairman in the First Division. To add to the confusion of having two managers, the club decided to have two captains as well. Colin Bell was announced as the team captain, with Tony Book being named club captain.

Matters were confused off the field, but on it the campaign was going steadily. Although City suffered a 3-0 reverse at Leeds, they inflicted early pacesetters Sheffield United's fourth loss of the month before taking a point at Huddersfield to finish the month in third.

October had started with a top-of-the-table clash between Manchester United and Sheffield United at Old Trafford. After a tight goalless first half, George Best opened the scoring with a memorable solo effort. Picking up the ball in the opposition half, he danced through the defence before firing into the far corner. The *Match of the Day* cameras were there to capture the iconic strike for posterity. Alan Gowling grabbed his fourth goal of the season to give Manchester United a 2-0 win. Sheffield United's first loss of the season allowed Manchester United to close the gap to a single point. United went top of the table for the first time in three years following their 3-0 win at Huddersfield. Best opened the scoring with a soaring header before Law and Charlton added the other goals. It would be the last time that all three would score in the same match. Best scored the only goal at home to Derby, and made it four in four with the winner at Newcastle, despite receiving a death threat from the IRA in the run-up to the game. A nervous wreck, he played superbly in the clash – possibly deciding that a moving target would be harder to hit.

United did falter at the end of the month to visitors Leeds. In the fifth minute, Johnny Giles squared a quick free kick to Lorimer, whose speculative shot from 35 yards sneaked under Stepney's body. 'The sort of mistake no goalkeeper would ever want to make,' Barry Davies sympathised. 'Poor Alex Stepney.' Best was unlucky not to score for the fifth successive game and level the scores. He had a shot saved by Sprake's leg, before striking the crossbar with a header. Despite the loss, United still finished the month two points clear of second-placed Derby.

The IRA death threat forced Best to withdraw from the Northern Ireland squad for their European Championship qualifier against the Soviet Union in Belfast.[1] Distillery's Martin O'Neill was called up to replace him. It had been Best's withdrawal against the Soviet Union two years before that cost him his best chance of appearing in a World Cup. Without him, Northern Ireland lost 2-0 in Moscow and finished runners-up in the group.[2] To the Irish FA's fury, his alleged injury cleared up by the weekend, allowing him to play for United. The following month's qualifier against Spain would be called off by FIFA because of the increasing troubles in Ireland, the game finally being played the following February in Hull.

Despite losing their unbeaten record to United, Derby moved into second in the table. The highlight of their month was the defeat of Arsenal. John O'Hare gave them a 10th-minute lead which George Graham cancelled out, before Alan Hinton converted a penalty awarded after Kevin Hector appeared to fall over his own feet.

Derby then dropped a home point against Tottenham, who finally looked to be running into form, after starting the month with an unconvincing 2-1 win over Ipswich. Spurs dutifully followed the draw at Derby with a 4-1 win over injury-hit Wolves, before making it ten goals in a week by thrashing Nottingham Forest. Alan Gilzean was superb against Forest before limping off on the hour, and was missed as Tottenham fell to two John Mahoney goals at Stoke the following week. Alan Mullery hobbled off against Stoke and wouldn't be seen in a Spurs shirt until the tail end of the season.

The defeat to Derby ended an Arsenal run of five wins as they started to recapture their title-winning form. They had begun the month by defeating Southampton 1-0 in a nasty game, although Hughie Fisher's broken leg was caused by an accidental collision with Bob Wilson. Charlie George recovered from his cartilage operation to make his first start of the season against Newcastle, setting up Arsenal's first two goals for Graham and Eddie Kelly. The Gunners extended their lead through Kennedy and George Armstrong before allowing Macdonald to grab a couple of late consolation goals.

Kennedy got both goals against Chelsea in Arsenal's first win at Stamford Bridge in a decade. The Gunners were fortunate in their next game when the Ipswich keeper, Laurie Sivell, caught a Radford header only to drop the ball over his own line. Although Mick Hill headed an equaliser, George lashed home a late winner.

Newcastle's five losses in October sent them to the bottom of the table and they capped a dreadful month by being humbled by Arsenal in the League Cup. In a bid to arrest their decline they signed Tony Green from Blackpool for £90,000 plus Keith Dyson.

Ipswich continued to struggle through October despite Mick Hill's four goals in three games, which earned him a call-up to the Wales squad. Although Hill was born in England, his father had been born in Wales. After the defeat at Spurs, Ipswich snatched draws with Nottingham Forest and Everton before Hill hit a brace in their win over Stoke, where Mick Lambert made his first appearance of the season as a substitute.[3]

Huddersfield won 2-1 at Nottingham Forest with goals from Jimmy Lawson and Frank Worthington to move up to mid-table, but the loss of their next four games sent them back into the relegation places.

Despite their home defeat to Arsenal, Chelsea were in decent form. They followed a 3-1 win over Wolves with a goalless draw at Anfield. John Motson made his debut on *Match of the Day* commentating on the match. The newspapers reported that at 26, Motson was the youngest man ever to work in television commentary.[4]

Chelsea comfortably beat Southampton, before Osgood's last-minute equaliser earned them a deserved point at Leicester. Keith Weller had a superb game against his old club. It was a foul by Ron 'Chopper' Harris on him that gave Leicester the free kick that led to their goal.

Palace had revamped their side in a bid to stay in the First Division. They used the money from the sales of Alan Birchenall and Steve Kember to sign John Craven, Bobby Kellard, Sam Goodwin, Bobby Bell, and Celtic pair John Hughes and Willie Wallace. Two goals from Bobby Tambling earned them a win at Newcastle, and Tambling's opener at Coventry looked to have won both points until fellow veteran Ian St John's third strike in five games. Palace were disappointed to lose at home to West Brom after dominating the game, and were well beaten by West Ham at the end of the month. Since their promotion in 1969, the Glaziers had faced London opposition 18 times and were still waiting for their first win.

An unbeaten October lifted West Ham to ninth and won Ron Greenwood the Bells Manager of the Month award. They started with the best of a goalless draw at Elland Road, in the first of three games against them during the month. They followed up with two more draws against Leicester and West Brom before Clyde Best's first-half goal sealed the points at home to Wolves. In their comprehensive 3-0 win over Crystal Palace, 17-year-old Ade Coker opened the scoring on his debut. Billy Bonds and Best got the other goals.

West Ham also progressed to the quarter-final of the League Cup by adding Liverpool to their Leeds scalp. Bobby Graham gave Liverpool the lead in the 33rd minute when his cross hit the underside of the bar and then the back of Bobby Ferguson's hand before going in. Just before half-time, Hurst fired home a deflected centre from Best to equalise. Liverpool had looked the more likely to get the winner before Redknapp crossed for Robson to outjump Ray Clemence and glance the ball home. True to tradition, West Ham managed to pick up just two points from their next seven games to drop down the table.

The only other fourth-round League Cup tie to be concluded was the Blackpool versus Aston Villa game, in which Tony Green inspired a 4-1 win in his last match for Blackpool.

Manchester City's conquerors, Bolton, looked well placed to cause another shock by taking Chelsea back to Burnden Park for a replay. Sheffield United were the better team in a nasty draw at Highbury. Stewart Scullion missed an open goal and also hit the underside of the bar with a shot. Charlie George can count himself lucky not to have been sent off after hacking at Geoff Salmons and later attempting to headbutt Tony Currie.

Norwich-Grimsby, QPR-Bristol Rovers, Tottenham-Preston and Manchester United-Stoke also had it all to do again. The replays would give Alf Ramsey selection headaches for the return match against Switzerland at Wembley. England had been fortunate to overcome the Swiss in Basle.

New manager Tommy Docherty made wholesale changes for Scotland's European Championship qualifier against Portugal. He ruffled a few feathers by including two English-born players in the squad – Hibernian's Alex Cropley and Arsenal's Bob Wilson. Their selection was made possible by the recent ruling that footballers could represent the country of their parents. It wasn't that long ago that the Scots frowned on picking players who *played* in England, let alone ones who were born there.

Chesterfield-born, Wilson's only previous international recognition had been in a schoolboy international for England against Scotland. Many accused him of being a Scotsman of convenience, given that Gordon Banks barred his way to the England side. But as well as both of his parents being born there, Wilson had some very distinguished connections to Scotland. His great-uncle was Sir John Ure Primrose, the second chairman of Rangers Football Club and former Lord Provost of Glasgow. It was Sir John who officially opened the third incarnation of Hampden Park in 1903.[5]

The selection of nine Anglo-Scots was picked up by reporters, but Docherty explained that for geographical reasons these were the players he was most familiar with. He promised that young home-based players would be given their chance. The 70s would be a rich decade for the Scottish national side and much of the credit must go to Docherty for kick-starting their rise.

Pat Stanton was the only survivor from the previous international as both Wilson and Cropley started against Portugal. Although Scotland could not qualify, a crowd of 58,612 turned up at Hampden Park to see Docherty's reign get off to a winning start. Derby County's John O'Hare and Archie Gemmill scored the goals in a 2-1 win.

In Belfast, Anatoli Byshovets equalised Jimmy Nicholson's opener after half an hour. A pulled muscle forced Derek Dougan to go off at half-time, and although the Irish were on the front foot for most of the second half, they couldn't overcome the lack of both Dougan and Best. The draw ended their hopes of qualifying.

Wales selected Yorkshire-born Trevor Hockey, their first Anglo, for the game against Finland. Alan Durban, John Toshack and Gil Reece gave Wales a comfortable win. Only Finnish keeper, Lars Nasman, stopped Wales hitting double figures. At the end of the month, Wales travelled to

Czechoslovakia for a must-win game. As the fixture coincided with the fourth round of the League Cup, they had to travel without eight regulars, including Mike England and John Toshack. Ladislav Kuna's goal from 25 yards on the hour was enough to beat the plucky Welsh, although they should have had a last-minute penalty when Dick Krzywicki was hacked down in front of goal.[6]

Despite a 2-1 loss to Millwall ending their unbeaten record, three wins and a draw were enough to keep Norwich at the top of the Second Division. Millwall began the month with 2-1 victories over both Carlisle and Cardiff before beating Bristol City 3-1 to leapfrog them into second place. Millwall's Barry Bridges harried the City defence into scoring two own goals, before Gordon Bolland got the third. The only blemish in the month was a last-minute defeat at Middlesbrough, but the Lions showed character in their next game by coming back from two goals down to snatch a draw at Orient.

Birmingham looked to strengthen their side by signing Tom Carroll on loan from Ipswich, with a view to signing him permanently, along with Bob Hatton from Carlisle. Carlisle replaced Hatton with Stan Bowles from Crewe.

Cardiff, one of the pre-season favourites for promotion, won at Preston to record what would be their last away win until December 1973.

Blackburn goalkeeper Roger Jones had to be replaced by centre-forward Don Martin during the 7-1 thrashing by Shrewsbury. Newly converted forward, Alf Wood, helped himself to five of the goals. Wood's ten league goals the previous season convinced Shrewsbury manager, Harry Gregg, to convert him from centre-half. Gregg, the former Manchester United goalkeeper and hero of the Munich air crash, plugged the gap in defence by promoting the raw Jim Holton from the reserves.[7]

Wood's 41 goals during the season would attract attention from several clubs, including Liverpool and Wolves, in the summer of 1972. Bill Shankly enquired about Wood and was told by Gregg the price was £75,000. However, the Shrewsbury board, fearing Wood might be a one-season wonder, had already decided to sell to Millwall. Bill Shankly was furious when he found out that his offer was far more than Shrewsbury agreed with Millwall, but their board refused to go back on their word and the deal with Millwall stood.[8]

Wood proved to be a big hit at Millwall, taking his career tally past 100 goals. After moves to Hull and Middlesbrough, he finished his league career at Walsall before moving into non-league football. Wood's final game was for Stafford Rangers at Wembley in 1979, where his two goals secured the FA Trophy. Sadly, he died in April 2020 after suffering from dementia. Known for his aerial power, Wood's case had chilling echoes of Jeff Astle and Tony Hateley's final years.

Wood's accuracy for Shrewsbury did mean less work for Fred Davies, a local coracle maker employed to sit in one of his boats during matches. Every clearance over the Riverside stand into the Severn that Fred recovered earned him 50p. Davies finally hung up his waders in 1986 when in his 80s. The widespread rumour that, on his death in 1994, Fred was treated to a fiery funeral on the river in the manner of a deceased Viking warrior is sadly untrue.

In the Third Division, Bournemouth remained top and Notts County second as they looked to repeat their Fourth Division one-two of the previous season. Ted MacDougall started the month goalless, but he hit his stride with seven in his next four games, including a strike in Bournemouth's comfortable win over Villa. His strike partner, Phil Boyer, also scored in the win. MacDougall and Boyer were one of the great striking partnerships of the decade. In the six seasons they played together (two at Bournemouth and Norwich and one each at York and Southampton) they netted more than 250 goals.

Notts County continued to pick up points despite missing the suspended Hateley for two games. He returned to score his first goal in eight games at the end of the month.

As well as the defeat by Bournemouth, Aston Villa also lost to Rotherham and Plymouth to drop to fourth. To add to their problems, midfielder Bruce Rioch was suspended for four weeks. His brother, Neil, replaced him and started well with two goals in Villa's 4-1 win over Blackburn. His second and last appearance of the season was in the 4-4 draw at Port Vale at the start of November. Although Neil had moved with Bruce from Luton in 1969, he remained a squad player, making just 22 appearances in his six years at Villa Park.[9]

October would see the busy FA disciplinary panels start to show some leniency, although Aston Villa were aggrieved that Rioch was the only player to have his suspension upheld. On 7 October, the PFA committee gathered in London with officials of the Football Association, the Football League, the Association of Football League Referees and Linesmen, and the Secretaries and Managers' Association. It was only the second time in 108 years that all of the bodies had been brought together, and the topic was referees.

The infamous 'Referees' Revolution' was launched after match officials received a memorandum through the post on the Monday following the opening games of the season. In it were detailed instructions aimed at eliminating foul play and gamesmanship. The following day, 32 players were cautioned in 15 games. On the Wednesday, seven players were booked in the goalless draw between Tottenham and Newcastle. Spurs manager Bill Nicholson complained: 'We have been told nothing about the new policy.'

Elsewhere, three players were sent off and a further 38 booked. By the end of the month, 715 players had been cautioned, and the number would hit 1,000 by mid-December. At the height of the clampdown, Bill Shankly observed: 'The trouble with referees is that they know the rules, but don't know the game.'

Previously, tackling was used to intimidate and soften up an opposition player. As Norman Hunter reflected: 'In those days, we never got booked for the first tackle.' All that had really happened was that referees had their power to use their own discretion taken away and players were being asked to play to the existing rules of the game.

Retired officials such as Mervyn Griffiths stepped forward to give their opinions in the press. Griffiths, who refereed 'The Matthews Final' of 1953, thought the clampdown was mad and spoke of his pride in never having sent a player off and only ever booking two. Given that he refereed in the era of Newcastle's Frank Brennan and Jimmy Scoular, Eddie Clamp of Wolves and the notorious Bolton full-backs, Roy Hartle and Tommy Banks, I can only assume the bookings were for murder and that sendings-off must have been reserved for genocide.

Because the clampdown ensured a record number of bookings and dismissals, players' appeals also multiplied. A normal season would see a dozen appeals in total, but now there were 140 by January. The disciplinary points system was introduced the following summer, but for now bans were still given in days rather than games. Depending on fixtures, it could lead to some huge anomalies in games missed.

The Referees' Revolution would have been more acceptable had the clubs been notified about it. Instead, they were left to read hints in the Sunday press given by Football League secretary, Alan Hardaker, about the campaign to come. PFA secretary, Cliff Lloyd, entered the argument with comments which illustrated the farce over a change that all parties agreed was, in principle, good for the sport. 'We know that the game can only be better for the removal of the tackle from behind and dissension,' he said. 'We've never argued against that. If there had been prior discussion of those points, there could have been no complaints.'

The players were denied the amnesty they sought for the early-season bookings, but the disciplinary committees did loosen up after the meeting. It was becoming clear that English football was a safer environment for the more skilful, less robust, players. Although George Kirby failed to lure Jimmy Greaves out of retirement, Stoke had more success enticing former England inside-forward George Eastham back from South Africa.

At the end of the season, the disciplinary figures reflected the Football League's get-tough policy. The total of 1,618 bookings was a rise of nearly 80 per cent from the previous season's 905 cautions. The following season, sendings-off doubled to 82 while bookings increased to 2,320. By the 2010/11 season there were 5,897 cautions and 370 dismissals.

For comparison, it is worth taking a closer look at the disciplinary record of one of the more notorious hatchet men of the day, Ron 'Chopper' Harris. Debuting in February 1962, Harris had picked up 18 bookings by the 1971/72 season. During the season he would pick up another two cautions in 57 league and cup appearances. His team-mates, Alan Hudson and Peter Osgood, picked up four and five bookings respectively. You might question a crackdown that merited Hudson picking up twice the cautions that Harris received. Osgood could certainly get involved in some unsavoury incidents, but surely the clampdown was designed to protect players such as Hudson and Osgood? In the four seasons from 1969 to 1973, Osgood collected 17 bookings in 191 games, whereas Harris collected just eight in 205 games.

Chopper played his last match in May 1980, finishing his career with 40 bookings and one sending-off in nearly 800 appearances. At the time of his retirement in the summer of 2020, Gareth Barry, who I wouldn't style as a hatchet man, had picked up 154 yellow cards and seven reds in 885 games.

After a third of the season, any four clubs from 14 looked as if they could win promotion from the Fourth, as teams struggled for consistency. Typically, Grimsby began the month with three wins and completed it with three losses, two of them at home.

John O'Mara was still amongst the goals for Brentford, as were Bill Garner and Billy Best of Southend. Tony Field's ten goals in ten games had fired Southport to the top of the table, so the decision to sell him halfway through the month to Blackburn was puzzling. Scunthorpe fell out of the promotion spots with a home loss to Grimsby and a 3-1 defeat at Bury. Future Liverpool great Terry McDermott scored two of the Bury goals.

McDermott had been a member of the talented 1967 Kirkby Boys team, which also featured Kenny Swain and Dennis Mortimer. Other players from the side who went on to have decent league careers included Jimmy Redfern, John McLaughlin and Gerry Farrell. Although every player in the team was quickly taken on by league clubs, McDermott and Mortimer were overlooked. Eventually Mortimer was signed by Coventry, and Bury's chief scout, Colin McDonald, spotted McDermott.[10]

In the UEFA Cup first leg, Wolves beat Den Haag 3-1 in Holland, while Tottenham got a goalless draw away to Nantes in a game only notable for Roger Morgan's first appearance in a year.

In Turin, Aberdeen took on tournament favourites, and Italian league leaders, Juventus. Much of the talk before the game centred on the Italian's new signing, Pietro Anastasi, the world's most expensive player at £440,000. The Sicilian-born striker took just five minutes to make his mark, ghosting past Willie Young before swerving a shot past Bobby Clark. Anastasi and Roberto Bettega caused the Aberdeen defence all sorts of problems, but a determined Dons held out to half-time without further loss. It was a different Aberdeen that came out in the second half, but just as they were forcing themselves into the game, Fabio Capello's effort was cruelly deflected past Bobby Clark by Steve Murray in the 55th minute.

Greek side Panionios were thrown out of the competition after just one leg of their tie because of the behaviour of their players during the 6-0 defeat to Ferencváros in Hungary.

In the Cup Winners' Cup, Liverpool could only manage a 0-0 draw at home to Bayern Munich. Bayern had lost 3-0 in the previous year's Fairs Cup at Anfield. The Åtvidaberg-Chelsea game also ended goalless. John Hollins, playing up front, should have had a hat-trick in the first half, but shot weakly each time he was put clear. To illustrate the thinness of the Chelsea squad, Cooke, Houseman, Kember and Webb were also deployed up front during the season.

Despite the absence of Willie Johnston and Colin Jackson, Colin Stein netted a double and Willie Henderson fired a superb shot into the top corner as Rangers raced into a 3-0 half-time lead against Sporting Lisbon. Rangers let the Portuguese side back into the match after the break and would have to travel to Lisbon defending a narrow 3-2 lead.

Kennedy got Arsenal off to a quick start in the European Cup by rifling home an Armstrong cross after four minutes. From then, Grasshoppers of Zurich completely outplayed Arsenal, who were flattered by Graham's goal two minutes from time.

Sliema Wanderers supplied Celtic's first-ever Maltese opposition when they visited Glasgow. Tommy Gemmell opened the scoring with his 69th and last goal for the club. Lou Macari added two more before Harry Hood needed two bites of the cherry from a penalty. For Celtic's fifth, Jim Brogan scored a rare goal. The game was so one-sided that the crowd took to cheering whenever Sliema won the ball. Sliema fought to keep the goal tally down with what can best be described as a 1-10-0 formation. In the second half Celtic fans were laughing at their side's missed chances and gave the Maltese side a fine ovation at the end.

Cruyff hit the winner in Marseille to give holders Ajax a 2-1 first-leg lead. The victory was the Dutch club's third on the trot, a run that would stretch to March the following year when a 2-0 win over DWS would give them their 26th consecutive win. It was a world record that lasted until November 2016, when East Kilbride posted their 27th consecutive victory. The Dutch club sent the Scottish Lowland League side 27 crates of beer to mark their achievement.

Borussia Mönchengladbach entertained Inter Milan in the second round of the European Cup. While they might have been a little past their best, Inter were still a formidable side. As well as the Brazilian Jair, the Italians featured Giacinto Facchetti, Sandro Mazzola, Tarcisio Burgnich, Mario Corso, Roberto Boninsegna and Gabriele Oriali. Although the Gladbach team contained Berti Vogts, Jupp Heynckes, Rainer Bonhof and Herbert Wimmer, its undoubted star was Günter Netzer.

After 20 minutes, honours were even. Jupp Heynckes' early goal, scored after being found by an inch-perfect Netzer pass, had been equalised by Boninsegna. Then, with Günter Netzer leading the charge, the German team scored five goals in a breathtaking half-hour. Netzer and Danish winger Ulrik le Fevre both scored two, and Heynckes added to his opener. Eight minutes from time, the Gladbach sweeper Klaus-Dieter Sieloff completed the incredible 7-1 scoreline from the penalty spot. Matt Busby, watching the match for UEFA, said: 'There is no cure against this Mönchengladbach side, what a fantastic team. Such pace, power and invention.'

Such a performance needed a poetic name and in Italy the match is known as 'Partita Della Lattina'. Sadly, that translates to 'Match of the Can'. In the 29th minute, Boninsegna was hit by a can thrown from the stands by a Gladbach fan. The forward was substituted after being carried off the pitch. The Dutch referee, Jef Dorpmans, believed Boninsegna made the most of his injury. 'I am still convinced that Boninsegna played at being unconscious, a mature acting performance. The can was open, not full, and thrown about 20 to 30 metres, which should not have had such an effect on Boninsegna.' Mazzola is said to have sprinted over to the touchline to collect the can and presented it to Dorpmans, squashed and empty, although another report has Netzer throwing the actual full can to the touchline where a German police officer collected it.

Inter finished the game in disarray, unable to replace the injured Jair, having used up all of their substitutes. With Corso sent off, they finished the game with nine men and were as good as out of the competition.

Three days later, Borussia Mönchengladbach faced the Bundesliga leaders, Schalke. The Schalke side was considered their best since the 1930s. In goal was Norbert Nigbur, who was well protected by a strong defence marshalled by captain, Klaus Fichtel. Nigbur's record of 551 minutes without conceding a goal was ended within four minutes by Heynckes. After a little over half an hour, Nigbur had conceded five goals, as many as he had conceded in the previous 11 games. Gladbach's performance in the first 35 minutes has to rate as one of the best ever by a Bundesliga side. They added a further two goals after the break, through Le Fevre and Netzer. As they did against Inter, Heynckes, Netzer and Le Fevre all scored braces, with Hartwig Bleidick this time getting the other goal.

After the game, Schalke's manager admitted: 'Today we looked like pupils although we gave our best. We could have attacked against Gladbach's class defence for hours and hours without result.' Gladbach's manager, Weisweiler, boasted: 'No one can play any better than we do at the moment.'

The games against Inter and Schalke illustrated that during the early 70s there wasn't a better midfielder in world football than Netzer. Due to the dearth of football coverage from abroad, Netzer was still relatively unknown in England. He would rectify that the following April.

The Schalke side quickly regained their composure and within three weeks of the Gladbach thrashing they were back at the top of the Bundesliga, where they remained until late March. From then on, they chased Bayern until the very last game of the season, when they lost 5-1 in Munich. A point behind Bayern, the game was in effect a play-off. League runners-up Schalke had lost just six games, conceding just 35 goals in 34 games, the lowest in the division. As a consolation they would win the German Cup by thrashing Kaiserslautern 5-0 in the final.

The following season, due to their involvement in the ongoing match-fixing investigations, Schalke struggled and finished 15th, just three points above the relegated Eintracht Braunschweig. While investigating the corruption scandal, the chief prosecutor of the DFB, Hans Kindermann, discovered that Schalke had thrown the game against Bielefeld in April 1971. Nearly all the players, including Klaus Fischer, Reinhard Libuda and Fichtel, were banned for long periods. The scandal ended the international careers of Fichtel and Libuda, and young hopefuls Fischer and Rolf Rüssmann had to wait until 1977 for the DFB to lift their international bans.

Inter appealed to UEFA to disqualify Gladbach over the Boninsegna incident, but rather than expel the Germans, UEFA decided that the match should be replayed in Berne. Although Gladbach appealed, the only concession they received was to play the replay on German soil in Berlin.

Before then, Gladbach travelled to Milan for what would have been a meaningless second leg, but which was now in reality the first leg. Inter were determined not to be outclassed again and brutally curbed Gladbach's attacking play to win 4-2.

The replayed game at Berlin on 1 December ended 0-0, so Gladbach – the only side that was arguably a match for Ajax – were out. Potentially one of the most fascinating European Cup finals ever – Borussia Mönchengladbach versus Ajax, Günter Netzer versus Johan Cruyff – was not to be.

As for the infamous Coca-Cola can, Dorpmans donated it to his local club, Vitesse Arnhem, where it was displayed in their museum. On the 40th anniversary of the game, Gladbach's CEO, Stephan Schippers, asked Vitesse if they could have the can for their planned museum. The Dutch club agreed and returned the can to its rightful resting place.

'In Scotland, it's League Cup Final day at Hampden Park, where Celtic meet Partick Thistle, who have no chance,' were Sam Leitch's closing words on *Grandstand's Football Preview*.[11] It was difficult to argue. Although Celtic would be without the injured Billy McNeill, they were competing in an eighth successive League Cup Final, having won six League championships in a row, whereas Thistle were newly promoted.

In the ninth minute Celtic failed to clear a corner and the ball fell to Thistle captain, Alex Rae, who fired past Evan Williams. Just 18 months earlier, Rae had been signed on a free transfer from Bury. Six minutes later, Bobby Lawrie's cross shot made it 2-0. In the 28th minute Frank Coulston's shot was blocked on the line before Denis McQuade stabbed the ball home from five yards. McQuade should have made it four in the 34th minute but delayed his shot after rounding Williams. It was only a temporary respite, as the Celtic defence stood like statues from a free kick and allowed Jim Bone the freedom of Hampden for the fourth.

In the second half, the 62,470 crowd was swelled by thousands of Rangers fans who had left Ibrox to witness their rival's humiliation. Celtic laid siege to the Thistle goal, but a combination of bad luck, poor finishing and inspired goalkeeping from Alan Rough, kept them out until the 70th minute, when Kenny Dalglish finally found the net. The Celtic onslaught grew even more ferocious in the last 20 minutes, but the Jags held on for their first silverware for 50 years. To confirm their status as the 'great unpredictables', Thistle lost 7-2 at Aberdeen the following week.

Of that Thistle team, Alan Rough, John Hansen, Alex Forsyth, Ronnie Glavin and Jimmy Bone would all go on to play for Scotland, although most had moved on to other clubs before being capped. Rough remained, however, to become Thistle's most capped player. Bone would move on in March and cap a remarkable season by winning promotion with Norwich. For John Hansen, older brother of future Liverpool great, Alan, the following season brought the first of five knee operations, which scuppered a potential move to Manchester United and would prematurely end his career at the age of 27.

Tommy Gemmell would only play two more games for Celtic before being offloaded to Nottingham Forest. Jock Stein bought John 'Dixie' Deans from Motherwell the following week, to strengthen his side.

For all the skill and endeavour of Manchester United, Borussia Mönchengladbach and Partick Thistle, the team of the month was undoubtedly *Quizball* winners, Dunfermline Athletic.

With Stuart Hall as the host, *Quizball* was consistently amongst the most-watched family shows of the era. It was the forerunner of *Question of Sport,* but unlike that light-hearted show, *Quizball* was deadly serious.

The teams of three footballers, together with a celebrity guest supporter, faced each other across a large replica football pitch that featured flashing lights indicating the chosen route to goal. There were four routes to goal, varying in difficulty, with route four requiring the team to answer four relatively easy questions and route one demanding the answer to a more brain-taxing poser.[12] Route one was the only method by which the opposition could not intercept with a tackle question. If a tackle question was answered correctly, the defending team gained possession and got to attack. An incorrect answer resulted in a goal.

Guest supporters included Tommy Trinder, Percy Thrower, Wilfred Pickles and Ted Moult. To say some of the guests had tenuous connections to the clubs they were supporting would be an understatement. In the 1969/70 competition, Kenny Lynch was the guest supporter for Manchester City, but would later pop up on the 1975 Cup Final *It's a Knockout* professing his undying love for West Ham. Another of these team jumpers, Leonard Sachs, guested for Sheffield Wednesday in 1966, but switched allegiance to Leeds in 1970.[13]

Dunfermline had a *Quizball* pedigree, having reached the 1967 final with their team of Willie Cunningham, James Fleming, James Fraser and guest supporter, Gordon Jackson.

Sadly, Jackson's hat-trick in the final was equalled by Arsenal's celebrity guest Jimmy Young, as they lost to Arsenal 7-3. The Arsenal team of Young, Bertie Mee, Ian Ure and Terry Neil won the Londoners' only silverware between 1953 and 1970.

Dunfermline still had Fraser from their 1967 line-up, with Alex Wright replacing Willie Cunningham as manager, both on the show and of the actual team. John Cushley, replacing James Fleming, would prove to be their secret weapon. In the final, they faced a Leicester side of John Sjoberg, Mike Stringfellow and Graham Cross. Leicester's guest supporter was Nicholas Parsons, host of new television quiz show *Sale of the Century* and leader of the notorious Leicester Baby Squad hooligan firm.[14] Not that Dunfermline could point the finger, having drafted in *Dr Who*, Jon Pertwee, to replace Jimmy Logan. I can only assume Pertwee qualified for Dunfermline because the Tardis stopped off there once, but he didn't prove a factor as Cushley's hat-trick was enough to win the trophy.

In their actual season, Dunfermline may as well have selected some of the wooden dummies used to decorate the *Quizball* pitch. Despite a strong defence, they finished the season bottom of the Scottish First Division. Cushley, Fraser and Wright all left at the end of the season. I have no idea if Jon Pertwee renewed his season ticket.

The show would stage a Home International series the following January, before disappearing from our screens forever. There was an attempt to revive it in 1998, when Frank Skinner hosted a pilot that was never broadcast. The *Quizball* trophy still sits proudly in Dunfermline's trophy cabinet, keeping their two Scottish Cups from the 60s company.

NOVEMBER

'Letters started arriving to prove that David Coleman aroused the same kind of perturbed reverence in other people as he did in me.'

Clive James

GLASGOW RANGERS had only qualified for the Cup Winners' Cup competition by default, Scottish Cup winners Celtic being otherwise engaged in the European Cup. It hadn't been a lucky competition for Rangers, having lost in the finals of 1961 and 1967. However, it looked their best opportunity of silverware given Celtic's domination of domestic football. A narrow 3-2 win in the first leg at Ibrox meant Sporting Lisbon were the favourites heading into the home leg. Rangers' cause wasn't helped when their journey to Lisbon took a day and a half due to a combination of delays caused by fog and a baggage handler strike.

Despite an intimidating partisan crowd of 60,000 being conducted by the stadium announcer, two Colin Stein strikes cancelled out goals from Héctor Yazalde and João Laranjeira, putting Rangers within sight of victory. With just three minutes left, Manuel Pedro Gomes got Lisbon's winner to equal the score of the first leg and send the tie into extra time. Willie Henderson equalised and put Rangers ahead on aggregate, but Fernando Peres scored with five minutes of extra time remaining to give Sporting a 4-3 win on the night. The aggregate score of

6-6 meant, in the opinion of Dutch referee Laurens van Ravens, that a penalty shoot-out was required.[1]

With the home supporters encroaching on the pitch, the pressure proved too much for Rangers, who proceeded to miss all their spotkicks. Davie Smith actually managed to miss twice after a retake. With the penalty shoot-out won, the Lisbon supporters completed their pitch invasion and carried their goalkeeper aloft from the pitch.

The Times reporter efficiently filed his story informing the next morning's readers that Rangers had lost on penalty goals. The only problem was, they weren't out of the competition. Referee van Ravens hadn't understood that away goals scored in extra time also counted double. Willie Waddell, the Rangers manager, had been alerted by journalist John McKenzie that his team had won on the away goals rule and Waddell wasted no time in making it known to the officials. A meeting between both of the clubs and the match officials confirmed that Rangers were through, despite heated Portuguese protests. A week later, UEFA suspended van Ravens for his error. van Ravens would be back to referee the second leg of the UEFA Cup Final between Tottenham and Wolves before retiring in the summer. Three days later, at St Johnstone, Willie Johnston came off the bench at half-time and showed how it was done by dispatching a hat-trick of penalties in Rangers 4-1 win.[2]

There was no confusion over the application of the away goals rule to end Chelsea's defence of the Cup Winners' Cup. When Chelsea were held 0-0 on a dreadful pitch in the away leg, everyone – including Åtvidaberg – expected Chelsea to run up a cricket score at home. The Swedish part-timers managed to keep things goalless by half-time, but in the first attack of the second half, Alan Hudson curled in a shot from the edge of the box to give Chelsea the lead. Shortly afterwards, they were awarded a penalty, but John Hollins hit the post with his attempt. The miss did not seem cause for alarm until the 68th minute, when the visitors mounted their first attack of the game. Roland Sandberg levelled the scores after being put through by Ralf Edström. For the last 20 minutes of the game, the Swedes defended desperately, knowing the score draw was good enough to put them through, in what would prove to be Chelsea's last European tie for 23 years.

Åtvidaberg boasted a solid back four and, in Ralf Edström and Roland Sandberg, had strikers who could unsettle any defence. The pair would be joint top scorers in the league in 1972 with 16 goals each. Although intrinsically a small-town club, for a short period they were the dashing cavaliers of Swedish football, breaking the dominance of Malmö by winning the Swedish title in both 1972 and 1973. Within two years of the Chelsea win, they were on the wane due to the advent of electronic pocket calculators. The club depended heavily on local company, Facit, for financial support. Facit had made a fortune in the 1950s and 60s manufacturing mechanical calculators, but their business collapsed when the Japanese company, Texas Instruments, developed the electronic pocket calculator. The club had no choice but to sell its biggest stars to survive. Edström and Sandberg both left in the summer of 1973, to PSV Eindhoven and Kaiserslautern respectively.[3] By the 90s, Åtvidaberg were in Swedish football's fourth tier, with attendances in the hundreds.

Bayern Munich got revenge for the previous season's Fairs Cup defeat by ending Liverpool's interest in the Cup Winners' Cup. The Germans didn't look back after Gerd Müller's two goals in two minutes midway through the first half. A wonder strike by Alun Evans reduced the deficit, but a goal by Uli Hoeness sealed the win on the hour. There was never really any doubt Müller would be confirmed as the world's best goalscorer at the end of a season in which he scored 50 goals in 48 matches for Bayern and 14 in eight games for West Germany.[4] His 85 goals in the calendar year of 1972 was a record until it was surpassed by Lionel Messi 40 years later, although Zambia's Godfrey Chitalu has strong claims to have surpassed Müller's total in the same year with 107 goals. Müller's career statistics were incredible – 566 Bayern Munich goals in 607 games, and 68 in 62 for West Germany. They are especially impressive when you consider they came mainly during the ultra-defensive 70s era.

Despite Müller being short and squat with massive thighs, he had superb acceleration over short distances and a low centre of gravity. He also had surprising agility, which enabled him to score a fair share of headers. Beckenbauer, who generally overshadows all Bayern and German players of the era, said on Müller's 50th birthday: 'Without Gerd Müller we'd still be in the wooden hut that was once our clubhouse.'

In the UEFA Cup, future Spurs centre-forward, John Duncan, scored a hat-trick in Dundee's 4-2 win over Cologne to join St Johnstone in the third round. Aberdeen could only draw 1-1 at home to Juventus and were out.

Tottenham and Wolves, England's remaining represen-tatives, won their home games to go into the last 16. Den Haag generously added three own goals to a seventh-minute opener by Derek Dougan to give Wolves a 7-1 aggregate win. While Spurs should have scored a hatful, they had to settle for a first-half goal by Martin Peters to give them a 1-0 aggregate win.

In the European Cup, Inter Milan beat Borussia Mönchengladbach 4-2 in the second leg, which was actually the first game played.[5] Celtic won narrowly in Malta to see off Sliema Wanderers 7-1 on aggregate. Arsenal beat Grasshoppers 3-0 to see them comfortably through. Holders Ajax lay in wait in the quarter-finals, following their emphatic win over Marseille. One-nil down, Johan Cruyff decided to take the game by the scruff of the neck, equalising from the edge of the box after a run from the halfway line. Sjaak Swart then put Ajax ahead with a simple finish from eight yards. Cruyff headed his second before Arie Haan finished the scoring with a long-range special for which he would become famous. Cruyff made headlines throughout November, grabbing the fastest goal of his career, after just nine seconds, against Telstar on the 21st and hitting six against AZ Alkmaar eight days later.

On 3 November, Leeds announced the signing of 21-year-old Asa Hartford from West Bromwich Albion for £177,000.[6] Revie had been after Hartford since 1969, and with Don Howe needing funds to freshen up his struggling side, he finally got his man. It seemed Hartford had been bought as a long-term replacement for Johnny Giles, but Revie still looked to incorporate him in his side. 'I'm not saying where I will play him,' Revie said when asked. 'But I can say that he will be playing for us against Leicester City at Elland Road on Saturday.'

Three hours before the game, it was announced that the transfer was off. During his medical, it was discovered that Hartford had a hole in his heart. On returning to West Brom, Hartford was immediately referred to a specialist in the Midlands, who informed him that, despite having a small hole in his heart, it would have no effect on his football career. Hartford played the following Saturday for West Brom, so missing just one game for the club all season. In May he would win the first of his 50 caps for Scotland, who he would represent at the 1978 and 1982 World Cups. Hartford would be the recipient of one of the greatest 'Colmanballs' when David Colman himself referred to him as 'a whole-hearted player'.

Despite the distraction, Bremner and Lorimer got the goals to enable Leeds to overturn Leicester's half-time lead. Revie's men then travelled to Southampton, looking for their fifth win on the trot, but fell to Ron Davies' first goal of the season. Southampton would be thrashed 8-0 by Everton the following Saturday. Leeds finished the month with wins over Stoke and Forest, but would have to wait until March to take revenge on Southampton.

On 6 November, one of the greatest Manchester derbies took place at Old Trafford. United took a 2-0 lead with goals from Brian Kidd and 17-year-old debutant Sammy McIlroy.

McIlroy had been Matt Busby's last signing and would be forever saddled with the epithet, the last of the Busby Babes. In the second half, Francis Lee flung himself to the ground in dramatic fashion to win a penalty, which he converted to reduce the arrears to 2-1. Lee then found Colin Bell, who rounded Stepney to equalise. Alan Gowling's shot was deflected past Joe Corrigan to restore United's lead, but Mike Summerbee made it three each with five minutes to go.

City were awarded a record number of 15 penalties during the 1971/72 season, all of which were converted by Lee. Many were won by his habit of tumbling from the slightest of contact in the box, which earned him the nickname of Lee Won Pen. His 15 spot-kicks would help him to become City's all-time record penalty scorer, although he also holds the record for the number of misses. Showing his ruthless attitude to spot-kicks on a pre-season tour in Sweden before the 1972/73 season, Lee psychologically destroyed one opposition goalkeeper, who approached him after one was awarded, saying it was his ambition to deny Lee from the 12-yard mark. 'OK,' Lee said, 'I'll put it to your right, and I won't hit it too hard.' The Swede duly dived to his right as Lee smashed the ball into the opposite corner. 'That,' he told the keeper, 'is how you score 15 penalties without missing.'[7]

In Manchester United's next game, Barry Daines replaced Pat Jennings for his Spurs debut. He was unable to stop Sammy McIlroy getting his second goal in two games, and Denis Law grabbed a brace to give the league leaders the points. Daines had joined Spurs as an apprentice in September 1969 and spent much of his early career understudying Jennings. His debut would be his only game of the season and, over the next four seasons, he would make just ten further appearances.

Hunter Davies illustrated the gulf between the footballers of the day and their managers, whose upbringing had been much tougher, in his book *The Glory Game*. 'You've not got to be hard on Dainesey,' assistant manager Eddie Baily was told

when the day's training was over. 'What do you mean?' asked
Eddie, all injured innocence. 'You upset him today. You've got
to be tender.' 'Tender! Christ Almighty,' said Eddie, looking
round, opening his eyes wide. 'At his age I had a bloody rifle
stuck in my hand.'

Spurs supporters of the early 1970s could always be
guaranteed to see Daines in action during the five-a-side
competitions held during the season.[8] The *Daily Express* five-a-
side was held in November and would be won by Southampton,
who beat Leicester in the final. After defeating Glasgow Rangers
2-0 in the first round, Southampton had to rely on goalkeeper
Eric Martin's skill in penalty shoot-outs to progress. He saved
from Tony Currie to send Sheffield United home, thwarted
Robson to defeat West Ham in the semis, and then saved from
Keith Weller and David Nish in the final. Holders Manchester
United had been the favourites until manager Frank O'Farrell
withdrew George Best, Dennis Law and Bobby Charlton. The
loss of Best, who had lit up the previous year's tournament, was
a huge disappointment for the crowd of 8,000.

Though London clubs had competed in the *Evening
Standard* event since 1954, it took the start of the *Daily Express*
competition in 1968 to spark television's interest. Scottish
clubs were invited to enter and the televised highlights on
Sportsnight proved popular viewing. By 1983, clubs were
unwilling to feature their star players, so teams were mainly
populated by reserves. The BBC decided that the tournament
was now not worth covering and, without TV exposure, the
sponsors withdrew to end the competition in 1986. The *Evening
Standard*'s competition carried on for a while, and in its latter
years was opened up to clubs outside of London to increase
interest. Wycombe Wanderers won the last tournament in 1994
to cap their first season in the Football League.

In the league, Law scored another brace in United's 3-2 win
over Leicester to give him nine goals in 17 games. Law hadn't
been an automatic choice at the start of the previous season but,

after Busby took back the reins from Wilf McGuinness, he hit seven goals in his last nine games and looked the player of old. Under new manager O'Farrell he looked back to his best and, alongside Best, was a major factor in United's rise to the top of the table. His return to form would earn him a recall to the Scotland team the following April. United finished November with a superb 5-2 win at Southampton. Best scored his second hat-trick of the season, McIlroy got his third in four games, and Brian Kidd completed the scoring.

Forest managed to claw their way out of the relegation places with a 4-1 win over West Brom after Jeff Astle had given the Baggies a half-time lead with only his fifth goal of 1971.[9] After replacing the disappointing John Robertson, debutant Martin O'Neill inspired Forest's comeback. He gave them the lead before Duncan McKenzie and Ian Storey-Moore put the game out of West Brom's reach.

As a schoolboy in Ireland, as well as excelling academically, O'Neill was a fine all-round sportsman, playing football, cricket, tennis and Gaelic football. He marked his debut for Lisburn Distillery in November 1970 with a goal. Although just 18 and still studying law at Queen's University in Belfast, he quickly established himself as the team's star player. In the Irish Cup Final against Derry City in April 1971, O'Neill opened the scoring. Three minutes after the break, he doubled the lead with what the *Belfast Telegraph* called a wonder goal. The report went on: 'O'Neill beat three men with a mazy run, actually changed feet and hit the ball hard into the net. A goal that was breathtaking and spectacular... it will long be remembered by the fans.'

A fortnight after starring in the Cup Winners' Cup tie against Barcelona, O'Neill made his debut for Northern Ireland, coming on for Bryan Hamilton against the Soviet Union. The following week he left Ireland to join Nottingham Forest. After his debut against West Brom he became a regular, although he was usually used as a substitute. The West Brom win merely provided a temporary respite for Forest, who lost at Newcastle and Leeds, where Sammy Chapman became the first Forest player to be sent off in a league game for 32 years. A week after a narrow defeat to Manchester United, in which O'Neill scored again, Forest beat Everton, but two points in their next ten games – and the sale of Storey-Moore in March – all but guaranteed relegation.

In the Second Division, O'Neill established himself under Matt Gillies and then Dave Mackay, but was in and out of the side under the next manager, Allan Brown. Brian Clough's arrival would revitalise the club and the careers of the transfer-listed O'Neill and John Robertson, the only survivors of their last season in Division One. While Clough always praised Robertson, he put O'Neill's contribution down at any opportunity. O'Neill believes Clough could have got another ten per cent out of him by being a little kinder. Nonetheless O'Neill, already a League and European Champion, crowned a fine career by skippering Northern Ireland at the 1982 World Cup.

After the Manchester derby, City visited London, winning at both Arsenal and West Ham before rounding off the month by firing four goals past Coventry.

Derby lost ground in the title race with defeats at Wolves and Huddersfield. The Huddersfield defeat was particularly galling, given it would be the Yorkshire club's last league win of the season. Given the thinness of Derby's squad, the decision to transfer Frank Wignall to Mansfield midway through the month seemed a baffling one, but Clough's record non-league signing, Roger Davies, was thriving in the reserves. Mansfield's supporters would certainly welcome some additional firepower; after eight home games they were still waiting to see their side score at Field Mill.

Sheffield United put a disastrous October behind them, moving back into the top four by thrashing Ipswich 7-0, with winger Alan Woodward scoring four in the rout.

For Everton, the 8-0 win over Southampton – where Joe Royle scored four and Dave Johnson three – followed their victory in the Merseyside derby and signalled they were back to their best following a poor 18 months. Unfortunately, it took them a further 14 league games to score their next eight goals and they had to wait until the last game of the season for Royle to net again.

One of the joys of Sheffield United scoring seven or Everton scoring eight was watching the score come up on the BBC teleprinter in both figures and words. It was as if the teleprinter decided viewers wouldn't believe a score just shown in figures. Sheffield United 7 (SEVEN) or Everton 8 (EIGHT) assuaged any doubts and spelt out the losers' humiliation.

The internet has spoilt a lot of tradition in football, but maybe none more than waiting for the final scores to come up on television. Obviously, having the games played at the same time on a Saturday afternoon helped. The results came from the Press Association, who would then provide a feed to the television studios. The football results would appear on BBC's *Final Score* via a device dubbed the teleprinter, whereby you would see the result typed out character by character.

No one carried the task of presenting the scores better than David Coleman. To listen to him as the results came in was to witness a master of his craft. Coleman was a great broadcaster, with the teleprinter as his party piece. The machine began chattering away at around 4.37pm with the Scottish results. Despite starting at the same time as matches south of the border, for some mysterious reason Scottish matches always finished earlier. Then came news from a couple of the lower leagues before the First Division scores began to filter through, and the urgency in Coleman's voice rose.

Occasionally the printer paused, chattering away so you knew it was still working, but seemingly keeping the scores to itself. As you desperately waited for your team's result, Coleman filled in, as if sensing your frustration. 'The last we heard from Spurs they were winning 1-0.' Coleman's successor in the *Grandstand* chair, Frank Bough, was full of admiration. 'Coleman was the only one who could tell you that a win had put Arsenal on top of Division One on goal average, or that was East Fife's first score draw in 19 consecutive games.'

Many might put the case for Brian Moore or John Motson being a better football commentator, but in the area of athletics Coleman had no equal. He had been a fine miler himself, tipped to grab an Olympic place before Achilles problems ruled him out of the 1952 British team trials.

It was the 1972 Olympics that would bring his finest hour, but sadly not for sports commentary. He had gone to bed at 5am and was woken four hours later to be informed that Black September terrorists had taken several Israeli athletes hostage in the Olympic Village. For the next 30 hours Coleman continued to broadcast live from the Munich studio as the horror unfolded.

For the best part of four decades Coleman was the country's sporting voice, covering 11 Olympics and six World Cups. He was a polarising figure who could inspire either admiration or antipathy. Sometimes both. Clive James, who started reviewing television programmes for the *Observer* in 1972, would write: 'Letters started arriving to prove that David Coleman aroused the same kind of perturbed reverence in other people as he did in me.' It was also James who wrote: 'The difference between commentating and Colemanating is that a commentator says something you may wish to remember; a Colemanator says something you try to forget.'

Arsenal, who had begun to find some form, had a tough set of fixtures for November. Their month started with a trip to Anfield, where they took a fifth-minute lead through Ray Kennedy, before Emlyn Hughes equalised just before the break. Arsenal were comfortable at 1-1 until Ian Callaghan scored with a clever lob in the 53rd minute. Arsenal managed to level with a Tommy Smith own goal, but Ian Ross grabbed Liverpool's winner four minutes from time.

The Gunners then hosted in-form Manchester City. A rare Sammy Nelson goal galvanised City into taking the initiative. A poor header from McLintock let in Ian Mellor to fire past Wilson, then Lee found Bell to slide the ball home for the deciding strike.

At Molineux, Arsenal, leading from a Kennedy goal, began the second half determined to close the game out. Wolves, like City the week before, started moving the ball around with more urgency, making it impossible for Arsenal to slow the game down. A quick equaliser by Dave Wagstaffe was followed by a second from Kenny Hibbitt. By the end, it was a rout. Two goals from Dougan and a Jim McCalliog penalty gave Wolves an emphatic 5-1 win.

Next up was the North London derby in front of 52,884. Chivers equalised Kennedy's opener to share the points. Arsenal ended a run of four defeats and a draw by defeating Crystal Palace 2-1 at the end of the month.

Tottenham moved into seventh after another mixed month. They began with a 3-0 win over Everton, Chivers scoring two and John Pratt the other. With Mullery injured, Pratt had an opportunity to stake a claim for a regular place in Spurs' midfield. He made his debut in April 1969 and would go on to make more than 400 appearances for the club over the next 11 seasons. While he always gave his all, he never won over the crowd, often being made the scapegoat when Spurs performed poorly. When asked by Pratt what he could expect in his first game at Old Trafford, manager Bill Nicholson replied that it would be just like playing at Spurs, except that 55,000 people would berate him, whereas at White Hart Lane it was only 45,000. Pratt was even booed at his own testimonial against Arsenal in 1978. Maybe the crowd were disappointed at his selection? He would earn his first medal at the end of the season, coming on for Ralph Coates in the first leg of the UEFA

Cup against Wolves. He marked the occasion by nearly scoring an own goal with his first touch.

After their defeat by Manchester Utd, Tottenham beat West Brom before the draw with Arsenal, then lost at Stamford Bridge to a Charlie Cooke goal.

At the bottom of the table, Macdonald's six goals during the month hauled Newcastle out of trouble as he thrived on the service from Tony Green. Newcastle would end the season in 11th place, thanks in part to Supermac's 30 goals, but mainly due to Green supplying the team's craft and drive. In September 1972, while playing at Crystal Palace, the 25-year-old Green damaged a cartilage in his knee. The kind of knock that would mean little nowadays forced him to retire in December 1973. Although Newcastle got their £150,000 back from the insurance, it was little consolation. Newcastle manager Joe Harvey rued: 'After they made Tony Green, they threw away the mould. I couldn't hope to buy a similar player, not even for twice the amount.' To this day, Green is revered on Tyneside despite making just 36 appearances, his final game for the Magpies coming just ten months after his debut.

Norwich and Millwall looked favourites for promotion as they both held a five-point lead over the chasing pack. Millwall had a good November, closing the gap on Norwich to a point. They made hard work of defeating Watford at The Den, before an efficient 2-0 win at Swindon. The highlight of their month was the 3-0 win over Birmingham. Their second goal by Derek Possee would be voted *The Big Match*'s Golden Goal for the season.

Their superb young goalkeeper, Bryan King, was well protected by a strong defence, marshalled by Barry Kitchener. With Gordon Bolland, Barry Bridges and Derek Possee they were always capable of getting goals, and were prompted in midfield by Irish international Eamon Dunphy. The hardworking Dunphy is now more famous as a journalist and author. His groundbreaking diary of the 1973/74 Millwall campaign, *Only a Game*, remains a classic.

Struggling Watford beat Luton 2-1 with goals from Keith Eddy and Colin Franks. They followed with a win over Burnley, by the same score, to lift themselves off the bottom of the table. A subsequent run of one win in their last 24 games would relegate them, 14 points adrift of the rest of the division. Their paltry tally of 33 goals remains a record for a 42-game season. Midfielder Keith Eddy was their top scorer with just six goals.

Eddy had been signed from Barrow in 1966 and Watford's relegation was the latest episode in what had been to date a fairly undistinguished career. The best was yet to come for the 27-year-old after Sheffield United signed him for £35,000 in the summer. His clever play and workrate were soon appreciated at Bramall Lane. Many supporters felt that when the Blades played well, Tony Currie played well; but when Eddy played well, the team played well. In December 1973, Eddy's old manager at Watford, Ken Furphy, took over and one of his first changes was to give Eddy the captaincy and penalty duty.

Together with Currie, Eddy was the heartbeat of a team which finished just four points behind champions Derby in 1975. However, the following season started disastrously, with just one win from their first 11 games. The board sacked Furphy at the start of October and the club were as good as relegated by Christmas. After Furphy was appointed coach of the New York Cosmos in January 1976, one of his first moves was to return to his old club to tempt the 31-year-old Eddy across the Atlantic. After Eddy clarified to his wife that the offer doubling his wages to £400 a week meant they were moving to New York, not Second Division York, off they went. Eddy captained the Cosmos, and, in spite of the presence of Pelé and Giorgio Chinaglia, took the penalties. He was voted an All-Star in 1976 and during the summer was selected for the American team competing in the Bicentennial Cup. He lined up alongside Bobby Moore, Chinaglia and

Pelé in the three matches against England, Italy and Brazil. He stayed in America after he finished playing, investing in real estate and a nightclub in Tulsa and getting involved in coaching.

On the 13th, Ricky Heppolette got the only goal in Preston's home win over Sheffield Wednesday. Preston's third consecutive win gave them an outside chance of pushing for promotion. While not prolific, Heppolette got his fair share of goals – none so important as the previous season's diving header at Fulham that pipped the London club to the Third Division title.

Born in Bhusawal, India, Heppolette made his debut for Preston in 1968 before going on to play for Leyton Orient, Crystal Palace, Chesterfield and Peterborough, where he settled and now owns a shop specialising in fancy dress outfits and partyware. An Anglo-Asian contemporary of his was the Norwich goalkeeper, Kevin Keelan. They played in an era when there were only a few black players. Today, although over a quarter of professional footballers are black, we still only have a handful with an Asian background. In the 2011 census, more than 3.5m people categorised themselves as Asian or Asian British, so where are all the footballers? Forty years after Viv Anderson was selected for an England side, we are still waiting for an Asian to have an impact on professional football. Unlike their grandparents or even their parents, young Asian men love football, but as Greg Dyke pointed out in 2014: 'The passion has not quite translated.' Over the last two decades only a handful of players have made the professional playing ranks. Players like Michael Chopra, Neil Taylor, Zesh Rehman, Anwar Uddin and Danny Batth have been the exception rather than the rule.

It looked at one time as if Leeds winger Harpal Singh would be the breakout star needed. In 1998, manager George Graham boasted: 'Liverpool may have Michael Owen, but we have Harpal Singh.' Undoubtedly talented, Singh never made the grade at Leeds and, despite playing a few games for Bury and Stockport, his career fizzled out.

English football isn't overtly racist, but maybe the grassroots coaches trying to find big athletes has hindered Asian players disproportionately? The English game needs to encourage this 15 per cent of its young population.

In the Third Division Brighton were the month's form team, winning all of their league games as winger Peter O'Sullivan started to get amongst the goals. He had made his Brighton debut in August 1970 after being given a free transfer by Manchester United. In January 1981, the 'Welsh Rivelino' would make one of his last appearances for Brighton at Old Trafford, the last survivor of their 1971/72 side.

Fourth-placed Aston Villa continued their stuttering start to the season with a 4-4 draw at Port Vale. The journey back would be far more fun in the future; three days after the game, the ten-route Spaghetti Junction motorway interchange was opened. Villa were still missing the suspended Bruce Rioch for their next game against Notts County. In front of a crowd of 37,000 and the *Match of the Day* cameras, Ray Graydon's goal was enough to sneak a 1-0 win against the run of play. Tommy Hughes had another unconvincing game, but his penalty save from Don Masson prompted Barry Davies to point out that after doing little right all day Hughes had earned Villa the points. By the next game, Hughes had been replaced by Jim Cumbes from West Brom. Cumbes would concede just 14 goals in the remaining 29 games.

Don Masson's sublime passing and 14 goals from midfield had inspired Notts County to the Fourth Division title in 1971. Despite his miss against Villa, he would convert four penalties among his 11 goals for the season, but County's early-season promise petered out to a fourth-placed finish. Masson was nearly 29 when he transferred to Queens Park Rangers midway through the 1974/75 season. The following season he was an ever-present as QPR came within a point of

winning the First Division title. At the end of the campaign
he made his debut for Scotland, scoring the winner against
England to seal the Home Internationals . For two seasons,
Masson formed one of the finest international midfield
partnerships with his one-time Third Division rival, Bruce
Rioch. In Scotland's World Cup opener against Peru, Rioch
and Masson were overrun by the 'old men' of Peru. Masson's
poor display was compounded when his weak penalty was
saved with the score at 1-1. The Peru match was Masson's
last for his country; at the end of the tournament he received
a life ban from the Scottish FA for his comments to the press.
Early the next season he returned to Notts County as player-
coach and inspired them to promotion to the top flight. He
had captained Notts County to three promotions from the
Fourth to the First Division, and for many supporters he is
Notts County's greatest player.

In the Fourth Division, Southend started the month with
a 3-1 loss to second-placed Workington Town, but a win over
Exeter kept them in contention. They went top with a 4-2
win over Stockport at the end of the month, Billy Best and
Bill Garner scoring two apiece. Southend's huge improvement
from last season could be mainly credited to their twin strikers,
Best and Garner. Garner's 25 goals would win the club's player
of the season award. In Southend's League Cup tie against
Chelsea the following season, he would impress enough to earn
a £100,000 transfer to Stamford Bridge.

England's draw at home to Switzerland as good as sealed
their quarter-final spot in the European Championship. As
League Cup replays robbed manager Ramsey of Gordon Banks
and Martin Chivers, Ramsey gave Peter Shilton his third cap
and recalled Mike Summerbee after four years. The two had
mixed fortunes in a dull game. Summerbee's early header was
equalised by a swerving strike from Karl Odermatt, which
Shilton should have stopped. The point left England needing
only to avoid a 3-0 defeat in Greece to qualify.

Although Scotland couldn't qualify, they beat Belgium with a John O'Hare goal to continue their revival. Belgium's draw in Portugal earned them a quarter-final place. A hat-trick from Johan Cruyff helped Holland to an 8-0 win over Luxembourg, but Yugoslavia had already qualified from the group.

In Group One, Romania beat Czechoslovakia, leaving them needing to beat Wales to pip the Czechs on goal difference. Terry Hennessey and Alan Durban were already out injured before a further eight players were withdrawn by their clubs, who preferred to retain them for their Texaco Cup matches. Wales lined up in Romania with what the press labelled the weakest Welsh side ever. Swansea's Herbie Williams had been recalled after six years, and five of his team-mates had less than three caps between them. Romania's comfortable 2-0 win was enough to seal their place in the quarter-final draw.

On 24 November, the Third and Fourth Division sides joined the remaining 32 non-league sides for the first round of the FA Cup. Hereford United had created a record by qualifying for the first round for the 17th successive season. Torquay managed to keep the amateurs of Nuneaton Borough confused enough to overcome them 1-0. The half-time substitution of Brian Hill for his namesake, Brian Hill, proved a masterstroke. The tie of the round was Southend United against Aston Villa. Billy Best struck the only goal of the game to give the Fourth Division side the win.

While the first-round ties were taking place, Oxford City and fellow part-timers Alvechurch were playing the fourth replay of their fourth qualifying round tie at Oxford United's Manor Ground. The game also ended in a draw, necessitating a fifth replay, to be held two days later at Villa Park. 'It was almost like going to work every day,' said one Alvechurch player. 'The same teams, the same players, the same result.' During the frequent stoppages for cramp or exhaustion, opponents chatted amicably on first-name terms. As the two teams kept using the same tactics, the tie became more a battle of stamina than skill.[10]

In the 18th minute of the sixth game, the Oxford City keeper fumbled a soft Bobby Hope header to settle the epic tie once and for all. *Oxford Mail* reporter, Jim Rosenthal, described Hope's winner: 'Shocked that he had been given a chance of saving the attempt, Peter Harris got his right hand to it, but the ball wriggled loose, hit him on the heel, and crawled like a scolded dog just over the line.' Two days after finally overcoming Oxford City, an exhausted Alvechurch meekly succumbed 4-2 to Aldershot Town. As consolation they would go on to win the Midland Combination Division One and the Combination Challenge Cup.

As well as joining Alvechurch in the *Guinness Book of Records*, Oxford had regained some respectability from the previous year's competition. They had come close to dumping Bournemouth out of the first round, before Ted MacDougall scrambled a late equaliser. It was a different story in the replay as MacDougall's double hat-trick fired Bournemouth to an 8-1 win. A year on, while Oxford and Alvechurch were playing their fourth replay, Bournemouth hosted Southern League side Margate on the 10th anniversary of Margate's sensational 3-0 FA Cup win on Bournemouth's ground. Bournemouth duly took revenge, routing Margate 11-0, with MacDougall scoring nine goals. The game was only in its second minute when MacDougall opened the scoring after Margate keeper Chic Brodie dropped the ball at his feet. He added another three before the break, and ten minutes into the second half pounced on another goalkeeping mistake for his fifth. With a quarter of an hour to go, Brodie only half-saved MacDougall's shot, the ball sneaking over the line for his sixth. In the last ten minutes, the striker rattled in his third hat-trick of the afternoon.

It was the latest calamity to strike Brodie, one of the unluckiest goalkeepers ever to play the game. A little more than a year before, his Brentford side visited Colchester. Having already conceded four goals, Brodie wasn't having a great afternoon when a black-and-white terrier invaded the pitch. As he bent down to scoop up a back pass, the dog sent him crashing to the ground, shattering his kneecap and effectively finishing his professional career. 'The dog might have been a small one, but it just happened to be a solid one,' Brodie lamented after conceding defeat in his battle to recover.

After Margate, Brodie wound down his football career with Wealdstone and Maidstone United before embarking on a new career as a London cabbie. While driving through Westminster, he swerved to avoid hitting a stray dog and hit another vehicle driven by former West Ham and England striker, Geoff Hurst.

Ted MacDougall had already met Hurst under happier circumstances. His goals against Margate had turned him into an overnight celebrity and when he went into training the following Monday, he received a phone call from Hurst inviting him to play in his testimonial. Four days after playing Margate, MacDougall would be rubbing shoulders with some of the greatest footballers in Europe.

Supplying the opposition to Hurst's West Ham was a European side managed by Tommy Docherty. Lining up alongside MacDougall were Dave Mackay, Tommy Gemmell, Jimmy Johnstone, Uwe Seeler, Eusébio, Rodney Marsh, Jimmy Greaves and … Tommy's son, Mick.

Hurst opened the scoring before the Europe select levelled with MacDougall's 29th goal of the season. The Europeans went 4-1 up with two from Marsh and one from Greaves, who had replaced Eusébio at half-time. West Ham managed to level the game with a brace from Robson and a goal from Clyde Best to end the game 4-4 in front of the 30,000 crowd.[11] Mordechai Spiegler came on as a substitute for MacDougall, but under different circumstances might have been lining up for West Ham.

Spiegler had made his name when Israel reached the quarter-finals of the 1968 Olympic football tournament. In 1970 Israel qualified for the World Cup finals and, although troubled by a stomach bug, Spiegler was declared fit enough to play in the 2-0 loss to Uruguay. Israel fared better against Sweden, where Spiegler's 25-yard left-foot strike earned them a draw. Although they played out a goalless draw against eventual finalists Italy, it wouldn't prove enough to take Israel through to the knockout stages.

Ron Greenwood had seen enough of the midfielder to invite him to join West Ham's pre-season preparations and play in their three friendlies. Spiegler was as keen to join as the club was to sign him, but the move was fraught with difficulties. West Ham would have to sign him on amateur terms for two years, after which he would complete his residential qualification. Though Spiegler was happy to play as a part-timer, there were still a number of issues to solve. The Israeli FA would have to approve the move, he would also need a work permit and the Football League management committee would also have to rubber-stamp the transfer. In the end the many 'technical reasons' deterred West Ham, although it was a close-run decision, as proven by the two pictures taken of the 1970/71 squad – one without Spiegler and a second with him standing in the back row alongside Bobby Moore.

Spiegler's appearance in Hurst's testimonial revived the potential transfer, but the Israeli FA threatened to impose a 12-month ban if he moved to London, forcing the player to decline the opportunity. He finally got his move abroad when he signed for Paris FC in 1972, and would play for the new Paris Saint-Germain side after the two Paris teams merged. He returned to Maccabi Netanya for the 1974/75 season before venturing to America to join the New York Cosmos. It was Spiegler who set up Pelé's debut goal for the Cosmos.

On the same evening as Hurst's testimonial, the Ron Harris testimonial was taking place at Stamford Bridge. If Hurst's opposition was a glittering array of European legends playing an entertaining high-scoring game, it was perhaps apt that Chopper's guests were from Glasgow and the game was gritty, full-blooded and anything but friendly.

Despite being at home, Chelsea wore their yellow away shirts, allowing Rangers to wear their traditional blue. Midway through the second half, goalkeeper Peter Bonetti was replaced by John Phillips, but after John Boyle, Chris Garland and Garry Locke all went off with injuries, Bonetti returned to play out on the pitch. Rangers got the only goal in the last minute when Sandy Jardine fired in from 25 yards. Harris lost his £50 bet on Chelsea to score at least once, but was compensated by the estimated £6,000 gate receipts. He also raffled the signed match ball, with tickets priced at 5p each.

Harris always had a good eye for business and would earn a tidy sum in the property market. In the mid-80s, he took a huge risk by selling his family home, cashing in all his savings and borrowing heavily to buy the Bremhill Golf Club for £400,000. Three years later, he sold it for £2m. Harris played at a time when footballer endorsements were still in their infancy, and I don't think it's unfair to point out that he wasn't renowned as a glamourous player. He was the logical candidate, however, to help promote the super cool bicycle of the era that bore his nickname. His fee for taking part in the subsequent advertising campaign was two free Chopper bikes.

Harris would get a second testimonial at Stamford Bridge in April 1980, when the Chelsea side of the day played a past Chelsea side for whom Jimmy Greaves netted the solitary goal.[12] Before the days of the six-figure weekly pay packet, the money raised from a testimonial was vital to a player contemplating a long retirement. The gate receipts were given to a player to launch him in his post-football life and thank him for long service to one club. Testimonials had begun in the days of strict wage restriction when occasionally one-off fixtures would be organised, but more typically clubs allocated a specific league game as a benefit match and sent stewards around the pitch holding a blanket for fans to throw money into. Players traditionally used their testimonial money to buy a pub or sports shop. Generally, a testimonial committee was set up to receive the money and, in turn, present it as a gift to the player, thus avoiding the attention of the taxman. Chancellor of the Exchequer, George Osborne, put an end to the loophole and from 2017 players would have to hand over half their takings to the Inland Revenue. I doubt many will shed a tear for the Premier League millionaires for whom testimonial matches are an opportunity for supporters to thank a player for his service, with charities generally the beneficiaries. Even if the likes of Harry Kane don't stay involved in football after retirement, it is hard to imagine them stringing tennis rackets or pulling pints.

NOTES FROM ABROAD

Across the Atlantic, Toni Fritsch was finding success in a different code of football. Fritsch had earned the nickname Wembley Toni due to his two late goals that gave Austria a famous victory over England at Wembley in October 1965.[13] By 1971, the Dallas Cowboys general manager, Tex Schramm, and chief scout, Gil Brandt, were looking to recruit a soccer player who could also grow the team's brand in Europe. After being tipped off about Fritsch, they took a trip to Vienna, accompanied by head coach Tom Landry. The Cowboys' contingent took Fritsch to a field where US soldiers had played American football during the Second World War. Kicking the oval-shaped ball through the goal posts proved little problem for Fritsch and a lucrative offer to sign for the Cowboys quickly followed.

After Mike Clark missed three field goals in the loss to the Chicago Bears, the 26-year-old Fritsch was handed his NFL debut against the St. Louis Cardinals on 7 November 1971. In a tight game, Fritsch's field goal, his third of the fixture, won the game 16-13. The following week he punted another four goals to help the Cowboys to a 20-7 win over the Philadelphia Eagles. Unfortunately, the following Friday, Fritsch pulled a hamstring in training. Clark replaced him and kept his place all the way to a Super Bowl win in January. Joining Clark in the

Super Bowl side was Bob Hayes, who had won the gold medal for the 100 metres at the Olympics in 1964.

Fritsch won back the starting role for the following season and set a club record of 21 field goals. During the 1977, 1979 and 1980 seasons, he converted the highest percentage of field goals in the NFL. By the late 1980s, soccer-style kickers, influenced by Fritsch, had raised the field-goal completion rate from less than 60 to around 80 per cent.

DECEMBER

*'They will remember this goal for
the rest of their lives.'*

Aldo Poy

THE 3-2 home win over Nottingham Forest enabled
Manchester United to open up a five-point lead at the top of
Division One at the start of December.[1] But from looking like
champions-elect, United started to struggle with draws against
Stoke, Ipswich and Coventry. George Best informed the press
that he was off form and sick about the way he was playing.
Bobby Charlton said, 'Players were just doing their own things,
there was no team cohesion, or confidence.'

Derby County moved to second following a 3-1 win over
Manchester City. Alan Hinton scored the opener from the
penalty spot, and it was his crosses for Ron Webster and Alan
Durban that gave Derby a 3-0 lead at half-time. Francis Lee
scored his 18th goal of the season from the penalty spot as
a consolation for City. Derby's poor away form continued as
they lost at Anfield, where John Toshack's replacement, Jack
Witham, scored a hat-trick. The hat-trick didn't kick-start the
injury-prone Witham's Liverpool career; he would score just one
more goal in the five games before Toshack returned.[2]

Derby made up a little ground with a 2-0 win over Everton,
but lost their final game of the year at Leeds to a couple of
Lorimer goals.

Manchester City bounced back from the defeat at the Baseball Ground with a comprehensive 4-0 win over Ipswich, before dropping a point at home to Leicester. They closed the gap on United to three points with a 3-1 win at Stoke.

Crystal Palace's 5-1 win over Sheffield United lifted them out of the relegation places. John 'Yogi' Hughes was magnificent, scoring two goals, one of which would be the runner-up for goal of the season. Hughes and Willie Wallace had moved in October from Celtic in a £30,000 joint deal. At 28, Hughes should have been approaching his peak but would only play a further 13 games before joining his younger brother, Billy, at Sunderland in January 1973.[3]

Another Celtic player, Tommy Gemmell, signed for Nottingham Forest for £40,000 after being on the transfer list for two years. Although he had swapped being a squad player at a club guaranteed to win trophies for one in a relegation fight, he did triple his wages to £180 per week plus £40 a point.[4]

The right-footed Gemmell, rated by many as the best left-back in the world in his prime, was a wing-back before they existed. In the 1967 European Cup final, with Inter leading 1-0, Gemmell pushed forward and fired the Celtic equaliser into the top-left corner. Ignoring Stein's touchline instructions to play for extra time, Gemmell kept pushing forward and was part of the build-up for Stevie Chalmers' winner.

The same year, Gemmell showed the hot-headed side of his personality in the Intercontinental Cup play-off in Uruguay against Argentinian side Racing Club. In a brutal match labelled 'The Battle of Montevideo', Celtic had three players sent off to Racing's two. The referee also sent off Bertie Auld, although he refused to leave the pitch and was allowed to play on. Gemmell was fortunate not to be the fifth Celtic player to be shown a red card when the officials missed his kick to the testicles of a Racing player who had spat on him.

Gemmell won just 18 caps for Scotland, frequently dropping out of internationals at Stein's request to keep him fresh for

Celtic's games. 'Back then, the international fee was £50, so you cleared around £36 after tax. Big Jock would add a sweetener, a £50 tax-free payment for not representing Scotland.'

In October 1969, while playing against West Germany in a crucial World Cup qualifier, the red mist descended again and ultimately led to him leaving Celtic. Germany were leading 3-2 with a minute to go when Gemmell prepared to shoot just outside the box. As he pulled back his right foot, Helmut Haller clipped his heels from behind. The furious Gemmell chased Haller and booted him up the backside in front of the referee, who sent him off.[5]

The pair's relationship had always been strained, but after that incident a furious Stein dropped Gemmell for the League Cup Final against St. Johnstone. The following day, Gemmell asked for a transfer. As well as being Jimmy Johnstone's partner in crime in the high-jinks stakes, Gemmell was the only player at Celtic willing to stand up to Stein over matters like pay. In Gemmell's two years on the transfer list, Stein knocked back all enquiries – including bids from Tottenham and Barcelona.

He worked his way back into the side, playing and scoring in the 1970 European Cup Final. Despite his goal, Gemmell took a fair share of the criticism for the loss to Feyenoord. As Stein started to introduce players from Celtic's prodigious reserve team of young players – known as the Quality Street Gang – into the side, Jim Brogan proved a more than capable replacement for Gemmell. One of Gemmell's handful of appearances during the season was in the humiliating 4-1 League Cup Final defeat to Partick Thistle.

Although financially better off at Forest, Gemmell missed being a Celtic player: 'That meant more than money.' At 28 he should have been at his peak, but he could do little to stop Forest being relegated. The loss of seven successive games in January and February all but doomed them, before Gemmell tried to rally them with five goals in nine games.

With Forest in the Second Division and results continuing to disappoint, manager Matt Gillies was replaced by Dave Mackay. Four games into Mackay's reign, Gemmell was dropped and wouldn't play for Forest again. He had been at the club for little more than a year. He moved to Dundee and got revenge on Stein by captaining the Dens Park side to a win over Celtic in the 1973 League Cup Final.

Gemmell was left to ponder what would have happened if he had hung on until the end of his three-year contract at Forest. By then Brian Clough had taken over and he would sign the 32-year-old Frank Clark from Newcastle and turn him into a European Cup winner.[6]

On Wednesday, 22 December Everton sold Alan Ball to Arsenal for a record transfer fee of £220,000. The sale caused outrage amongst the Everton supporters, especially after manager Harry Catterick had stressed earlier in the year that he would 'consider offers only in the region of £1m and then say no'. Catterick felt Ball wasn't the same player as he had been between 1966 and1970. He seemed to be suffering from the World Cup after covering every blade of grass in the rarified atmosphere of Mexico.

After the sale, Catterick said, mysteriously, 'Aspects of the deal will never be told.' Rumours of gambling debts and friction in the dressing room swept Merseyside. There was no doubt that Ball had caused some discontent at the club. He had done a great job replacing Brian Labone as captain for the last few games of the 1969/70 season, but when given the job full time, due to Labone's injury problems, Ball started to infuriate his fellow players.

Howard Kendall believed that the final straw for Catterick was a training-ground incident when an exasperated Ball turned to one of the coaches and asked: 'How can I play with this lot?' However, Ball insisted: 'I was sold purely and simply for business reasons. Harry Catterick called me to his office and told me it would be a good move for me and that I'd make some money out of it. It was then that I realised what this game of football really is, it's a business.'

'I think we all knew a great era was over the day Bally was sold to Arsenal,' Joe Royle reflected. 'Once he'd gone things began to crumble.' Harry Catterick had a heart attack two weeks after the transfer and, although he returned, it was as a much-diminished figure. He would be replaced by Billy Bingham at the end of the following season. A mixture of injuries and poor judgement by both Catterick and Bingham ensured that the team Alan Ball boasted would dominate the English game for the next five years all left Goodison.

Gordon West would be replaced by David Lawson the following season and would only play a further four games before retiring.[7] Labone would retire at the end of the season with an Achilles problem. Tommy Wright also had an injury-interrupted season and would retire in 1974 before the age of 30. The third Everton defender who had played in Mexico, Keith Newton, had been dropped in October 1971 and moved to Burnley on a free transfer in the summer.

Colin Harvey began to be troubled by a hip problem during the summer of 1971, which would limit his appearances and form until he left for Sheffield Wednesday in 1974. By then, the third of the holy trinity, Howard Kendall, had already moved to Birmingham as part of the Bob Latchford deal. After the arrival of Latchford, Royle was never certain of his place and left for Manchester City at the age of 25. Royle's partner up front in the title-winning side, Jimmy Husband, was sold to Luton as Bingham rebuilt the side.

Young forwards, Alan Whittle and David Johnson, were moved on within weeks of each other due to off-field problems. Whittle never lived up to his early promise, but Johnson flourished, going on to play for England and haunt Everton as a Liverpool player.

The early break-up of the 1970 side and their replacement by poor signings doomed Everton to a decade of underachievement just as Liverpool began to dominate English and European football. Everton's victory at Anfield in March 1970 was their last win there for 14 years. In the same period, they would only manage two derby wins at Goodison.

For Arsenal, the signing of Ball seemed like a great piece of business, but did raise two significant problems. Firstly, his record transfer fee – along with dressing-room speculation about the size of his salary – created friction among the players. Secondly, his playing style didn't gel with the well-drilled Arsenal game plan. One of Arsenal's chief tactics during the Double-winning season had been to bypass the midfield with long balls to Radford and Kennedy, who would hold the ball up. Ball was used to play repeatedly going through him as he set the tempo.

While Ball played well at Arsenal, they only really saw the best of him after ditching the style that had won them the Double. A little over three years after Ball's signing, Arsenal were flirting with relegation.

On Boxing Day, over one million fans packed into England's grounds. The 11 First Division matches attracted an average crowd of 43,903.[8] Given the modern attendance restrictions, it's a record unlikely to be beaten.

In their last game before Christmas, Chelsea's Peter Bonetti had been carried off with an ankle injury after a collision with Coventry's Quentin Young, leaving centre-back David Webb to cover in goal for the last hour.

Bonetti had not recovered by Boxing Day and his usual stand-in, John Phillips, slipped a disc getting out of bed on the morning of the home match against Ipswich. Chelsea called up the other keeper on their books, Steve Sherwood, who was spending Christmas with his family in Yorkshire. Sherwood didn't leave until 11am and, missing the arranged police escort, got stuck in traffic on the M1. The Ipswich boss, Bobby Robson, sportingly agreed that Chelsea could put in two team sheets – one with David Webb in goal and one with Sherwood, in case he made it to the ground in time. When Sherwood arrived just three minutes before the kick-off, Robson insisted Chelsea had to play with Webb in goal.

In the corresponding fixture the previous season, Ipswich had lost 2-1 after Alan Hudson's 20-yard shot, which hit a stanchion behind the net, was given as a goal. With a defender in goal, Robson must have thought Ipswich's luck had changed.

Peter Osgood recalled in his autobiography: 'At the beginning of the game Webby dropped to his knees in the goalmouth, placed his palms together and feigned praying. It was a very funny moment, but he need not have worried.' Webb kept a clean sheet in a comfortable 2-0 win. To rub it in, when Chelsea visited Portman Road in April, Webb played up front and scored both goals in Chelsea's 2-1 win.

Alan Ball and Tommy Gemmell made their respective debuts for the Boxing Day visit of Arsenal at Nottingham Forest. In the 14th minute, Ian Storey-Moore scored Nottingham Forest's greatest ever goal – or, as the cameras were not in attendance, the greatest goal seen by the 42,000 at the City Ground.

I will describe the goal using reports from the game.

'Gemmell sent a headed clearance to Storey-Moore just inside the Arsenal half. With Ball a pace behind him he evaded three Arsenal tackles before beating the onrushing Wilson from 15 yards.'

Alternatively: 'Jim Barron collected the ball and rolled it to Tommy Gemmell, waiting outside the left-hand edge of the penalty area. The Scottish full-back, newly arrived from Celtic, pushed it a few yards upfield to Ian Storey-Moore, who set off on a winding 70-yard run that took him through and past the entire Arsenal defence, Pat Rice, Peter Simpson, Bob McNab and Frank McLintock, and into a one on one against the goalkeeper. When Bob Wilson was left grasping at thin air, delirium ensued on the terraces.'

A third version recounted: 'The Forest striker received the ball from goalkeeper Jim Barron and ran about 70 yards before depositing it firmly inside Wilson's right-hand post from eight yards out.'

In another version, 'he broke free on the halfway line, left four opponents scattered in his wake and finished with a low shot past Wilson.'

So, Storey-Moore either collected the ball from Jim Barron or Tommy Gemmell, and, if from Gemmell, from a header or a pass. He then ran from between 55 to 70 yards, beat three or possibly four opponents, before dribbling around or shooting past Wilson from a distance of between eight to 15 yards. Personally, I prefer Arsenal keeper Bob Wilson's description of what he called the greatest ever goal scored against him. 'Storey went one way, Moore went the other, and I was left with the hyphen in the middle.'[9]

George Graham equalised in the 33rd minute and the game ended in a 1-1 draw. Tommy Gemmell's other contribution was a booking for body-checking Alan Ball.

In August 2014, the *Nottingham Post* listed the ten greatest Forest goals of all time; Storey-Moore's solo effort against Arsenal didn't even feature. According to the *Post*, it wasn't even the greatest goal Storey-Moore scored. Apparently, that was in the hat-trick in 1967 in the FA Cup quarter-final against Everton. Although it was an iconic game in a great season for Forest, none of the goals was outstanding. And if the importance of the game was a factor, then one would expect the winners from Forest's European Cup finals to feature in the top 10.

The article might have been better titled 'the ten greatest Nottingham Forest goals you can see online', as I doubt that a club formed nearly 150 years earlier, scored five of their ten greatest goals within five years of the article. But back in the seventies, only the highlights of a minority of top-flight games were televised. As none of the Boxing Day fixtures was televised, for all we know Storey-Moore's goal might not have even been the best that day.

BBC's *Match of the Day* only started showing two matches from the 1970/71 season, a revamp that included the new and now-familiar *Match of the Day* theme tune, written by Barry Stoller.[10] The ITV regions covered the matches that fell within their particular geographical area. In my area, covered by London Television, Brian Moore introduced *The Big Match* on a Sunday afternoon and also supplied the commentary on a London side's home match. The London match would be the main feature together with brief highlights from two other games selected from the other ITV regions. Jimmy Hill, football's first pundit, would supply his analysis on the games in the studio, utilising the new technology of slow-motion replays.[11]

Although action replays had first been seen during the 1966 World Cup, the BBC only had one HS100 instant slow-motion recorder, which was generally reserved for the horse racing. It was only during the 1971/72 season that slow-motion replays were utilised on *Match of the Day*. Even the top teams of the day enjoyed less coverage than you might think, as both the BBC and ITV were contracted to broadcast a quota of games from the lower divisions. To see your team with any regularity you had to physically go along to watch them. Nowadays you have to drop pretty low in the football pyramid to find a game that isn't being broadcast in some form. Even a Sunday morning pub game often has someone recording bits on their phone to post online.

Back in the 1970s you would be thrilled to see a television broadcast van outside the ground. It meant you could have a half-time wee, free from the fear of missing an early second-half goal as you would be able to see it later that weekend. Usually when you missed a goal, it was gone forever.

For superstitious supporters – like my cousin, Greg – it was important who was actually covering the match. When his team, Tottenham, were in the Second Division during the 1977/78 season, they had their best campaign for a few years, eventually being promoted in third place after 20 wins, 16 draws and just six defeats. Despite being in the Second Division, they still got a fair bit of television coverage, no doubt helping to fill some of the broadcaster's lower-division quotas. On the five occasions *Match of the Day* covered them, they won four and lost one. However, when *The Big Match* featured them, they seemed to mine deeply for the lowlights of their season, televising one win, five draws and two defeats. He would always tell how it took many years for his heart not to sink when he saw a London Weekend Television van parked outside White Hart Lane.

The television companies, when paying tribute to the players and teams from the 1970s, always fall back on the same clips because there is such a limited choice. The reason we keep seeing George Best's goal against Sheffield United is that the BBC cameras happened to be there when he scored it.[12] It wasn't necessarily the best of Best, but the cameras weren't always there to capture his greatest moments.

That said, Manchester United were on the television an awful lot, so nothing has changed there. Of their 42 league games during the season, the highlights of 21 were shown somewhere. Eleven of George Best's 18 league goals were captured by the cameras.

Other clubs were not as well served. United's neighbours, City, were on television 14 times and just nine of Francis Lee's 33 goals were broadcast. Ipswich Town did not appear on *Match of the Day* at all during the season. After being featured at home to Liverpool on 24th October 1970, they next appeared at home to Stoke on 16 September 1972. They did appear nine times on Anglia during the season, but they were the region's only First Division side. Newcastle wouldn't make their season's debut on *Match of the Day* until the cup tie at Hereford in February.

As for televised midweek league games, they were as rare as unicorns. The previous season, the only televised highlights when Arsenal clinched the title with a 1-0 win at Tottenham had been a two-minute clip on Monday's evening news.

If you want to research how good a player was via old clips, even for the players active in the 1960s and 1970s, film is fairly scarce. Jimmy Greaves is still the highest goalscorer in the history of English top-flight football, but I doubt whether you will find more than 50 of his goals online. Michael Owen is more than 200 behind Greaves, but as he played in the Premier League era you will find all of his 262 goals somewhere. On the other side of the coin, some players' reputations may be enhanced by only living on in newspaper reports or in the rosy retrospection of supporters. I have little doubt that some legendary wingers survived their whole career with just one trick. Without the glare of the cameras and defenders examining their party piece in slow motion from ten angles, they could go their whole career skinning full-backs with a step-over.

Although modern television's wall-to-wall coverage ensures that we will never miss a goal, it has also robbed us of a rite of passage. My father would swear blind that he saw Tommy Lawton head the concrete ball of the day 40 yards on to a crossbar, which reverberated for minutes after. Years later, I would similarly bore my son describing Wyn Davies doing the same.

Lawton's old team-mate Joe Mercer's view of television is worth repeating. 'Nothing is being left for the supporter to make up his own mind about. Football has much to do with memories. The memory can play tricks, but supporters love to look back, think a certain player did this or that in a game, that a certain goal was scored from 30 yards. It may not have happened exactly like that, but supporters love to believe it did. Television logs everything and as such disproves the memory. It's robbing football of its romance.'

In the Second Division, Sunderland's Derek Forster replaced the injured Jim Montgomery for the visit of Fulham. It was only Forster's eighth game in the seven years since he became the Football League's youngest ever goalkeeper. After he had conceded ten goals in three first-team matches, newspapers of the day felt that at 15 he was too young and too small and that it was cruel for Sunderland to continue to play him.[13] In what proved a busy season for him, Forster would make 11 appearances, but wouldn't play again before moving to Charlton in July 1973. At Charlton he made just nine appearances before finishing his career with three games for Brighton. Forster never played a league game after the age of 25.

In Forster's second game, Millwall grabbed a 3-3 draw at Roker Park to get back on track after their 4-0 loss at Preston. A 4-1 home win over Fulham at the end of the month gave them a three-point cushion over third-placed QPR.

Queens Park Rangers, inspired by Rodney Marsh, beat Swindon 3-0. Marsh scored two to add to his goal in the 2-1 win over Sunderland and his brace in a 4-1 win at Carlisle, before QPR's momentum was slowed by a 2-0 reverse at Orient.

Marsh had scored over 100 goals since his £15,000 transfer from Fulham in March 1966. His goals helped the then Third Division side to the 1967 League Cup and successive promotions to the First Division. His broken foot, incurred during pre-season training, was a key factor in QPR's immediate relegation to the Second Division with only 18 points. In the summer, Manchester City appeared to have agreed a £140,000 fee for Marsh, but a disagreement over who paid the VAT caused Joe Mercer, who had not been keen on the player, to advise the board not to proceed. Marsh subsequently signed a new contract on the understanding that he could leave in the summer if the club didn't win promotion.

The shock of the month was Norwich falling to a Stan Bowles hat-trick at Carlisle.[14] Norwich were recovering from the disappointment of a home draw to bottom side Watford when they ran into an inspired Bowles.

In September 1967, the 17-year-old Bowles scored two goals on his debut for Manchester City against Leicester City. Three days later he scored another two in the league win over Sheffield United. Mercer recalled: 'Straightaway we realised that Stan was something special as a player, but what we didn't know was that by the time he was 21, he would be impossible to handle.' Bowles was eventually sacked by Manchester City for missing a flight to Amsterdam to play Ajax in a friendly. 'I told them I was on my way, but what I didn't know was that the flight was delayed for three hours. I didn't actually try to go at all.'

'He had brilliant ability,' said Allison, 'but I couldn't control him', – a point Bowles didn't argue with. 'I got the sack from City because Joe Mercer and Malcolm Allison thought I was barmy. It was in my wild days and they couldn't stand it.' After a short spell on loan at Bury, Bowles moved to Fourth Division Crewe. Their manager, Ernie Tagg, was a gambler (like Bowles) and took a chance on a player every other club was scared of signing. Bowles buckled down and his 18 goals in 51 games alerted the big clubs, but Tagg wisely steered him towards Carlisle.

In September 1972, Gordon Jago paid £110,000 for Bowles to take over the QPR number ten shirt worn previously by Marsh. To some it would have been an impossible burden, but Bowles always believed he was a better player than Marsh. The QPR fans would eventually agree, voting him the best player in their history. While at QPR, Bowles would join the group of 70s mavericks with just a handful of international caps, winning just five under three different managers.

Aston Villa, welcoming Bruce Rioch back from suspension, beat Bradford, Bolton and Swansea, making it five wins on the bounce to finish the year a point behind leaders Notts County.

Ted MacDougall scored two goals against his former club, York, to earn Bournemouth a home draw, but failed to score in the 3-1 win over Halifax. Bournemouth missed the chance to finish the year top by losing 2-0 at fellow promotion chasers, Brighton.

In the Fourth Division, Barry Noble made his first and only appearance in goal for Hartlepool. Over the next three games Hartlepool would field another three keepers – Mick Gadsby,

Eddie Naisbet and Ron Hillyard. Even with today's bloated squads, it would be quite a feat for a Premier League club to rustle up four different goalkeepers in four games.

Rod Fletcher scored for the fourth consecutive game to give Scunthorpe seven out of eight points and push them to second, just a point behind Brentford. Fletcher's burst of 13 goals in 16 games would propel Scunthorpe to the top of the table by mid-March.[15] They had finished in 17th place the previous campaign and, after selling Kevin Keegan, must have expected another season of mid-table obscurity or worse. However, the payment of £3,000 of the Keegan fee to Lincoln for Fletcher proved a masterstroke, as his 19 goals fired Scunthorpe to promotion.

Fletcher had turned professional at Leeds in 1962. During his two years at Elland Road he began a teacher training course. Unable to make the breakthrough, he left football for a couple of years to concentrate on gaining his teaching qualifications. He would return to the game with Crewe in his final year of college. While taking up his first teaching post, Fletcher moved to Lincoln on a part-time basis. He established himself in the first team towards the end of the 1968/69 season and finished the following season as the club's top scorer with 17 goals.

He continued to combine his football and teaching careers during the 1971/72 promotion season. Although he top-scored for Scunthorpe again the following season, his ten goals were not enough to save them from relegation. He finished his professional career in 1975 after two injury-plagued seasons at Grimsby Town before going on to a career in teaching. He retired in 2003 as Deputy Head of Humberston Comprehensive School in north east Lincolnshire. Coincidently, another member of the Scunthorpe promotion-winning team, Mick Atkin, also pursued a career in teaching. With Fletcher and Atkin in the side, I'm sure the question you are asking is why Scunthorpe didn't try their hand at *Quizball*?

On the 18th, the 3-3 draw between Peterborough and Exeter started a record eight consecutive draws that made Peterborough the darlings of pools punters. Their draw at Chester on 4 March would help Cyril Grimes to the first £500,000 jackpot. Grimes, aged 62 and earning £900 per year as a wages clerk, was handed a cheque for £512,683 by Littlewoods.

It was Littlewoods who started the pools in 1923, selling them outside Manchester United's Old Trafford ground. The football pools did not fall under gambling legislation because they claimed to be a competition of skill. When Leeds factory worker, Viv Nicholson, and husband, Keith, won £152,319 in 1961 and promised to 'spend, spend, spend', they captured the spirit of the new consumer age. Keith Nicholson died in 1965 and by the end of the 60s Viv had spent the lot.

In 1973, to capture any spare money the public wished to gamble on football, Littlewoods introduced a Spot the Ball competition. Although it was played by three million people a week in its heyday, it was small potatoes compared with the pools. At its peak in the 70s and 80s, Littlewoods, Vernons and Zetters had 15 million regular punters served by an army of door-to-door coupon collectors, who earned 12.5 per cent commission on the money collected.

Such was the importance of the pools that in 1963, after a particularly harsh winter stopped football for three weeks, a panel was formed. Now, when more than 25 matches were postponed, the panel would meet to adjudicate on their results. After the winter of 1962/63 the panel weren't required again until February 1969. By the start of the 1971/72 season, they had only been called on four times since 1969.

The Pools Panel was made up of former players Neil Franklin, Stan Mortensen, Raich Carter and George Swindin, joined by one-time Scotland manager Ian McColl and Arthur Ellis. Generally, they had an expenses-paid get-together, but when called upon, it was rumoured they shared £1,000 between them – small beer considering the pools companies were attracting revenues of £124m annually at the time. From 1988 the panel ruled on all postponed games, and in 1996 it was decided that they would also adjudicate on any of the summer Australian matches that were postponed.

Even though the football pools had peaked by 1994, ten million players still took part before the National Lottery started. In its first year, four times as much was gambled on the Lottery than had been wagered on the pools in the previous 12 months. Nowadays 300,000 people spend an average of just over £3 a week in the hope of scooping the maximum prize of £3m. Spot the Ball has fared even worse. By January 2015 there were just 14,000 players who were dismayed to learn that the £250,000 jackpot hadn't been won since 2004.

On the international front, England, in their best performance of the campaign, won their last European Championship qualifying tie 2-0 in Greece, with goals from Hurst and Chivers, to secure a quarter-final place. The Greeks were much improved under their new manager, Billy Bingham.

Scotland lost in a friendly to Holland. With three minutes to go, Bob Wilson missed his punch from a corner kick to allow Barry Hulshoff to score the winner. It marked Wilson's last appearance in his short but controversial international career.

On Wednesday, 8 December, 17,000 watched the 88th Varsity Match at Wembley. It was the 20th Varsity match played at Wembley since its move there in 1953.[16] Just as in the first Wembley fixture, we had a goalless draw. It was a far cry from ten years earlier, when Malcolm Allison coached Cambridge to an exciting 5-2 victory. The opposition coach that day was current Manchester United assistant manager, Malcolm Musgrove. For Oxford, the draw meant they hadn't won the fixture since 1964, when Bobby Robson coached them to a 3-1 win.

Peter Phillips of Fitzwilliam College had contributed to Cambridge's recent dominance by scoring in each of his three Varsity matches from 1966–1968. In the summer of 1971, he joined Cambridge United to give him the unique claim of being the only Varsity player to ever play for the city's professional team.

On the evening of the eighth, Wolves navigated their way into the quarter-final of the UEFA Cup with a 3-0 home win over Carl Zeiss Jena.

Tottenham beat Rapid Bucharest 5-0 on aggregate to join them in the last eight. Goals by Jimmy Pearce and Martin Chivers were enough in a vicious game in Romania. Pearce, a second-half substitute for Alan Gilzean, had an action-packed 10-minute cameo. He scored a goal, had another disallowed, and was sent off for retaliation.

Dundee outplayed AC Milan at home, but their 2-0 win wasn't enough to overhaul their 3-0 loss in Milan.

At the Potteries, West Ham won 2-1 in the first leg of the League Cup semi-final. Stoke were leading through a Peter Dobing goal, when West Ham were awarded a penalty after Clyde Best appeared to go to ground rather easily. Despite Banks getting his fingers to the ball, he could do little to stop Hurst's powerful spot-kick. As Hurst explained after the game: 'If you connect properly, no goalkeeper should be able to save it.' West Ham, led by a magnificent Bobby Moore, survived the Stoke pressure before Clyde Best volleyed home West Ham's winner.

In the second leg at Upton Park, Stoke managed to take the semi-final to a replay in dramatic circumstances. Stoke were hanging on to a 1-0 lead with just three minutes of extra time remaining when Banks brought down Harry Redknapp. In round two of the Hurst–Banks penalty duel, Hurst once again 'connected properly' but his England team-mate hurled himself to his right and palmed the ball over the bar. With away goals not counting, the teams would travel to Old Trafford in the New Year to settle the tie.

In the other semi-final first leg, Chelsea beat Tottenham 3-2 at Stamford Bridge. Peter Osgood opened the scoring, but Spurs hit two in three minutes through Terry Naylor and Martin Chivers in the second half. Chelsea staged a great comeback, scoring twice in the last 15 minutes through Chris Garland and John Hollins.

My main Christmas present for 1971 was new football boots. Football boots back then were uniformly black, with the choice of moulded or screw-in studs. My father thought any boot that wasn't black and resembling a weathered Doc Martin, was worn by potential homosexuals, so actually getting a new pair on my Christmas list had been an ongoing battle.

Moulded and screw-in boots both had their pros and cons. The screw-ins meant you got a stud key, which could give you many hours of pleasure on Christmas Day, screwing and unscrewing the studs while you waited to get out to play in them. On the downside, by Boxing Day the studs had cross-threaded, sheared off or removed the threaded hole you actually put the stud into, so your eight studs were now four. The moulded boot, on the other hand, was more maintenance-free, but eventually the studs wore down and gave you zero traction.

By the late 1960s the embryonic marketing in football had seen some movement in the boot world. Christmas 1969 had seen me debut my George Best-approved Stylo Matchmakers. These had the revolutionary concept of side lacing, which as well as making the boot appear like a slip-on, also provided a smooth surface on top for shooting. That was the theory anyway. The reality was that there was a very good reason why laces were on the top of a boot, because if you put them on the side, the stress on the non-laced side meant the boot separated from the sole. Thus, you needed a new pair by the New Year.

Christmas 1970 brought the white Hummel boot, as endorsed by Alan Ball. I was quite a fan of Bally until he signed for Arsenal. I think it was a mixture of his energy and being an irritating git. Also his voice hadn't broken, so I could see a lot of myself in him.

Coloured boots are a risky strategy, even now. Luminous green or pink boots on a modern pub football pitch are an incongruous mix. The choices in 1971 were black, red or white.

I was a Tottenham fan, and with Charlie George as the face, or feet, of red boots, that eliminated them – so white it was. The problem with white is that it's not an immensely practical colour in a game that takes place, for the most part, on muddy pitches.

This year it was the turn of the Hummel Tufspin©. To give us amateurs the body swerve of Best, they came up with the ingenious idea of having the front four studs on what can best be described as a turntable. The back two studs, on the heel, were still rigid. The first game I played there was some improved hip movement. I wouldn't say I was now a jinking Eddie Gray, more like my grandfather after he had his hips replaced. Second game my feet swivelled, but completely separately to the rest of my leg. For the next few months, both legs from the knee down were encased in plaster. On a positive note, the plaster did actually stay white, unlike the Alan Ball boots.

The quest for your own Billy's Boots to improve your game never leaves you. Even as I hurtled towards my 40s I was one of the first in the queue for Predator boots, which didn't enable me to swerve free kicks around a wall into the top corner, but did enhance my slice when taking a goal kick. I still put the ball into touch, but now could give away a corner rather than a throw.

By 1971, Christmas Day fixtures in England were a ghost of Christmas past. After a full programme in 1957, the number of matches declined dramatically due to a lack of public transport and the wish of fans to stay at home on Christmas Day. The last Christmas Day match played in England was back in 1965.

North of the border, the Christmas Day fixtures lasted a bit longer, finally ending in 1976. Christmas Day 1971 saw the last full programme of fixtures as the Scots enjoyed Celtic versus Hearts, Falkirk against Aberdeen and Hibernian versus Rangers, among others.

NOTES FROM ABROAD

Atlético Mineiro clinched the first National Championship of Brazil on 19 December. In the final play-off match,

Dário's goal was enough to beat Jairzinho's Botafogo and seal the title. Botafogo were missing their other World Cup-winner, Brito, who was serving a one-year suspension after knocking the referee out with a haymaker in an earlier match against Fluminense. Twenty teams took part in the competition, which ran from August until the end of the year. It fitted in well with the military regime's goal of national integration, and a place in the league became a powerful political tool. From 1971–2001, the format of the league changed every year and the number of clubs eventually numbered nearly 100.

On the day Atlético Mineiro clinched the championship, the most celebrated goal of all time was scored in Argentina; Maradona's second goal in the 1986 World Cup against England doesn't even get close. For the first time in history both Rosarian clubs, Newell and Rosario Central, played each other in a cup match when they met in the semi-final of the Argentinian Nacional championship. After a goalless first half, Aldo Pedro Poy scored the only goal of the game for Rosario Central with a 'palomita', a diving header. Three days later, Rosario beat San Lorenzo 2-1 in the final to clinch their first national trophy, a victory made all the sweeter for the final taking place at Newell's stadium.

Poy's goal is a good goal, as the grainy footage online testifies. Diving headers are usually spectacular, but I doubt it's the greatest diving header you've ever seen? But I never said it was the greatest goal, just the most celebrated. Poy had said immediately after the game, 'They will remember this goal for the rest of their lives.' When he got a call two months later from a group of Central fans asking him to recreate the goal, he obliged, thinking nothing more of it. The same fans then called him again, ahead of the first anniversary of the goal. Poy was unaware at the time, but an annual ceremony had been born. Every year, on 19 December, the palomita is recreated – with Aldo, of course, playing himself.

The reconstructions are staged by the Organisation Canalla Anti Leprosa, a shadowy secret society. Made up of Central fans, OCAL originated years before Poy's goal and is – according to Jose Vazquez, the organisation's minister for information – a 'footballing version of the masons'.

The annual celebrations take place shrouded in secrecy for fear of disruption from Newell fans. Sometimes Poy repeats the goal in Rosario, sometimes elsewhere. In 1997 the palomita was recreated in Cuba, where Ernesto Guevara, the youngest son of Rosario fan, Che, supplied the cross. The following year, 2,000 fans turned up in Rosario wearing Poy masks. In addition to Cuba, the celebration has also been held in Chile, Uruguay, the United States and Spain, as every year, on 19 December, fans from all over the world put on their Poy masks, recreate the goal and send their videos to OCAL.

Another sign of the messianic worship afforded to Poy is that OCAL members celebrate Christmas not in December, but on 28 July – Poy's birthday. The weirdest tribute can be found at the OCAL museum, alongside the ball Poy scored with in 1971 and every club T-shirt worn by Poy for the reconstructions dating back to 1972. 'One day, Ricardo Di Rienzo, the player that was marking me during that game, fell ill and was taken to the hospital,' recounts Poy. 'He was suffering from appendicitis and went to the operating room. The surgeons instantly recognised him. After performing the operation, they didn't throw the appendix away, but saved it in a jar, then donated it to OCAL.' And there it sits to this day, labelled 'the closest appendix to Aldo Pedro Poy, the day of his palomita against Newell's Old Boys.'

JANUARY

*'I have always resisted the temptation to
describe any match as the most exciting I have
ever seen, but this was the exception.'*

Peter Batt

ON NEW Year's Day, visitors Leicester outplayed Sheffield United
for much of the game and deservedly led through John Sjoberg's 58th-
minute goal. With Currie anonymous, Trevor Hockey had to do the
work of two players to compensate. Currie did, however, contribute
a sublime pass to Bill Dearden for the equaliser.

An interesting subtext to the game was the duel of Sheffield
United's Ted Hemsley and Graham Cross of Leicester in
opposition at Bramall Lane. Hemsley started playing cricket for
Worcestershire in 1963 and would help them win the County
Championship in 1974. He left the Blades for Doncaster Rovers
in 1977, where he played for two seasons before retiring. He
continued playing cricket for a further three years, earning
£5,000 in his benefit season in 1982. Graham Cross made a
record 599 appearances in all competitions for Leicester City
in addition to playing cricket for Leicestershire from 1961–76.
It was his cricket career that would be responsible for ending
his time at Filbert Street. After helping Leicestershire win the
County Championship in 1975, he was suspended for failing
to curtail his cricket in time to report for pre-season training.
He joined Third Division Brighton and helped them win

promotion from the division, repeating the feat with Preston the following season.

Joining Cross in Leicestershire's Championship-winning side of 1975 was Chris Balderstone. Balderstone started his footballing career under Bill Shankly at Huddersfield Town before moving to Carlisle United in 1966. It was Balderstone's penalty against Spurs that briefly sent Carlisle to the top of the First Division in August 1974. His cricket career was even more successful, winning the Benson & Hedges Cup for Leicestershire in 1972 and the County Championship in 1975, as well as playing two tests for England in 1976. He was unfortunate to come up against the West Indies just as they were beginning to hit their peak. In his second test at the Oval, he was bowled twice for a duck, but did manage to collect a wicket during his only international bowl. Middle-order batsman, Collis King, attempting to club one of Balderstone's deliveries out of the ground for a six, was caught by Mike Selvey at long-on. The delighted Balderstone congratulated Selvey: 'That has put them in the shit.' The scoreboard at the time read 647 for 7.

Balderstone scored 1,000 runs in the County Championship in eight out of ten seasons between 1972 and 1982. By September 1975 he had moved to Doncaster Rovers, where he showed the effort needed to balance the two sports. He ended a day's cricket on 51 not out against Derbyshire before driving to Belle Vue to play for Rovers against Brentford. The next day he was back in his whites to complete his century. Balderstone was still opening the batting in 1985 when Leicestershire won the Benson & Hedges Cup Final, his sixth major honour with the county. Players could earn around £1,000 playing cricket during the summer, which – at a time when players such as Ted Hemsley and Jim Cumbes were earning £60 per week – wasn't to be sniffed at.

Aston Villa goalkeeper Jim Cumbes was a fast-medium bowler who played for Lancashire, Surrey, Worcestershire and

Warwickshire from 1963 to 1982. In May 1972, Cumbes joined Hemsley at Worcestershire and was part of the Championship-winning side of 1974.

Another goalkeeper who had played for Worcestershire was Jim Standen. His last match for Portsmouth came in November 1971, two years after his final first-class cricket match. In 1964, he completed the unique double of winning an FA Cup winner's medal with West Ham United and a County Championship medal with Worcestershire.

Other cricketer–footballers from the era included Ray Bailey of Northampton and Northamptonshire, Len Hill of Newport and Glamorgan, and Harold Jarman of Bristol Rovers and Gloucestershire. While our versatile footballers were holding down two jobs, others were not so fortunate. There were angry demonstrations in the House of Commons on 20 January when the jobless total was confirmed as 1,023,583. It was the first time that the number of people out of work and claiming benefit had risen above one million since the 1930s.

There were other footballers who certainly had the talent to play cricket professionally. Ipswich's Mick Lambert did a sterling job as 12th man for England against Australia in 1968, but scoring two ducks limited Geoff Hurst to a solitary first-class match for Essex against Lancashire in 1962. Hurst played for many years under the captaincy of Bobby Moore for West Ham and England, but they actually first played together in an Essex schools cricket match.

Chelsea's Ron Harris also had the talent to play first-class cricket. He'd been offered terms by Middlesex after being the first London under-11 to score a century in a competitive game. According to a friend, 'He decided that football offered more opportunities for violence.'

By the 1980s it became almost impossible to play both sports because of the expanding football fixture list, which – together with the disparity in wages between cricket and football – meant that dual sportsmen were a thing of the past.

In the modern era, Phil Neville could certainly have played both sports; many believe he was a better cricketer than footballer. As the youngest ever player for Lancashire's Second XI, he played alongside Andrew Flintoff, who recalled: 'Phil was our team's superstar when we were growing up. To give you an idea of his level, he captained England Under-15s at cricket, while I didn't even get in the squad.' Neville also captained the England Under-15s at football.

Hemsley and Cross facing each other at Bramall Lane was particularly apt as it was the last football ground still hosting cricket. In the summer, two months after helping the Blades win promotion, Hemsley had been back at Bramall Lane walking out to bat for Worcestershire against Yorkshire. 'It was uncanny how we always seemed to play Yorkshire in Sheffield. I played there four times and every year my United team-mates came along to fire the flak in my direction.' Graham Cross had visited Bramall Lane the previous summer, taking a tidy three for 34 off 14 overs. One of his victims was Yorkshire wicketkeeper, David Bairstow, who made his footballing debut for Bradford in December 1971.

Most football grounds have a history, but few can equal that of Bramall Lane. Opened in 1855, it hosted its first representative county cricket match between Sussex and Yorkshire seven years before it hosted its first football match. Yorkshire County Cricket Club was formed at Bramall Lane in 1863.[1] In 1878, the ground staged the first football match to be played under floodlights, and five years later hosted the first international between England and Scotland to be played outside of London or Glasgow. In 1888, the largest ever crowd for a cricket match in England saw the match between Yorkshire and the touring Australians. A year later, the largest ever crowd at an FA Cup semi-final saw Preston North End defeat West Bromwich Albion. In July 1902 Bramall Lane was awarded the third test of the Ashes, and ten years later, after hosting 12 FA Cup semi-finals, finally got to host the final – albeit a replay, between Barnsley and West Bromwich Albion.

By the start of the 70s the ground was only hosting three or four county games a season and had been subsidised by the football for many years. The pavilion had grown shabby and from the football stands the ball was hard to follow against a background of stone and steel. As for the football, the new grass cultivated every year for the cricket made for unusual bounces and changes of pace and sometimes direction.

During the summer of 1971, the board of the Sheffield United Cricket and Football Club felt that if the newly promoted football club were to compete at the top level, they needed a modern ground, and they voted to expel cricket from Bramall Lane. Given the ground's history, it was like a baby evicting its mother from the home. After the Yorkshire versus Lancashire match was played in August 1973, the cricket pitch was dug up to end 118 years of history.

With the South Stand opening in August 1975, Bramall Lane lost its unique three-sided appearance. The new stand would all but bankrupt the club and lead to the sale of Tony Currie and others and the club's subsequent relegation. Within five years of the South Stand opening, United were in the Fourth Division for the first time in their history.

The previous 12 months had been good for Manchester United. Their 59 points from 42 league games in 1971 was just one less than their title-winning total of 1966/67. After last Boxing Day's 4-4 draw at Derby left United in 18th place, Busby took back the reins from Wilf McGuiness and steadied United to an eighth-place finish. Frank O'Farrell took over in the summer and revitalised United with the same players McGuiness had struggled with.

Although United still had a three-point lead at the start of 1972, three successive draws at the end of the previous month had shown their frailties. After Manchester City's defeat by Derby at the start of December, Malcolm Allison said: 'We've no need to worry when there's a bad team at the top.' Derby's manager Clough added: 'I am surprised Manchester United have stayed the course for so long.'

United had been driven on by talented but badly ageing legs and now, instead of the team revolving around Best, it depended on him. Best had become the eighth footballer to appear on *This Is Your Life* in November.[2] Although he was only 25, it was as good a time to reminisce about his career as any. The run of form that had brought him 16 goals by the end of November would be the last of its kind. The pressures of carrying Manchester United had begun to weigh on Best and, coupled with external pressures, made him crack. After the threat to his life in October, he remained under police guard, and the business interests that contributed the majority of his income were also going through a downturn.

On New Year's Day, United lost their third game of the season at West Ham. Harry Redknapp, who gave Francis Burns a torrid time all afternoon, made the opener for Keith Robson. It was from Geoff Hurst's clever pass that Clyde Best added a second, before Hurst wrapped the game up from the penalty spot. Best had a bust-up with O'Farrell after the game and didn't report for training the following week, preferring to visit the London home of Miss Great Britain, Carolyn Moore.

Wolves took full advantage of his absence, winning 3-1 at Old Trafford. Derek Dougan scored Wolves' opener and made the second, nodding down Kenny Hibbitt's corner kick for John Richards. In the second half Jim McCalliog converted a 75th-minute penalty before Sammy McIlroy scored a consolation for United. Determined to make a stand, O'Farrell fined Best two weeks' wages and ordered him to train mornings and afternoons with no days off for five weeks.

Best was restored to the side for the FA Cup third-round match at Southampton. In the 37th minute, Law's header, dummied by Best, ran on to Charlton to drill in an unstoppable shot for the opener. Southampton equalised 20 minutes later,

Ron Davies – troubling United in the air, as always – headed down Terry Paine's free kick for Jimmy Gabriel to sweep the ball home.

Southampton dominated the replay for the first hour, leading through a Mick Channon header, but in the second half Best came to life. In the 68th minute, he turned the defence inside and out before firing home from 12 yards. David Sadler put United in front five minutes into extra time as Best continued to terrorise the Southampton side. He hit a post, brought a great save out of Eric Martin and went close with another couple of efforts before he scored a deserved second. John Aston added United's fourth two minutes before the end. Little did the United supporters know that this would be Best's last great performance for them. In the league, United dropped to fourth after losing to Chelsea and West Brom.

Wolves' win over Newcastle at the start of the month was their third victory in a row, and they moved to sixth. Their unchanged side had taken 16 points from their last nine games. Although the Old Trafford win took them to within two points of fourth-placed Derby, it would prove to be their high point in the league. At the end of the month, Manchester City would put them to the sword 5-2.

Wolves' momentum suffered a major blow when Mike Bailey was injured against Leicester in the FA Cup. He wouldn't play again until the last game of the season. Already missing Bailey, Derek Dougan failed a late fitness test as Wolves' cup hopes ended in the replay at the hands of the Foxes. Bailey's long absence, coupled with their progress in Europe, spoilt any chance Wolves had of at least equalling the previous season's fourth place.

The following season, Wolves finished fifth and in 1974 would win the League Cup. They repeated their League Cup win in 1980 when finishing in sixth place, before financial problems led to a freefall through the divisions. On 8 January

1987, 15 years to the day after their win at Old Trafford, the once mighty Wolves sat 17th in Division Four.

In his programme notes for Chelsea's New Year's Day visit, Brian Clough stated that he wanted Derby to toughen up away from home, where they had lost five of their last six games. With Peter Bonetti and John Phillips still injured for Chelsea, 18-year-old Steve Sherwood made his debut.[3] The young keeper had a superb game and was unfortunate when Gemmill's shot was deflected past him by Webb for the only goal.

Sherwood would make only 16 appearances for Chelsea and, after two loan spells with Brentford, he signed for Fourth Division Watford in 1976. In his 11-year stay at Vicarage Lane, Watford rose to runners-up in Division One and Sherwood would be in goal when they lost 2-0 to Everton in the 1984 FA Cup Final.

Brian Clough's criticism seemed to galvanise Derby into snatching a 2-1 win at Southampton before their 2-0 cup win over Shrewsbury set up a return to the Baseball Ground for Willie Carlin. Carlin had scored the winner for Notts County at Bolton on the eighth to keep his side top of the Third Division.

To any side seeking promotion, Carlin was a must-buy. He helped Carlisle win promotion to the Second Division in 1966 before Clough signed him from Sheffield United. It was his goal that sealed Derby's promotion in 1969. After helping to establish Derby as a force in the First Division, he moved to Leicester who he then helped gain promotion in 1970/71.[4]

Derby's away frailties returned when they threw away a two-goal lead to draw at Upton Park. West Ham could have pinched the win at the death when Clyde Best had a goal disallowed after Robson drifted offside.

Although challenging for the title with a paper-thin squad, Clough played seven regulars in the first leg of the Texaco Cup Final at Aidrie. Despite the strong Derby side, the part-timers held Derby to a goalless draw in front of a 16,000 crowd. Making his debut for Derby was Tony Parry, who Clough had recently signed from his old club, Hartlepool. His £2,500 fee was paid directly to the taxman to save Hartlepool from being wound up. Despite predicting that Parry would be in the first team before the end of the season, it was obvious Clough was doing his former club a favour by easing their dire financial situation. It has to be said, it was a generous gesture with Sam Longson's money.

Parry had been Clough's first signing as manager at Hartlepool. It was said that Clough curbed the nightlife-loving Parry's excursions by using him as a babysitter. However, it was a drunken incident on a pre-season trip to Mallorca that pretty much finished Parry's prospects at the Baseball Ground. He would make just four starts at Derby and, after moving, a substitute appearance for Mansfield Town. Although his transfer had saved Hartlepool from bankruptcy, it would ultimately be at the cost of his professional career.

A 1-0 win over Coventry at the end of the month lifted Derby into third, two points behind new leaders Manchester City. Allison's side had started the year by dropping a home point to struggling Nottingham Forest, but were happier with their draw at White Hart Lane the following week. Martin Peters opened the scoring for Spurs with a spectacular scissor kick to register his 100th league goal before a defensive mix-up allowed Wyn Davies to equalise in the 77th minute.

Davies' goal was his eighth and last of the campaign. His partnership with Francis Lee had been a key factor in City's title challenge, but strangely, in the many autopsies of City's collapse, no weight is placed on Davies' run of 16 games without a goal.

City were knocked out of their second cup of the season by lower-division opposition when Middlesbrough beat them after a replay to end their interest in the FA Cup. After their cup disappointment, City travelled to Selhurst Park where, despite Tambling giving Palace an early lead, goals from Lee and Summerbee lifted City into second place. The capital had proved a happy hunting ground for City, with four wins and two draws for the season. The following week they took the top spot with an emphatic 5-2 win over Wolves. John Richards got both goals for Wolves, but was outgunned by Lee's hat-trick. Tommy Booth and Tony Towers got the other goals to put City two points clear of Leeds.

On New Year's Day, Leeds moved ominously into second by ending Liverpool's unbeaten home record, which stretched back to March 1970. Leeds secured a famous 2-0 victory with goals from Clarke and Jones. A 4-1 win over Bristol Rovers meant Leeds would have to return to Anfield in the FA Cup fourth round.

A week after their Anfield win, Leeds had to battle back from 2-0 down against Ipswich for a point. Allan Clarke's brother, Frank, had scored Ipswich's second goal, and he joined his team-mates in protesting that Allan's 84th-minute equaliser did not cross the line.

All five of the Clarke brothers played professional football, and all but Kelvin were forwards. Although Allan was the most prolific, collectively the Clarke brothers scored more than 600 goals. Allan's first-half strike at home to Sheffield United was enough to seal the win and send Leeds top, but at the end of the month Spurs' first win in six league games knocked them from the summit.[5] Roger Morgan, starting his first full league game for 16 months, was magnificent and vied with Gilzean for man of the match.[6] Chivers got the only goal after a mix-up between Sprake and Lorimer.

Morgan was one of three Tottenham players whose careers would be prematurely ended by injury over the next two seasons. Peter Collins would only make a dozen or so appearances over the next two seasons before retiring[7]. His final game against Sheffield United in May 1973 would also be Jimmy Pearce's last.

Before the win against Leeds, it had been a poor month for Tottenham. They started the month with draws against Crystal Palace and Manchester City before a trip to Newcastle gave us a duel between the current holder of the England number-nine shirt, Martin Chivers, and his potential heir, Malcolm Macdonald. Macdonald's long throw set up Irving Nattress's first league goal to open the scoring. After Gilzean equalised in the 54th minute, a draw looked likely until Macdonald outpaced the Spurs defence to hammer home Newcastle's second. John Tudor wrapped the game up four minutes later after a mistake by Cyril Knowles.

In a month of tough fixtures for Crystal Palace, they found some respite with a vital win at fellow strugglers Nottingham Forest. Willie Wallace scored the game's only goal with a diving header. The game found Wallace and Tommy Gemmell on opposite sides in a relegation dogfight, less than two years after playing in the European Cup final for Celtic.

Palace finished the month with a trip to Anfield, where Liverpool welcomed back Larry Lloyd and John Toshack for their first games since early November. Liverpool were in tenth, seemingly out of the title race as their lowest league crowd of the season saw them win 4-1 to end a run of five league games without a goal. The win would start a run that nearly snatched the title and was the first of 21 consecutive home wins that continued into the following season and became the foundation of their 1972/73 title win.

The line-up against Palace included six players – Clemence, Smith, Hughes, Keegan, Heighway and Callaghan – who would play in their European Cup win five years later.[8] Liverpool would first challenge, and then overhaul, Leeds as the best team in England, winning eight championships over the next 12 seasons.

Chris Lawler's two goals started a scoring run of five in ten games for him. He'd been one of the few players to survive the Shankly rebuild of his 60s side. Another to survive the cull was Peter Thompson, who had replaced Steve Heighway for their third-round win over Oxford earlier in the month. Thompson had only missed 12 league games in seven and a half seasons, before suffering an injury in December 1970. He started the first seven games of the season before another injury sidelined him. A week after the Oxford tie, Thompson made what would be his final appearance for Liverpool in the goalless draw with Wolves. His knee injuries would stop him from making a single first-team appearance over the next two years. He contemplated retirement before moving to Burnden Park in December 1973, where he enjoyed a renaissance, helping Bolton back to the top flight before retiring in 1978.

After their loss at the Baseball Ground, Chelsea dropped a point against Huddersfield. Osgood's diving header gave Chelsea a 2-1 lead, but Huddersfield rescued a much-needed point when Steve Smith took advantage of a defensive slip-up seven minutes from time.

Unlike in 1965, the bright lights of Blackpool didn't distract the Chelsea players. A John Dempsey goal was enough to put them into the fourth round of the cup. They then added to Manchester United's woes with a win at Old Trafford before rounding off the month by trouncing Everton 4-0. Osgood nodded the opener and Hollins added a penalty. Dempsey powered home a Cooke corner before Osgood sealed the win with the goal of the game, killing a Hollins pass before steering his shot wide of West.

The highlight of their month was reaching the League Cup Final after a 2-2 draw at White Hart Lane. Martin Chivers' half-volley had levelled the tie a minute before the break. Chris Garland equalised on the hour, firing past Jennings from 30 yards. The Chelsea defence, with Webb superb, repelled the Spurs pressure until the 81st minute when Alan Hudson inexplicably handled in the area from a Chivers throw. Martin Peters coolly slotted home the penalty to put Spurs back in front on the night and level the tie on aggregate. In the last minute, Chelsea won a disputed free kick for a Mike England foul on Osgood. Hudson's free kick to the near post slipped under Knowles' foot and rolled past the unsighted Jennings into the net. It was a cruel way for Spurs to lose a magnificent semi-final. Knowles would be dropped for Spurs' next game as punishment.

Peter Osgood overenthusiastically celebrated the win and was arrested on a charge of being drunk and disorderly in the early hours of the morning. After Osgood had spent a couple of hours in the cells, a policeman gave him his car keys and told him to go home. He was bailed until 4 February. When his case went to court the magistrate asked the arresting officer, 'Was he drunk?' 'Oh, yes. He was very drunk,' the policeman replied. 'So why did you hand a very drunk man his car keys and send him on his way just one hour and 47 minutes after his arrest?' Case dismissed.

Chelsea would have to wait a little longer to find out who they would meet in the Final as the Stoke-West Ham tie needed a fourth act after a 0-0 draw in the replay. Stoke, prompted by Eastham, shaded an exciting game but were unable to break down a West Ham defence superbly marshalled by Bobby Moore. After watching the game, Harry Catterick, the Everton manager, suffered a heart attack while driving home. He spent several days in intensive care and wouldn't return to Goodison Park for ten weeks.[9]

Seven weeks after the first leg, the epic tie was finally settled at Old Trafford on a bog of a pitch in the pouring rain and a biting wind. Stoke overcame West Ham 3-2 to reach a Wembley final for the first time in their history. It is food for thought that, as we are no longer allowed multiple cup replays, this game wouldn't even have taken place in the modern era.

'I have always resisted the temptation to describe any match as the most exciting I have ever seen, but this was the exception,' wrote Peter Batt in *The Sun*. 'This really was the greatest.' The drama started when West Ham keeper Bobby Ferguson was concussed by a poor challenge from Terry Conroy. Ferguson finally went off after receiving seven minutes of treatment on the pitch, but West Ham held back their substitute in the hope that he might be able to resume. Clyde Best was the player briefed to take over in goal in emergencies, but he looked away, saying: 'No man. Not me.' Moore surveyed a team of averted eyes and told them: 'I'll go in.'

He'd already seen a Mike Bernard shot hit his left-hand post when John McDowell's attempted back pass got stuck in the mud. John Ritchie took the ball and McDowell took his legs and the referee pointed to the spot. Moore saved Mike Bernard's poor penalty only for Bernard to follow up and score. Bonds equalised and Brooking put the ten men ahead, before Ferguson returned after 19 minutes off the pitch. He would finish the game but would remember nothing of the night and was still in a daze when Peter Dobing equalised in the eighth minute of first-half injury time.

Ten minutes into the second half Terry Conroy gave Stoke a 3-2 lead. Chances continued to come at both ends. Redknapp twice hit the post for West Ham, while Dobing went around Ferguson only to run the ball out of play. Stoke looked like they would get a fourth when George Eastham's long pass caught West Ham square, but Jimmy Greenhoff was stopped by a desperate tackle. West Ham should have had their own penalty when Best was pushed over in front of goal, but Stoke held on to reach Wembley for the first time. Gliding across the bog of a pitch, the veteran Eastham was superb. It was hard to reconcile that he and Dobing had played for the England Under-23s back in the 50s.

The epic semi-final had so many subtexts to it, but it was ultimately the tale of penalty kicks. Geoff Hurst's penalty in the first leg at Stoke gave West Ham a 2-1 lead to take back to London. Gordon Banks' remarkable save from Hurst's penalty in the dying minutes at Upton Park was enough to keep Stoke in the tie.[10] After both sides took a breather at Hillsborough, the other World Cup-winner, Bobby Moore, saved a penalty when standing in as an emergency goalkeeper, and Clyde Best should have been awarded a penalty that might have levelled the game.

Moore might not have been one of the long-haired mavericks of the era, but he was the epitome of cool. One of the enduring images of the 1966 World Cup win was Moore wiping his hands before shaking hands with his Queen. The following tournament, he went from house arrest to be the best defender in the 1970 World Cup. Five months later it was Moore who calmly picked up and blew the referee's whistle to stop play when Gerard Lewis was knocked out in a match against Wolves. I doubt anyone was too surprised that Moore saved Bernard's penalty; just shocked that he got muddy in the process.

The League Cup had been introduced in 1960 to replace the Southern Professional Floodlit Cup. While the smaller clubs embraced the competition, the First Division clubs, with one eye on Europe, were not so keen. As the initial attendances were only slightly higher than the Third Division average, the press speculated it would last no more than three seasons. After Aston Villa won the first competition, the next three finals saw the trophy won by clubs who had never won a major trophy before.

To generate more interest, from the 1966/67 season the Football League decided that the Final should be a one-off game at Wembley, and from 1968 a position in Europe was also on offer for the winner, UEFA agreeing to allocate a place after Alan Hardaker had threatened them with a boycott of the Fairs Cup. As a result, only European Cup-holders Manchester United declined to participate in the 1968/69 competition. Everton were the last side to opt out before entry was made compulsory from 1971.

For the first time all four semi-finalists were from the top division and both ties were classics. Average attendances throughout the season were a record for the competition. The four West Ham–Stoke games attracted 171,334 fans and firmly cemented the League Cup's place in the football calendar. Sadly, the season also signalled its peak. In the modern era, its popularity has plummeted and it's rare for a Premier League side to play anything resembling their first XI until the final.

Arsenal's Alan Ball returned to Goodison Park on New Year's Day, for his new club's 1-1 draw with Everton. The defensive, tough-tackling Everton were a world away from the stylish team that won the title with Ball just two years before. The following week he found himself totally bypassed by Arsenal's long-ball game during a goalless draw with Stoke. He must have been hoping that Charlie George's four goals for the reserves would bring him back from exile. George had been dropped after the thrashing by Wolves for a 'lack of sufficient effort and application'.

Arsenal travelled to Swindon for the start of their FA Cup defence. Swindon hoped the bog of a pitch would help them to repeat their 1969 League Cup Final win. Their starting line-up included seven survivors from that game. Unfortunately for Swindon, Alan Ball chose this game to start to earn his reported salary of £12,500 a year. Armstrong stroked in Arsenal's opener after 30 minutes from Ball's pass before Ball himself got a deserved goal in the 71st minute.

Arsenal's fourth-round opponents would be Reading, who thrashed Blyth 6-1 in a replay to book themselves a home tie. During the replay, only half of the turnstiles were operational and large crowds formed, desperate to buy one of the 3,000 programmes from inside the ground that contained a voucher for the Arsenal game. Supporters broke down a gate 15 minutes before the kick-off, which enabled hundreds to watch the game for free.

Despite suffering with food poisoning, Alan Ball had another good game against Huddersfield before being replaced by Charlie George in the 80th minute. Gary Pierce totally misjudged Kelly's 12th-minute cross to allow Armstrong to score the game's only goal.

George replaced the injured Radford for the next game against Sheffield United and scored two first-half goals in a

5-0 win. George Graham, Peter Simpson and Ray Kennedy completed the scoring as Arsenal stretched their unbeaten run to 11 games. Arsenal's display was as good as any during their Double-winning season, but their arrogance upset Sheffield United. Charlie George continually baited them verbally, and Alan Ball, having another superb game, sat on the ball in front of the main stand when they were four goals up.

It was 45 years earlier, at the Arsenal and Sheffield United game at Highbury, that the BBC had made its first live radio broadcast of a football match. To help the listener visualise the game, the *Radio Times* had published a diagram of a football pitch, divided into eight numbered squares. The commentators described the square in which the action was taking place. It has been suggested the term 'back to square one' came about when the commentator described a back pass to the goalkeeper. I'm guessing it was by Arsenal.

Keeping busy off the pitch, Ball set a competition in his *Daily Mirror* column. The challenge was to spend up to £1m creating the best team in his opinion. The prize in this Fantasy Football-type competition was a lavish £100. Ball modestly omitted himself from selection along with Colin Harvey and Howard Kendall, the other members of Everton's Holy Trinity. Ball seemed to be upset with Everton over his recent transfer, hence the complete absence of any of their players in his squad.

His loyalties were obviously now with Arsenal, but there were some pretty eclectic selections from them too. No Bob Wilson? As he omitted Peter Shilton, I guess Wilson didn't have much chance. Bob McNab, Charlie George and John Radford were also missing, although you could argue that none of them was having an outstanding season. John Roberts was included at the expense of Frank McLintock and Peter Simpson, which – considering Roberts only played if either was injured – was an odd choice. Few could argue with the inclusion of Rodney Marsh, Ted MacDougall or Don Rogers from outside the First Division, but I can only surmise that Arsenal's upcoming tie against Reading accounted for the inclusion of Ray Flannigan. Flannigan had only played nine games in the season to date, generally filling in for injuries, and would leave Reading on a free transfer at the end of the season. That said, I doubt Ball's managerial selections will surprise the blue half of Manchester.

It took another 20 years for Fantasy Football to catch on in Britain, although the season would see Bernie Donnelly forming England's first league. At the time of writing, Bernie's league is still going strong.

Ball was always keen to expand his commercial profile, most famously by wearing white boots. Brian Hewitt, who had previously worked for Slazenger, was tasked with the UK launch of Hummel, a largely unknown German football boot manufacturer. To try to get some publicity, they decided to sell white boots and offered Ball £2,000 a year to play in them. He wore them for the first time in Everton's 1970 Charity Shield match against Chelsea. Well, when I say he wore them, Hummel didn't actually have any boots that were right for him to use. Hewitt recounts: 'We took the Adidas boots that Alan was wearing for matches and had them sprayed goodness knows how many times, then added the Hummel chevrons on.' As it was the first time a pair of football boots had been worn that weren't black or brown, they were frequently mentioned by the commentator, Kenneth Wolstenholme, as the TV camera featured close-up shots of the boots. The Monday after the game, 12,000 pairs of white boots were sold, more than doubling Hummel's sales in one morning. Before long, several other players began wearing Hummel's coloured football boots, including Charlie George, who favoured a red pair. In the two years of Ball's endorsement, Hummel sold around 50,000 pairs.

Also included in the Ball endorsement portfolio was *Soccerama*, a football management board game first produced in 1968. It was a rudimentary version of the later PC phenomenon, *Championship Manager*. Like *Monopoly*, each player was given money to spend, but rather than buy property

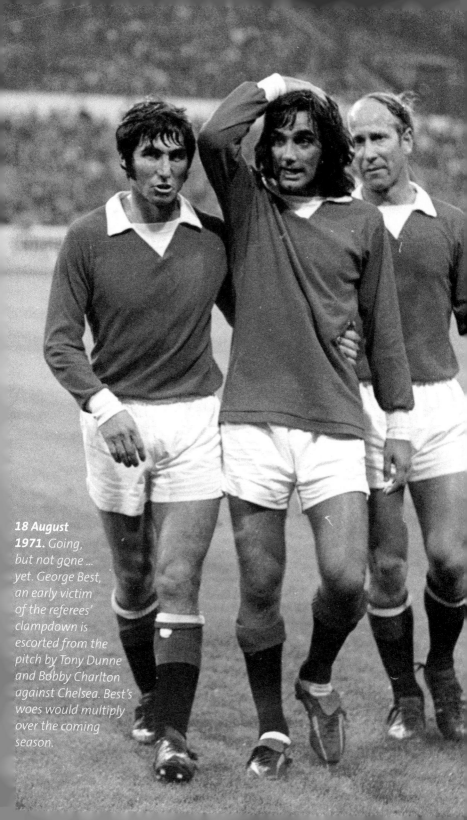

18 August 1971. Going, but not gone ... yet. George Best, an early victim of the referees' clampdown is escorted from the pitch by Tony Dunne and Bobby Charlton against Chelsea. Best's woes would multiply over the coming season.

30 October 1971. *Clyde Best and debutant Ade Coker to kick off against Crystal Palace. Best's contribution to inspiring a generation of black players cannot be measured.*

November 1971. *Toni Fritsch revolutionising another code of football. Six years after scoring two goals to help Austria beat England at Wembley, he crossed the Atlantic to star in the NFL.*

27 December 1971. *David Webb gets a goalkeeper's jumper for Christmas. The centre-back started in goal for Chelsea against Ipswich. Three months later he played as a forward in the return fixture, scoring a brace in Chelsea's 2-1 win.*

January 1972. *Sheffield United's Ted Hemsley on the attack during his summer job, playing cricket for Worcestershire.*

5 February 1972. *Cue John Motson. Ronnie Radford celebrates the Goal of the Season against Newcastle. As you can see, Parkas were the must-have jacket for cold afternoons in Hereford back in 1972.*

February 1972. *Bobby Moore preparing to dig himself into a financial disaster with the ill-fated venture to turn Woolston Hall into an exclusive country club.*

21 February 1972. *Pele and the Santos Globetrotters star at Aston Villa. Could any other player have dragged 55,000 people to a Third Division club on a cold February evening during a power cut?*

8 March 1972. *Hollywood royalty partying with Celtic supporters in Budapest. The most famous couple in cinema, Richard Burton and Elizabeth Taylor, threw a party for the fans.*

March 1972. *Some of The Clan. The Clan was an early attempt to maximise players' off-field earnings. David Webb top row left, Geoff Hurst top row centre, Terry Venables top row right, Alan Ball middle left, Alan Hudson middle right, Terry Mancini bottom left, Rodney Marsh bottom right.*

29 April 1972.
Gunter Netzer in green starting the beginning of the end for Sir Alf Ramsey and a quarter century of German penalty heartache for England as he beats Banks to make it 3-1 at Wembley.

June 1972. What might have been? Frank Worthington signing for his aborted transfer to Liverpool in the summer of 1972, with Reds boss Bill Shankly and his assistant Bob Paisley looking on.

June 1972. *Eight years after receiving a life ban from football over the betting scandal in the 60s, the pardoned Peter Swan and David Layne are welcomed back to Hillsborough by Sheffield Wednesday boss Derek Dooley.*

the player accumulated star players to build his team. They helped the manager to rise from lowly Division Four to the First Division, hopefully, and eventually lift the European Cup. What particularly dates the game is the £40,000 prize money for winning the First Division, which wasn't a great deal larger than the prize money for winning any of the lower divisions. More tellingly, the winner of the cup competitions was awarded a full £10,000 more than the winner of the First Division.

Probably the most exciting day of the season was 15 January, for the third round of the FA Cup. The weekend didn't get off to a good start when non-league Hereford's tie at Newcastle was called off on the Friday due to a waterlogged pitch, much to the disappointment of the 5,000 travelling Hereford fans.

On the Saturday morning, Norman Gillier wrote that it was 'virtually certain' that one of Reading, Portsmouth, Derby, Leeds, Liverpool, Ipswich, Stoke, Arsenal, West Ham or Tottenham would be subject to a giant-killing. Despite casting a fairly wide net, all the teams Gillier selected got through to the next round, although some were a little fortunate. Boston were unlucky not to get something out of their game against Portsmouth, where their player-manager, Jim Smith, would later enjoy managerial success. They dominated the first half, carving out six clear chances, and had two penalty appeals turned down, before Nick Jennings scored against the run of play for Portsmouth.[11]

Spurs could also count themselves very fortunate to still be in the FA Cup. Alan Gilzean's scrambled shot gave them the lead, but Carlisle's Stan Bowles equalised in the 31st minute with a lovely shot on the turn. In the replay, Spurs went one down after nine minutes when Bowles flicked a pass to Dennis Martin to fire Carlisle ahead. Five minutes later Martin spurned an easy chance to extend the lead. At this point, Alan Gilzean took the game by the scruff of the neck, setting up an equaliser for Chivers before nodding in the second. The game was decided when Chivers converted another clever pass from Gilzean. A pastime I'd highly recommend is to look at old footage of game shows from the 70s and guess the ages of the contestants. You will confidently identify someone as being in his late 50s only to discover he is 31. The 33-year-old Gilzean could easily have passed for a 58-year-old headmaster.

At Everton, Crystal Palace's John Hughes was sent off for a late tackle on David Johnson as the teams shared four goals, five bookings and a pitch invasion. Joe Royle was booked in the 28th minute, but the game might have been less volatile had he been booked for his earlier foul on Palace keeper John Jackson. Bobby Kellard, Hughes and Gerry Queen joined Royle in the book, as did Everton's Alan Whittle. Willie Wallace put Palace ahead in the 44th minute, but Whittle equalised just after the break. Wallace scored his second in the 75th minute, but within a minute Colin Harvey shot through a crowd of players to equalise.

John Jackson would recover from his bruised thigh to play in the replay and continue his run of 222 consecutive appearances. He didn't miss a single league or cup game for five seasons from 1967/68 to 1971/72. After he was sold to Orient in 1973, he rattled off a further 210 successive appearances.

The replay was carried out in a far better spirit than the original tie, Everton overcoming Crystal Palace 3-2 despite Tambling's two goals. Unlike Peter Knowles, Tambling was able to reconcile his football career with being a Jehovah's Witness. After quitting Crystal Palace, Tambling moved to Ireland in 1973 to take up evangelical duty in Cork. On the advice of his former Chelsea team-mate, Paddy Mulligan, he signed for Cork Celtic and helped them to their only league title in 1974. He would play for them in the following season's European Cup and serve as their player-manager from 1974–77.

Despite Bobby Moore being carried off after eight minutes with a damaged right ankle, West Ham dominated the first half against Luton to lead 2-0 through goals from Hurst and Best. After the break, the outstanding Chris Nicholl kept

Hurst quiet and Luton were unlucky not to add to Don Givens' goal.

West Brom lost 2-1 at home to Coventry and felt the game's turning point was when Bobby Parker punched away Tony Brown's goal-bound shot in the ninth minute. Referee Keith Styles, one of the few people in the ground not to see the incident, awarded a corner.

Ipswich took some revenge for twice falling victims to giant-killers Peterborough during the 1950s with a comfortable 2-0 win.

Inevitably, four of the six First Division teams playing lower-division sides that Gillier *didn't* pick – Nottingham Forest, Sheffield United, Manchester City and Newcastle – were knocked out. Forest's woeful season continued as they lost to a Millwall side looking to replace them in the First Division.

On Monday, 24 January, 39,000 were at St James' Park for the visit of Hereford United. The match had been postponed twice due to the atrocious weather in the north east. It had been eight years since Newcastle had last entertained non-league opposition in the FA Cup. On that occasion, they lost 2-1 to Bedford Town.

In the finest 90 minutes in their history, Hereford managed to take the tie to a replay. Brian Owen gave Hereford the lead after just 17 seconds, but Macdonald equalised in the third minute from a disputed penalty. Tudor put Newcastle ahead on 24 minutes, only for Colin Addison to equalise two minutes later. After an action-packed first half-hour, the game settled down, with Hereford defending stoutly to force a replay. The replay was scheduled for two nights later, but would be postponed four times due to the Herefordshire weather. Apart from squeezing in a 0-0 draw at Huddersfield, Newcastle's players spent most of the next ten days in a Worcester hotel, fighting boredom and shopping for more clothes.

Colin Addison had only been appointed player-manager of Hereford the previous November. The outgoing player-manager, John Charles, had left for Merthyr Tydfil just before the fourth qualifying round of the FA Cup. Charles took charge of the Welsh Under-23s against England at the start of the month after Dave Bowen chose to miss his first game in eight years to concentrate on his struggling Northampton side. In front of an 18,000 crowd at Swindon, Toshack caused the English defence all manner of problems before goals from Macdonald and Channon sealed a win for an underwhelming England.

England's senior side were drawn against West Germany in the quarter-final of the European Championships. The first leg at Wembley was due to be played on 29 April. As a bonus should England get through, they would host the semi-finals and final in June.

Due to a full league programme that day, the FA unsuccessfully tried to move the tie to the 26th. Clubs with players involved were allowed to postpone their matches, causing further chaos as teams scrambled around to rearrange the fixtures. Alan Hardaker confirmed that due to the league programme the international wouldn't be screened live.

Because of the European Championships, Sir Alf Ramsey turned down an invitation to the Independence Cup due to be held in Brazil in June. There was press speculation that Sir Matt Busby would manage a Great Britain side in the tournament. Although Scotland were already sending a squad of 17, Tommy Docherty felt there was a deep enough well of talent to supply some players for a British team.[12]

Details of the replacement for the Jules Rimet trophy, won outright by Brazil in 1970, were announced. The trophy would be known as the FIFA World Cup and the 11lbs of pure gold valued it at almost £8,000.

On Sunday, 9 January, Granada screened the brilliant Jack Rosenthal drama, *Another Sunday and Sweet F.A.* A week later, BBC2 screened the play, *They Don't All Open Men's Boutiques*, as part of their *Thirty-Minute Theatre* broadcasts.

If that wasn't enough, Watford's home ground, Vicarage Road, featured in an episode of *The Persuaders* at the end of the month. *The Persuaders*, featuring Tony Curtis and Roger Moore, was one of the top shows on television, costing an incredible £100,000 per episode. Vicarage Road was used as a meeting place for Curtis and a spy. The series was very 'on trend' for the era, Frank Muir calling it 'the best bad series ever made … absolute hokum.' Sadly, they only made one series. Shortly after the first series was aired, Moore was offered the James Bond films.

To reinforce football's domination of television, *Quizball* returned with a seven-week series of Home Internationals. One cannot help but suspect that John Jackson and John Osborne were selected for England due to their skill at *Quizball* rather than a premonition that they would be selected for the national side any time soon. Scotland no doubt used the same rationale when selecting Dunfermline's John Cushley.

For those still struggling to grasp the importance of *Quizball*, I can only point out that Sir Stanley Rous was scheduled to present the trophy to the winners. Football was moving into the entertainment mainstream. As well as plays, dramas and quizzes, the following month would premiere a movie, *The Goalkeeper's Fear of the Penalty*. Made in Germany, the film was an existentialist feature in which the central character fails to save an easy penalty for no apparent reason. He then goes on to commit a senseless murder. Football as a metaphor for life, or life as a metaphor for football, was the theme. Unless you are particularly pretentious, I think you'll probably find *Escape to Victory* a little more accessible. In March we'll look at football's attack on the pop charts.

Millwall's loss at Luton enabled Norwich to extend their lead at the top of Division Two with a win at Oxford. Foggo's injury-time winner against Fulham extended their lead to five points. QPR closed to within a point of Millwall with a 3-1 win over Burnley.

The month saw Europe's first all-weather pitch opened in Islington. Costing £130,000, it was heralded as the future; it was expected that it would eventually become the standard playing surface throughout the game.

In 1981, QPR were the first to dig up their grass and replace it with an artificial pitch. Under their innovative manager, Terry Venables, they flourished on the new playing surface, reaching the cup final in 1982 and winning the Division Two championship in 1983. Coincidentally, in 1971 Venables had a novel published, with Gordon Williams, called *They Used to Play on Grass*. The novel predicted the end of grass as a playing surface, and that plastic pitches would become the norm in football. Their example was followed by Luton, who spent the rest of the decade in the top division and won the League Cup in 1988 (then known as the Littlewoods Cup). In 1986, Oldham installed their own plastic pitch and also achieved some success, reaching the First Division and enjoying some exciting cup runs.

The future would be consigned to history after QPR abandoned their Omniturf pitch in 1987, and by 1991 plastic pitches were being phased out by the FA. Luton's pitch would be donated to Whipsnade Zoo.

Birmingham began the year with a 1-0 defeat at Bristol City to leave them still waiting for their first away win of the season. Goalkeeper Dave Latchford broke his finger and would be out for six weeks as he joined his stand-in, Mike Kelly, and third-choice keeper, Ritchie Blackmore, on the injury list. The crisis forced full-back Ian Osborne to play in goal for the third team, as the only fit keeper at the club was 17-year-old Paul Cooper.

Cooper's debut against Portsmouth couldn't have got off to a worse start when his team found themselves two goals down after just 20 minutes. Cooper had little chance with McCann's perfectly hit strike for the first, but he did get his fingers to George Ley's free kick before it went in off the underside of the bar to put Portsmouth two up. However,

Birmingham rallied to lead 3-2 at half-time before Cooper's lack of concentration gifted Portsmouth an equaliser. Not to be denied, Birmingham City scored three times in the last seven minutes to win the game.

The following week, an unlucky Watford lost their ninth game on the trot to allow Birmingham to break their away duck. At the end of the month, Birmingham skipper, Stan Harland, faced his old club Swindon for the first time since his November transfer. Four goals in 17 minutes either side of half-time gave Birmingham the points.

Harland had been Swindon's captain when they won the League Cup and promotion from the Third Division in 1969. The next season he led them to the Anglo-Italian Cup. After Dave Mackay took over at Swindon, there was a tactical reshuffle to accommodate the new player-manager in his specialist role in the back four. Harland's move into midfield was not a success so he became surplus to requirements. Following his £15,000 sale, Harland was made captain at Birmingham and his defensive partnership with Roger Hynd gave Birmingham the stability they had been lacking.[13] A 3-0 cup win over Port Vale earned them a fourth-round home tie with Ipswich.

While Birmingham and Aston Villa were pushing for their respective promotions, their youngsters faced off in the Youth Cup at St Andrews. The strong Birmingham side already had Cooper in goal, Joe Gallagher in defence, and Kenny Burns and Steve Phillips[14] up front before manager Freddie Goodwin allowed Trevor Francis to play in the game. Against them was an equally strong Villa side, including John Gidman, Brian Little, Bobby McDonald and Jimmy Brown. An attendance of more than 21,000 saw Tony Betts give Villa the lead after 22 minutes. Four minutes after half-time Kenny Burns headed down a Trevor Francis cross for Steve Bryant to hammer home the equaliser.

Jimmy Brown was by far the most experienced member of the Villa team, and his duel with Trevor Francis was fascinating in its own right. Brown had made his Villa debut two weeks before his 16th birthday in 1969. Despite playing nearly 90 matches in his six years at Villa, he never truly fulfilled his potential. After three years at Preston, he moved to Greek club Ethnikos before returning to English football with Portsmouth. After a season with Hibernian, he ended his senior career in 1981 aged just 27. I cannot help but feel that there was an opportunity missed by Aston Villa in 1969 when they could have played a midfield of Jimmy Brown, Oscar Arce and Barrie Hole.

Without Trevor Francis, the Birmingham side lost the replay at Villa Park 2-1.

The Third Division top three – Notts County, Aston Villa and Bournemouth – all began the year with wins. Bournemouth's 4-0 win over Wrexham moved them above Villa into second. Although MacDougall wasn't on target, his partner, Phil Boyer, got a hat-trick. The 17-year-old Micky Thomas came on as a substitute to make his debut for Wrexham.

Over the next seven seasons, Thomas helped Wrexham to promotion and to establish themselves in the Second Division before moving to Manchester United for £300,000. After playing for Everton, Derby, Chelsea, Leeds, West Brom and Stoke (amongst others) over the next 13 years, the 37-year-old Thomas asked former team-mate Brian Flynn, now the Wrexham manager, for a trial. When he had left in 1978, Wrexham were in the Second Division, a couple of points off a promotion place. Now they were bottom of the Fourth Division. Thomas helped them to mid-table respectability, but the highlight of the season was the FA Cup third round.

Almost exactly 20 years after Thomas had made his debut, Wrexham hosted reigning First Division champions, Arsenal. With his side trailing 1-0 and with just eight minutes left, Thomas fired a stunning 25-yard free kick past David Seaman to equalise. Two minutes later, Steve Watkin snatched the winner to complete one of the biggest shocks in FA Cup history.

Within a fortnight, Thomas was arrested for passing counterfeit £10 notes. Although banned from training with his team-mates, he continued to play for Wrexham. He remained on Wrexham's books for the promotion-winning 1992/93 campaign before being released ahead of his courtroom appearance. In July 1993, he was found guilty of passing £800 in counterfeit notes to apprentices at Wrexham and sentenced to 18 months in prison.

Aston Villa bounced back from their defeat at Rochdale to beat Shrewsbury and move within one point of leaders Notts County. They followed up with wins over Barnsley and Tranmere to go top after Notts County lost at Bournemouth. Man of the Match Phil Boyer put Bournemouth ahead and Ted MacDougall completed the scoring with his first goal in six matches.

In the Fourth Division, the year began with a punch-up when the clash between Grimsby and Southend was marred by a brawl involving 16 players. Grimsby manager, Lawrie McMenemy, both linesmen and three policemen ran on to the pitch to break up the fights. Referee Derek Mapp could have sent six or seven players off, but satisfied himself by erroneously booking Billy Best, one of only a handful of players not involved. Grimsby comfortably won 4-1, although top scorer Matt Tees drew a blank, as he would throughout January.

Southport remained in third with a 1-0 win over a Barrow side for whom 20-year-old Peter Withe made his debut. While the game marked his only appearance for Barrow, Withe probably remains their most famous player. After being released by Barrow, Withe, unable to find another club in England, moved with his wife to South Africa. While playing for Arcadia Shepherds in Pretoria, he impressed guest player Derek Dougan, who informed Wolves manager, Bill McGarry, that he had found his own successor.

Although Withe scored on his Wolves debut, he struggled to win a regular place and at the end of the season he dusted off his passport to sign on loan to play in Portland Timbers' inaugural NASL season. In his second game Withe scored the first goal in Timbers' history, and by the end of July his 15 goals had fired them to the 1975 Soccer Bowl Final. His form had drawn the attention of several clubs back home and Birmingham jumped in to sign him from Wolves. Withe had a season at Birmingham, scoring nine goals in 35 appearances, before Brian Clough took him to Notts Forest for a fee of £44,000.

Withe was the top scorer when Forest won promotion from the Second Division, and joint top scorer when they won the title in 1978. The following season, Clough surprisingly sold him to Second Division Newcastle, where, despite being a huge crowd favourite, his goals couldn't fire them to promotion. On the eve of the 1980/81 season Ron Saunders took him to Aston Villa for a club record fee of £500,000, which he repaid by scoring 20 goals to help them win the First Division title. The following year he had his greatest footballing moment when he scored the winner in the European Cup Final. He would win 11 England caps. Together with league titles for two different clubs and a European Cup-winning goal, it wasn't a bad return for a player who couldn't break into Barrow's team.

Trying to break their run of drawn games, Fourth Division Peterborough played a midweek friendly against factory side, Perkins Diesel, but were predictably held to another draw. Peterborough continued with a further five consecutive draws in the league to equal Torquay and Middlesbrough's record of eight. Sadly, the Perkins Diesel match couldn't be included to enable them to snatch the record outright.

Brentford scored six goals in an 18-minute spell in the second half to defeat Darlington. John O'Mara's blistering 20-yard goal was described by manager Frank Blunstone as one of the greatest ever goals to be scored at Griffin Park. On 21 January, Brentford discovered they would lose O'Mara's services for five weeks after he lost an appeal against his third booking in 12 months. He had already been under a three-week suspended sentence, imposed while still at Wimbledon. He would miss five matches, including vital games against Southend and Scunthorpe. The lower-league clubs did feel there was one rule for the big clubs and another for them, pointing out that First Division clubs often had television evidence to back up their appeals.

At the end of the month, Reading's 2-1 win over Brentford knocked the Bees off the top of the table and made it four games unbeaten since Charlie Hurley had taken charge. Back-to-back wins at the end of the month gave Northampton an outside chance of challenging for a promotion spot. Northampton legend, Frank Large, hit the club's first hat-trick for two years in the 4-2 win over Chester, and scored another in their 2-0 win at Aldershot. Aldershot sacked their player-manager Jimmy Melia two days later.

After winning promotion from the Fourth Division in 1960/61, Northampton quickly rose to the First Division by 1965. But by the end of the decade they were back in the bottom division. To complete their fall from grace, two wins in their last 20 games meant that Northampton would need to seek re-election at the end of the season for the first time in their history.

The month ended with British soldiers shooting 28 unarmed civilians protesting against internment in the Bogside area of Derry. Fourteen people died on 'Bloody Sunday', after which contributions to the IRA increased three-fold between January and July.

FEBRUARY

*'It was common knowledge that Mr Heath
was a danger to us youngsters, but luckily for
me, he never came near me.'*

Alan Hudson

DURING FEBRUARY energy was evenly divided between
the league and navigating the fourth and fifth rounds of the FA
Cup. The month's games were played against the background
of an ongoing state of emergency brought on by the dispute
between the National Coal Board and the National Union of
Mineworkers. Electricity was being switched off on a rota basis,
forcing more and more factories and businesses to close.[1]

The miners' strike was the most high-profile industrial
dispute as unions began to flex their muscles. In 1970, 11 million
working days had been lost to strikes, the highest since 1926. In
1972 this more than doubled to 24 million days. For football,
the energy crisis meant a few glorious weeks of midweek games
in the afternoon, played in front of surprisingly large crowds.

On the eve of the FA Cup fourth-round ties, QPR spent
£750 advertising their Friday night friendly against West
Brom. Despite it being the first time an English club had used
television to advertise a game, only 7,000 supporters turned up.

The Derby versus Notts County tie was due to have its
highlights featured on Sunday before Derby banned the ATV
television cameras. Brian Clough felt that Derby had already

172

been overexposed and the £87.50 disturbance fee they would receive was insufficient compensation given that they would have to lose 250 spaces on the terraces to accommodate the cameras.[2]

The figures involved seem laughable now, but televised football was only beginning to hit its stride as clubs were still figuring out whether it was a force for good. *Match of the Day* was first screened in August 1964, featuring highlights of the game between Liverpool and Arsenal. Because BBC2 was not transmitted outside London and could only be picked up by the newer television sets, the programme's audience was estimated at just 20,000 – less than half of the attendance at the actual game.

The agreement between the BBC and the League was that 36 matches per season would be broadcast at a cost of £20,000. A couple of years later, the BBC increased the fee to £60,000 to head off competition from ITV. After ITV introduced their regional football programmes in 1968, the two broadcasters soon realised they could work together in an informal cartel to secure the football rights cheaply. Between 1968 and 1979, the cost of the rights to English league football rose from £120,000 a season to £534,000. The money went equally to all the league clubs, irrespective of their league status and whether or not they actually appeared on television.

During the 1971/72 season, clubs earned just over £1,500 each from the TV pool, even though *Match of the Day* was getting 12 million viewers and ITV eight million for their Sunday highlight shows. The cartel temporarily broke up in 1978 after ITV offered £5 million to the League and its clubs for three years of exclusive rights for League and League Cup football. After the Office of Fair Trading decided the deal should be considered null and void, the two broadcasters drew up a new joint agreement for £10m over four years.

If anything united the leading football clubs throughout the 1980s, it was the belief that the broadcasters weren't paying them the true value for the television rights. In 1985 the two broadcasters refused to raise their offer and when the clubs persisted with their demands, they simply withdrew coverage. The clubs were warned that, 'Football rates itself far too highly. It has no God-given right to be on television. It's not our job to underwrite and subsidise the game.' The withdrawal had an immediate impact; the lesser clubs lost their vital share of television revenues, around £50,000 a season, and the gates at the bigger clubs fell dramatically. After 20 years of speculation, the clubs finally discovered that television actually promoted attendances rather than reduced them.

The Premier League was created in July 1991 'to prevent the top clubs from losing income to the lower leagues'. It wanted to maximise the clubs' bargaining position for when the next television contract was up for renewal. By now the BBC had removed themselves from the market for live rights, but just when ITV felt they had a clear field, BSkyB entered the negotiations.

By 1991, BSkyB had reduced its losses from £14m per week to £1.5m per week, but were still £2bn in debt. To try to arrest the decline, the company decided to offer its subscribers exclusive sporting events and targeted the Premier League. Their bid of £191m for the Premier League rights over five years, in Alan Sugar's words, 'blew ITV out of the water'.

From 1992 the cost of the television rights to football exploded as Premier League football turned Sky from potential bankruptcy into a very successful business. In 2015, competition between Sky and BT drove the overall value of the live TV rights to more than £5.14bn over three seasons. Even by a conservative estimate, the total raised, once international rights were factored in, was likely to top £8.5bn over three years from 2016/17. The champions would receive £156m and even the bottom club would collect around £99m. We have come a long way from an £87.50 disturbance fee.

A key part of Sky's coverage nowadays is their Super Sunday, where up to three matches are televised live. During the energy crisis, Halifax's request to switch their games to a Sunday were refused by the Football League, who pointed out, 'No League match has ever been played on a Sunday.'

Football had to wait a couple of years to have matches played on Sundays, and it took another energy crisis to bring it about. The Yom Kippur War led to the Arab members of OPEC suspending deliveries of oil to Western nations and the subsequent energy crisis in late 1973 was escalated by a miners' strike. A state of emergency was declared, incorporating a three-day working week to save electricity. To assist with the fixture backlog, permission was finally granted to play matches on Sundays.

Sunday, 6 January 1974 saw four FA Cup third-round ties played and, two weeks later, a dozen grounds staged league football on a Sunday for the first time. The Sunday Observance Act of 1780 prevented an admission charge being made for events on the Sabbath, but clubs got around it by allowing free admission with a paid-for programme. Pushing the loophole to the limit, programmes cost different amounts, depending on what part of the ground supporters entered.

On the day of the fourth round of the FA Cup, there was still unfinished business from the third round. Hereford's quagmire of a pitch still wasn't really fit enough, but after three postponements the replay against Newcastle had to go ahead. The 16,000-plus crowd was joined by the BBC cameras. *Match of the Day* had sent an outside broadcast unit and junior commentator to capture the novelty of watching a major First Division side trudge through the mud at a non-league ground for a four-minute filler at the end of the programme.

John Motson had made his *Match of the Day* debut back in October, but the events of the afternoon ensured that the game was promoted to the main match. The programme was watched by more than 14m viewers, ensuring that Hereford, Ronnie Radford and John Motson would become instant household names.

Tony Gough captained Hereford despite being told earlier in the week to quit football due to arthritis in his right knee. Gough had made his debut for Bristol Rovers in April 1959, but after that one appearance he drifted into non-league football. In July 1970, Swindon's Fred Ford, who knew Gough from his time as assistant manager at Bristol Rovers, brought him in to help with the reserves. Although employed as a coach, Gough was given the opportunity to prove himself as a player and made his Swindon debut against Sunderland in August 1970 for only the second league game of his career.[3] He scored in Swindon's 2-0 win and kept his place until seven months later in the return match at Roker Park, where he was stretchered off with a knee injury. It would be his last game for the club. After being released at the end of the season, he joined Hereford.

Newcastle, playing all in red, attacked Hereford from the start, but the non-league side kept them at bay. With eight minutes left, Newcastle's pressure finally told when Macdonald leapt above Roger Griffiths to head home at the far post. Needing a goal, player-manager Colin Addison replaced Griffiths with the attacking Ricky George.[4] In the 86th minute Ronnie Radford played a one-two with Brian Owen. As the return bobbled on the well-ploughed pitch, it hit a divot and sat up nicely for Radford to thunder a 30-yard strike into the top corner of the Newcastle goal.

Commentator John Motson screamed, 'Radford again … Oh, what a goal! WHAT A GOAL! Radford the scorer, Ronnie Radford!' Supporters run on to the pitch to join Radford in the celebrations. Hereford withstood late Newcastle pressure to take the match into extra time. Thirteen minutes into extra time, Radford and Dudley Tyler combined to free Ricky George to fire past McFaul.[5] The ball crept into the far corner of the Newcastle goal, triggering another pitch invasion. A stunned Newcastle couldn't force an equaliser during the remaining 15 minutes of extra time and the final whistle signalled a third pitch invasion.

Ronnie Radford's thunderbolt goal was voted the Goal of the Season and remains one of the most famous FA Cup moments of all time. It would be featured in the opening titles of *Match of the Day* for years afterwards. John Motson would claim: 'The game changed my life because my boss realised I could be trusted to commentate on a big match.'

Although Hereford had a race to get goalkeeper Fred Potter fit for their fourth-round tie against West Ham, they did have David Icke standing by. Yes, *that* David Icke. Hereford had signed the 19-year-old Icke from Coventry during the summer. As an arthritis sufferer he could no longer play full time, so jumped at the chance to move to Hereford. He started the season as first choice until injury forced him to watch the cup run from the sidelines. He would win a regular place the following season, helping Hereford to win promotion from the Fourth Division, until his worsening arthritis forced him to retire for good at the end of that season.

Needing a new career, he found a job as a reporter at the *Leicester Advertiser* before moving into broadcasting. He quickly rose from regional sports coverage to become a sports presenter on *Newsnight*. Two years later, on 17 January 1983, he appeared on the first edition of BBC's *Breakfast Time* and later that summer co-hosted *Grandstand*.

Still suffering with arthritis, Icke began to flirt with alternative medicine and then New Age philosophies. This led to him joining the Green Party, and within six months he was one of its principal speakers. *The Observer* called him the Greens' Tony Blair.

In 1990, Icke experienced an awakening when he began to receive messages from the spirit world. The following year he announced that he was a Son of the Godhead, and that the world would soon be devastated by tidal waves and earthquakes. When he repeated the predictions on Terry Wogan's chat show, he pretty much killed his broadcasting career. For those who think that Gary Lineker spouts off a bit on political matters, do bear in mind the alternative had David Icke's career trajectory continued.

Hereford managed to get Potter fit and their fairy tale continued with a goalless home draw with West Ham, who – in manager Ron Greenwood's words – were 'bloody lucky'. The replay on Valentine's Day was brought forward to 2.15pm, because of the power restrictions. Even so, a crowd of 42,271 – just 1,000 less than West Ham's record – filled Upton Park. Thousands were locked out, leading many to believe that the crowd was much larger, but that West Ham couldn't very well admit that their record attendance was for a game against a non-league side on a Monday afternoon. A Geoff Hurst hat-trick, the last of his career, was enough to win the match 3-1 and end Hereford's FA Cup adventure in their tenth cup tie.

In a remarkable case of déjà vu, West Ham drew Hereford in the Cup again in 1974 when Britain was again suffering a power crisis. Hereford took revenge for 1972, beating the Hammers 2-1 in a replay, which kicked off at 1.30pm on a Wednesday afternoon. The game would be Bobby Moore's last for West Ham.

Before Hereford's heroics against Newcastle, the main feature on *Match of the Day* was due to be the tie between Liverpool and Leeds. Thousands were locked out when the gates closed on a capacity crowd of 56,598, Anfield's biggest for nine years. Liverpool were the slightly better side, but Leeds weathered all Liverpool could throw at them to achieve a goalless draw.

Despite the replay being played on a Wednesday afternoon, almost 46,000 supporters packed into Elland Road. Leeds seized the initiative midway through the first half with an outstanding goal. Terry Cooper began the move, which was taken up by Johnny Giles and Paul Madeley. When the ball came to Billy Bremner, he flicked it on to Allan Clarke who lifted the ball over Ray Clemence. Liverpool came close to an equaliser minutes before the break when Larry Lloyd nodded a free kick from Emlyn Hughes against an upright. In the second half, Liverpool came out strongly and forced the home side back. For 20 minutes, with their goal under siege, Leeds gave an exhibition of defensive play. After weathering the storm, they doubled their advantage in the 63rd minute with another wonderful goal. Giles passed to Clarke out on the touchline near the halfway flag. As Lloyd converged, Clarke skipped past him before his sudden turn left the advancing Clemence on the ground, allowing him to finish.

Although Everton won 2-1 with goals from David Johnson and Alan Whittle, Walsall's Bernie Wright impressed enough for Everton to sign him four days later for £30,000. The signing of Bernie the Bolt, as he was affectionately known, would be a disaster. He played for Everton ten times, scored twice, had four fights, and got sent off twice, before having his contract terminated for serious misconduct.

Just before Christmas 1972, a hungover Wright had come into training and spotted a leftover hamper that had been given to the players by John Moores. He was drinking a bottle of whisky when trainer Stewart Imlach challenged him.[6] Bernie hit him before charging up the stairs to look for Harry Catterick. Fortunately, the manager had been tipped off and made himself scarce. Wright eventually left the training ground on the back of a passing coal lorry, still swigging from the bottle of whisky. After just 11 months his contract was terminated, and he moved back to Walsall. When he retired from playing, he worked as a forklift operator and became a part-time referee in the Warwickshire Sunday Leagues.

Reading looked good value to win a replay at Highbury until Arsenal right-back Pat Rice scored seven minutes from time. Tottenham had a more comfortable afternoon at home to Rotherham, with Gilzean and Peters giving them a 2-0 lead within 17 minutes.

Bolton were unable to get revenge for their League Cup defeat by Chelsea. They faced an uphill struggle after the referee gave a very weak penalty, which John Hollins dispatched. Peter Houseman and Charlie Cooke got the other goals to extend Chelsea's unbeaten run to 23 games.

Second Division Birmingham beat First Division Ipswich 1-0 with a Bob Latchford goal, and in another shock result Orient won 2-0 at Leicester. Leicester manager Jimmy Bloomfield, hosting his old club, saw Ian Bowyer – who he had signed for Orient two weeks before he left – snatch an opener. Orient got a huge slice of good fortune when 17-year-old goalkeeper Carl Jayes made a dreadful error on his debut to allow Peter Allen to score. Jayes wouldn't make another appearance until November 1974.[7]

The draw for the fifth round gave us three all-First Division ties – Derby v Arsenal, Everton v Tottenham and Huddersfield v West Ham. We also had a London derby, Orient v Chelsea, and a couple of other interesting First versus Second Division ties. Middlesbrough's Nobby Stiles would return to Old Trafford, and Stoke would host Hull City in a rematch of the previous season's classic quarter-final clash.

After the draw, the bookies named Chelsea and Leeds as 11/2 joint-favourites for the Cup. After only just squeezing past Hereford in the last round, West Ham crashed out of the cup to struggling Huddersfield. Tottenham eased into the sixth round with a 2-0 win over Everton, who offered little threat except the physical intimidation that saw six Tottenham players in need of treatment the following day.

In the other all-First Division tie, Arsenal travelled to the Baseball Ground. Charlie George's two goals made it seven since his return to the first team, but he was criticised in the papers for putting two fingers up to the Derby supporters. Alan Hinton equalised George's first from the penalty spot and Alan Durban headed Derby's second equaliser two minutes from time. Arsenal's biggest crowd for more than a decade, 63,000, saw the replay at Highbury end goalless. The only incident of note was the collapse of a crash barrier in the 13th minute.[8]

Angry fans claimed that they warned police an hour before kick-off that the barrier was loose. The second replay would be played at Leicester in March.

In the shock of the round, Orient came back from a two-goal deficit to defeat Chelsea 3-2. Chelsea were coasting until Phil Hoadley pulled one back a minute before the break with a long-range screamer. Five minutes into the second half, a mix-up in the Chelsea defence allowed Mike Bullock to level, before Barrie Fairbrother snatched an injury-time winner.

The Stoke-Hull rematch was a formality for the First Division side after Jimmy Greenhoff's two-goal burst in the last two minutes of the first half. Terry Conroy and John Ritchie added two more in the last 11 minutes.

Nobby Stiles led his Middlesbrough side to a well-earned draw at the Old Trafford ground he had graced for so many years. In truth, Stiles had not been treated well by United after 14 years of loyal service. Middlesbrough had bid £25,000 for Stiles in 1971 and told him that if he could persuade United to accept less then he could pocket the difference. Considering Stiles was due a testimonial in 12 months, it was a reasonable request, but Sir Matt Busby turned it down flat. Sadly, Manchester United did not have the best record of looking after their old players.

Munich survivors, Jackie Blanchflower and Johnny Berry, were both evicted from their club houses when it was clear they wouldn't be able to play football again. Blanchflower's wife was heavily pregnant at the time. Stiles, George Best and Shay Brennan should all have been granted testimonials, but missed out. Tony Dunne eventually got one after he left the club, but its organisation was horribly botched. All of them were at Old Trafford for longer than Pat Crerand, who was granted a testimonial.

Before the replay, Frank O'Farrell clinched the £135,000 signing of Martin Buchan from Aberdeen. Buchan was only their fourth signing since June 1964. The Dons needed the money to help rebuild the stand that had been burnt down the year before.

Willie Morgan's penalty gave Manchester United an 11th-minute lead, and Best added a second five minutes after the break, before Bobby Charlton wrapped the game up to earn United a tie against Stoke. After the exertions of their tie against Liverpool, a Johnny Giles double comfortably saw off Cardiff to secure Leeds a quarter-final berth.

In the First Division, there was no change at the top as Manchester United continued to implode. Manchester City, Leeds and Derby led the way, with Liverpool moving to fifth. The best game of the month was at Maine Road between league leaders Manchester City and Sheffield United, and it was captured by the *Match of the Day* cameras. By the 33rd minute City seemed in complete control, leading 2-0 with goals from Lee and Bell, against a Blades side who had not won a game since 27 December. Bill Dearden reduced the arrears, but just before the interval Trevor Hockey was carried off with a broken leg after an accidental clash with Mike Doyle. The second half began with a flurry of goals. In the 50th minute Alan Woodward made it 2-2 from the penalty spot before Tony Currie put the visitors ahead two minutes later. United's joy was short-lived as debutant Mick Speight handled Lee's 58th minute shot. Speight was booked for his full-length save before Lee blasted home his 13th penalty of the season.

At the end of the game, Malcolm Allison was generous in his praise for the Blades. 'United are the best side to come up from the Second Division in ten years.' Liverpool, Leeds, Derby or his own City side might have contested his claim, but few could argue with the impact Sheffield United had made. Any hope they had of qualifying for Europe, however, ended with Hockey's injury. They would win just two of their next 12 outings.

Hockey's signing from Birmingham midway through the previous term had been a key factor in their promotion and flying start to this season. While Currie was labelled the maverick of the side, off the field he was an introverted family man. Hockey, however, was a true eccentric and one of the characters of 60s and 70s football. In 1968, while at Birmingham, he released a song called *Lucky Cos I'm Blue*.[9] To assist his singing career, he purchased a pink piano. Also while at Birmingham, he covered his Triumph Herald in blue suede. While it might have been trendy, it did mean that he couldn't drive it in the rain, and washing it proved an ordeal. During Christmas 1971 he polled 29 per cent of the vote to win a competition in *Shoot* magazine to determine which footballer would make the best Father Christmas. After recovering from his broken leg, he struggled to regain his place and United swapped him for Norwich striker, Jim Bone, in February 1973.

Manchester City followed their point at Sheffield United with a 1-0 win over Huddersfield, Tommy Booth getting a rare goal with an even rarer overhead kick. They then ran into the in-form Liverpool and lost 3-0 to goals from Larry Lloyd, Kevin Keegan and Bobby Graham.

Despite losing their last five games, Manchester United were still fifth, just two points behind second-placed Leeds, when the teams met at Elland Road. Although Leeds dominated the game, it somehow remained goalless at half-time. Two minutes into the second half, the floodgates opened. Alex Stepney managed to touch Eddie Gray's shot on to the post, but Mick Jones was on it in a flash to touch home. Allan Clarke got the second, deflecting a shot from Jones. Francis Burns reduced the arrears in the 57th minute, but within a minute Jones nodded home from two yards before completing his hat-trick five minutes later. Peter Lorimer smashed the ball into the roof of the net for the fifth with 16 minutes left.

In the middle of their cup-tie marathon, Derby and Arsenal met in the league. Arsenal won 2-0 with goals from Charlie George. His first came from a diving header before he was brought down for a penalty, which he converted himself.

Arsenal then moved into fourth with a 1-0 win at Ipswich in a game best remembered for the punch-up late in the second half. The incident, which involved almost every player on the pitch, started after Colin Viljoen kicked Bob Wilson in the chest while trying to equalise Charlie George's sixth-minute header.

Since George had returned from the reserves, he had scored seven goals in five games and embroiled himself in controversy at Derby and Ipswich. The maverick label fitted George like a glove; he courted controversy wherever he went. His bust-ups with managers, players and fans saw him loved and hated in equal measure. An early insight into George's fiery temperament came when he was expelled from Holloway Comprehensive School – although not before he was discovered by Arsenal goalkeeper, Bob Wilson, who taught there.

In May 1966, George signed for Arsenal and turned professional within 18 months. A supporter and rebel at heart, he once missed a youth match to travel to Bristol to watch the first team in an FA Cup tie. He made his debut in the opening fixture of the 1969/70 season and by the end of the season he had scored 15 goals and helped break the club's 17-year wait for silverware when they picked up the Fairs Cup. A broken ankle at the start of the 1970/71 season kept him out until the New Year, and when he returned he dropped back to an attacking midfield role due to the form of Ray Kennedy. His creativity blossomed and he finished the season with 15 goals, the pick of which was his FA Cup Final winner to seal the Double. His celebration, lying on the ground with his arms outstretched above his head, is one of the most iconic images in the history of Arsenal and the FA Cup.

His role in the Double-winning season should have been the launchpad to greatness, but injury and inconsistency dogged him. The following season saw ill-discipline continue to fracture his relationship with Bertie Mee. A dispute over a new contract led to him being placed on the transfer list on the eve of the 1972/73 season. Although Charlie stayed for another three years, he never rediscovered his best form until moving to Derby County in the summer of 1975 for £90,000. He recaptured his form for Derby, but in the first game of the following season he was sent off against Newcastle. Injury-prone at the best of times, he even picked up a smashed cheekbone when the taxi he was travelling in crashed.

It was at Derby that he won his only England cap against the Republic of Ireland, at Wembley. Played out of position, when George was substituted on the hour he told manager Don Revie exactly what he thought of him as he exited the pitch. Having burnt his bridges with Revie, in 1978 he snubbed an opportunity to play for Ron Greenwood's England B team. He took the invitation as an insult and effectively ended his international career. Moving to Southampton in 1980, he lost his index finger and the tip of another while trimming the garden. 'I lifted the mower up to clear some grass from the blades when it moved and chopped off my finger. I won't be able to take a throw-in. Or put two fingers up at people.' It was at Southampton where an accidental clash with former team-mate, Ray Kennedy, now at Liverpool, destroyed the cartilage in his left knee and ultimately finished him as a top-class player. Moves to Nottingham Forest, Bournemouth and Brighton followed, with little success.

After retiring in 1983, George undertook a couple of unsuccessful business ventures as a pub owner and garage manager until finding peace at his beloved Arsenal as a tour guide at the stadium.

At the bottom of the table, West Brom's wins over Leicester and Southampton gave them 11 points from their last seven games to get out of trouble. Derby's comfortable 4-0 win handed Nottingham Forest their fifth straight loss. Five points from safety, Forest looked doomed.

In the Second Division, points were shared in the top-of-the-table clash between Norwich and Millwall. Norwich took the lead against the run of play when Dennis Burnett diverted a Doug Livermore shot past his own keeper three minutes before half-time. Millwall equalised through Derek Possee, and Gordon Bolland got a second equaliser after David Cross had put Norwich back in front. Making his debut for his fourth club of the season was Norwich's on-loan Bobby Bell.

Bell had played the first seven games of the season for Ipswich before being transferred to Blackburn as part of the deal that took Alan Hunter in the opposite direction. He played just two games before moving to Crystal Palace. After six appearances he lost his place and, unable to displace John McCormick, went on strike just before Christmas. After three weeks he returned to join Norwich on a two-month loan with a view to a £50,000 transfer. With Bell in the side, Norwich drew two matches and lost 4-0 at Birmingham. Unsurprisingly, they decided against making his transfer permanent.

Millwall took advantage of Norwich's stuttering form to go level with them at the top. Bolland got the winner from the penalty spot against Orient before scoring the only goal at Watford. The loss left Watford 11 points adrift at the bottom.

Birmingham's involvement in the FA Cup restricted them to just two league games – a goalless draw at Preston and a home win against Burnley. They strengthened their squad by signing Mike O'Grady on loan from Wolves, where he had made 28 appearances since his 1969 transfer from Leeds.

O'Grady had started his career under Bill Shankly at Huddersfield. While he was there he made his debut for England against Northern Ireland in 1962. Although he scored twice, he had to wait six years for a second cap, scoring again in the 5-0 win over France. O'Grady has been described as a walking set of quiz questions. He was the only man signed by both Bill Shankly and Don Revie, he scored Leeds' first goal in Europe, and he scored more goals for England than he won caps over a seven-year, two-game international career.

Possibly distracted by recent transfer speculation, Rodney Marsh hadn't contributed much for QPR in recent weeks. The club missed the opportunity to close on the top two when they lost to Blackpool and Portsmouth. They suffered another blow when Terry Venables limped off with a groin strain against Blackpool and would be out for the rest of the season.

In the Third Division, Aston Villa beat York 1-0. Willie Anderson pulled a hamstring minutes after netting his eighth penalty of the season and would miss the top-of-the-table clash with Bournemouth.

Ted MacDougall's 33rd goal of the season gave Bournemouth the points at home to Plymouth. While Notts County were being thrashed 6-0 at Derby in the cup, Brighton closed the gap on them with a 2-1 win at Wrexham.

On the day Norwich and Millwall faced off in their top-of-the-table clash, a crowd of 48,110 packed into Villa Park to witness the crucial match between Aston Villa and Bournemouth. The visitors were second in the table, two points behind with a game in hand. Pat McMahon replaced Willie Anderson for his first game since fracturing his leg in the opening game of the season.

After Ted MacDougall gave Bournemouth a deserved first-half lead with a diving header, Villa had to wait until the 72nd minute for Geoff Vowden's equaliser. As the incessant noise level reached a crescendo, George Curtis hit a free kick into the Bournemouth penalty area and on to Andy Lochhead's head. The ball bounced up and Lochhead reacted first to volley the dropping ball into the corner of the net to give Villa the win. Lochhead also netted an equaliser the following week to give Villa a hard-fought draw at Blackburn before a glamour friendly against Santos.

The Villa board had arranged the match, hoping that the game would turn a profit as well as giving their supporters the opportunity to see Pelé live. The £12,000 fee to Santos guaranteed Pelé would play and, due to the power crisis, Villa bought a £5,000 generator to power the floodlights. The game drew an attendance of 54,000 which, together with the Bournemouth game, meant that more than 100,000 had attended the Third Division side's last two home games. Thousands were still queuing to get in when McMahon gave Villa a fifth-minute lead. Pelé dropped deep to stroke passes from midfield. Although the Brazilians were treating the game as a friendly, Pelé still showed the touches that made him the greatest player in football.

The generator was only strong enough to power three of the four floodlights, so the start of the second half saw a hold-up when Santos objected to Villa switching the position of the floodlights. It would mean that Santos would again be defending the darkest half. Referee Jack Taylor agreed to the request of the visitors and the lights were changed back.

Villa went two up just before the hour mark, when Ray Graydon converted a penalty, before Edu's banana shot from 25 yards gave Santos a consolation goal. Much to the home crowd's disappointment, their side refused to let the Brazilians display their skills, quickly closing down Pelé. His every touch was cheered and he left the pitch to a tremendous ovation. Villa could boast they had beaten arguably the world's best team, but would have to admit that the opposition hadn't extended themselves. The record receipts of £35,000 gave Villa a nice return on their investment. An added bonus came when canny Doug Ellis sold the generator for a large profit a few days later.

After the glamour of Santos, the visit of Port Vale brought Villa back to Third Division reality. Making his debut for Villa was new signing Ian Ross, purchased from Liverpool in the week for £60,000. After a drab first half, an inspired six-minute spell midway through the second half saw Villa score twice through Lochhead and Pat McMahon. The win extended Villa's points tally to 28 from a possible 32 and made them near certainties for promotion.

Villa had more to celebrate when their youth team beat Chelsea in the quarter-final of the Youth Cup. Brian Little's header in the last ten minutes equalised Mike Brolly's opener to earn a replay. Back at Villa Park, Steve Sherwood's heroics took the game to extra time before Tony Betts set Villa on the road to victory just 45 seconds into the second period of extra time. Doug George added two more in quick succession to the delight of the 11,000 crowd.

Chelsea had a strong youth policy during the 70s, overseen by chief scout, Eddie Heath. As well as Sherwood in goal, their 1972 side included future first-teamers, Steve Finnieston, Ian Britton, Gary Stanley and Graham Wilkins, the eldest of the four Wilkins brothers. Mick Brolly didn't establish himself at Chelsea, but would become a legend at Grimsby with his clever wing play. In the replay, Chelsea clearly missed the presence of Gary Locke, who would enjoy a 12-year career at Chelsea after being discovered by Heath.

Heath would leap to front-page news 30 years after his death, as part of the child sexual abuse scandal that rocked football at the end of 2016. The scandal broke when former Crewe defender, Andy Woodward, alleged in an interview that he had been the victim of sexual abuse by former coach Barry Bennell in the 1980s. Bennell had been a youth player at Chelsea under Heath, which may or may not have been coincidental. Within the week, six other people had contacted the police. It was clear that, like showbusiness, football had ignored years of systematic abuse.

On 29 November 2016, Chelsea announced it was investigating allegations of historical sexual abuse, including a secret payment to Gary Johnson. Johnson said he was paid £50,000 not to go public with allegations that Heath had sexually abused him. *The Independent* reported an allegation by former youth team goalkeeper, Derek Richardson, that Dario Gradi, Chelsea's assistant manager, visited another player's family home in 1974 to smooth over a complaint of sexual assault against Heath. Alan Hudson alleged in the *Daily Mirror*: 'It was common knowledge that Mr Heath was a danger to us youngsters, but luckily for me, he never came near me.'

Heath was known to inspect players as they showered and would pull down a player's shorts to massage injuries. He diagnosed pretty much all injuries as a groin strain, no matter what the symptoms. Richardson told the papers: 'There were a load of people who knew what was going on. If anyone had come out and said anything, they would have disappeared. You would never see them again at the club. He was responsible for either bringing you in or throwing you out. You had to be very careful back then. If you said the wrong thing, you would end up not having a career.'

After being sacked in 1979 by Geoff Hurst, who had not been impressed by the standard of the youth players, Heath worked at Millwall and then Charlton Athletic, before dying in December 1983, aged 54, of a heart attack.

Scunthorpe's 1-0 win over Newport at the end of January took them to the top of the Fourth Division. Starting the month with a goalless draw against Stockport, Scunthorpe beat struggling Barrow with two goals from Rod Fletcher. They then travelled to Brentford for the Fourth Division's own top-of-the-table clash. Brentford's suspended striker, John O'Mara, watched from the stands as Fletcher's brace inspired the visitors to a 3-0 win. Without O'Mara Brentford picked up just two points throughout the month to drop out of the promotion spots. Scunthorpe rounded off the month with a comfortable 3-0 win over Exeter, Fletcher grabbing his fifth goal in three games. Grimsby moved into second place and Lincoln third after picking up six and seven points respectively.

Two days after their friendly at Villa Park, Pelé and the Santos 'globetrotters' returned to Hillsborough to play Sheffield Wednesday. They had previously played there during their first visit to England in 1962. In order to raise the funds to keep and add to their star-studded squad, Santos constantly played exhibition games all over the world. The Santos hierarchy were conscious that Pelé's contract expired in 1974, so they continued to cash in on him and his team-mates.[10] The Villa and

Wednesday games were part of a five-week tour of Honduras, Costa Rica, Columbia, Guatemala, England, Ireland, Belgium and Italy.

The huge number of friendly matches does need to be taken into account when looking at Pelé's goal-scoring record. Of the 1,115 games he played for Santos, from 1956 to 1974, 456 were friendly or exhibition games, and 526 of his 1,283 goals were scored in those games. That still leaves more than 750 goals, which isn't too shabby, but it doesn't quite have the same ring as 1000-plus goals.

The Sheffield Wednesday game had been scheduled for the evening, but the energy restrictions made a kick-off under floodlights impossible. Unlike Aston Villa, Sheffield Wednesday decided against incurring the expense of buying a generator. The crowd of nearly 37,000 was proof that the chance to see the world's greatest player overtook any other responsibilities. So many children were expected to play truant that many headmasters closed their schools for the day. One fan, whose headmaster wasn't as understanding, fondly recalls his father's threatening words: 'If I find out you've been to school, and not to see Pelé, then there'll be trouble.'

Unlike the classic 1962 match, the game itself was a bit of a damp squib, and it was apt that it was a fluke that gave Santos the lead. Wednesday keeper, Grummit, drop-kicked the ball at Nene and it rebounded off his backside into the net. The game's only bit of Brazilian magic, from Ferreira, sealed victory. King Pelé, as the headlines crowned him, had a header cleared off the line, but did little else.

The Santos team was not a patch on the 1962 vintage, when they had been the reigning World Club champions, but in fairness neither were Wednesday. Their 1962 side contained the prolific David Layne in attack and England internationals Peter Swan and Tony Kay. By the time of the 1972 return, the three were awaiting a decision from the FA as to whether their life bans from the game would be rescinded.

A couple of weeks after the 1962 Santos game, Jimmy Gauld approached Layne to identify a game he could influence for his betting syndicate. Layne suggested Wednesday were likely to lose their match against Ipswich on 1 December. Shortly afterwards, Layne recounted to his team-mates, Swan and Kay, what Gauld had told him about the money to be made if Wednesday were to lose at Ipswich. The pair agreed that the team generally lost at Portman Road and each gave Layne £50 to pass on to Gauld, to place a bet on Ipswich winning at odds of 2/1.[11]

To illustrate their naivety, even though they were aware that Gauld had fixed two other games, they only bet on their own game rather than an accumulator. Wednesday subsequently lost 2-0 to Ipswich, although Tony Kay was named by the *Sunday People* as the man of the match. The three thought no more about it until a year later, when Gauld's betting syndicate tried to fix the result of the match between Bradford Park Avenue and Bristol Rovers, to farcical results.[12]

The *Sunday People* got wind that a number of lower-division games had been fixed and approached the ringleader. Gauld, in search of a final pay day, sold his story to *The People* and served up Swan, Layne and Kay to satisfy the paper's need for bigger names.[13] Gauld arranged to meet with Layne and Kay separately in his car and raised the subject of the fixed match while recording the conversations. *The People* broke the story and the taped conversations would be used to convict the players in January 1965.[14] Despite the corruption, which mainly involved lower-league games, it was the Ipswich/Wednesday match that captured the headlines. The three players were found guilty of bribery, corruption and defrauding the bookmakers, and were sentenced to four months' imprisonment and a fine of £100. On their release from prison, Layne, Swan and Kay – together with the other players involved in the scandal – were banned for life from any further participation in football.

At the time of his ban, Swan had won 19 caps for England and at 28 was at his peak. The older Charlton, Jack, hadn't made his England debut yet and many are convinced that had Swan not been banned, he, rather than Charlton, would have partnered Bobby Moore in defence in 1966. Some also believe that the redhead in England's midfield that day might have been Tony Kay rather than Alan Ball.

Member of Parliament, Joe Ashton, a Sheffield Wednesday fan, took up their case, backed by Sir Matt Busby and Cliff Lloyd, the PFA secretary. In January 1971, the FA announced that players and officials under permanent suspension would be able to appeal after seven years and, thanks to the lobbying of Ashton, Busby and Lloyd, 34-year-old Peter Swan and 32-year-old David Layne had their bans lifted in June 1972. As Tony Kay was living in Spain, Football League President Len Shipman said it was impossible to deal with his case in his absence.[15] Two days later, Sheffield Wednesday confirmed that they would take back Swan and Layne.

On 12 August 1972, Peter Swan played his first game in eight years against Fulham. As the players went down the tunnel, they held back to let Swan run out alone to receive a tremendous ovation from the Hillsborough crowd. Swan would play 13 games and make a couple of substitute appearances, but by November had lost his place.[16] Layne was unable to break into the team and went on loan to Hereford, making his debut in December. He played just three more games before retiring from professional football.

The following summer, Swan signed for Bury, who offered him the captaincy and guaranteed first-team football. Within 95 seconds of his Bury debut, Swan scored the first goal of a career that had begun 18 years earlier. He played 35 games for Bury, netting another goal, as he helped them win promotion from Division Four. After only being offered a month-to-month contract, he left Bury in the summer of 1974 to become the player-manager of non-league Matlock Town. In his first season at the helm, Swan took Matlock to the final of the 1975 FA Trophy. Nearly 13 years to the day since Peter

Swan last played at Wembley, he returned to lead his side to a 4-0 victory.

German football spent the season coping with its own match-fixing scandal. The resulting investigation discovered that Eintracht Braunschweig players had been promised a bonus by a third party if they beat Oberhausen. Despite the fact that they had been incentivised to win, Eintracht Braunschweig were punished, if anything, even more harshly than the other clubs involved. Lothar Ulsab and Max Lorenz were suspended for the season and ten other players, as well as the club itself, were heavily fined.

Although they are now in the second tier of the German league system and relatively unknown, at the time Eintracht Braunschweig were one of the biggest names in German football. Unlike Bayern Munich and Borussia Mönchengladbach, they had been one of the original 16 teams selected to play in the inaugural Bundesliga in 1963, and they won the title in 1967. Their title-winning side was hit by tragedy the following year, when their 29-year-old forward, Jürgen Moll, and his wife, the actress Sigrid Mollwitz, died in a car accident.

In the aftermath of the match-fixing scandal, their results slumped, and fans stayed away in their droves. More than 6.3 million people had watched Bundesliga games live in 1970/71, but the figure dropped to 5.5 million in 1972, and barely five million a year later.

Unlike most teams in the league, Braunschweig owned their stadium and as the crowds fell the upkeep of the stadium pushed them to the brink financially. Günter Mast, the chief executive of Mast-Jägermeister, became aware of his local club's financial plight and arranged a meeting with their chairman, Ernst Fricke, to formulate a plan that would eventually revolutionise world football.

The German Football Association (the DFB) had strict anti-commercialism rules, and an initial approach in August 1972 to put the Jägermeister name on Braunschweig's shirts was immediately rejected. However, the rule that only a club's badge could be displayed on a team's shirt had left a loophole, that allowed for a symbol that bore a resemblance to the club's official crest. After some heavy petitioning by Fricke, the Braunschweig members agreed to change the club's lion badge to the Jägermeister deer's head. Reports of the figures involved vary from an initial payment of 90,000 Deutschmarks to a deal worth 800,000 Deutschmarks over five years.

The DFB looked at ways they could stop Braunschweig from sporting the new badge, but could only find one point of contention: the club had increased the size of the new badge to 18cm and placed it in the middle of the players' chests. Braunschweig happily complied with the DFB's demand that the club reduce the size of the crest to 14cm. On 24 March 1973, the kit was worn for the first time against Schalke, after the referee checked every badge with a tape measure.

Within seven months, under the weight of a huge number of similar requests, the DFB officially sanctioned shirt sponsorship. The English FA eventually gave in to pressure and allowed shirt sponsorship in June 1977. The television companies eventually relented from their initial refusal to show teams with company names on their shirts and the full potential of shirt sponsorship became evident for all to see. By the mid-80s, nearly every team in Europe had a sponsor.

Revenue from shirt sponsorship is now a huge money-spinner for clubs. Manchester United wear the Chevrolet name on their shirts, for which the car company is delighted to pay £53m a year for the duration of the seven-year contract. And now, unlike the early 70s, Manchester United do not even have to buy their own kits. Adidas is happy to remove that burden and pay United £75m a year for the privilege.

Prior to 1971, United had worn the same kit for ten years, but at the start of the 71/72 season, the club introduced three new kits. The first-team shirt was red with a white solid v-neck infill collar and white cuffs, with white shorts. The second kit was the same design but in all white. Unusually for the era, they added a third strip of yellow shirts with blue collar and cuffs and blue shorts. The kits were quite cutting-edge for the time and would be worn for the next three seasons, the only change being the addition of the club badge the following season. Including second kits, United had essentially only worn eight different kits in the 32 years from 1939; over the last 32 years, they have showcased 72 different kits.

Back in 1971, replica kits were only available in children's sizes. Umbro marketed selected replica kits for children, which sold for £2.30.[17] The badge was an extra 30p and had to be sewn on. The kits were not specifically linked to a club, but were offered in the 'club colours of ... ' and so the clubs didn't receive any revenue from them. Neither manufacturers nor football clubs had yet copyrighted kit designs or club badges, so there was nothing to stop multiple companies producing and selling the same club's kit. Both Umbro and Admiral manufactured replica Manchester United children's kits during the 1973/74 season. In reality, they were just unbadged red shirts with a white infill collar and cuffs, matched with white shorts and black socks. The minimalism of kit designs often meant one kit would suffice for several teams. Admiral's 1973 advert for a replica kit of white shirts and navy shorts was referred to as representing Spurs, Derby and England.

It was Admiral who became the first company to link up with a football club when it established a licensing arrangement with Leeds in 1973. The specifics of the deal were that Admiral redesigned the kit and, after copyrighting the design, became the sole legal supplier to retail outlets. In return, the company paid Leeds a fee believed to be £10,000, offset against a five per cent royalty on sales of the club's Admiral clothing and leisurewear. The immediate success of the partnership encouraged almost all English Football League clubs to sign similar deals as other kit manufacturers joined in the scramble for contracts.

Change strips, or away kits as they are now called, were being worn even when team colours did not clash, in order to promote and popularise them among potential consumers. The kits – or specifically the shirts – now available in adult sizes, would eventually be marketed in a different way. Whereas previous adverts depicted famous players, or children dressed in the full kit playing the game or within a team photo, replica shirts would be shown in combination with jeans as the manufacturers tried to rebrand sportswear as leisurewear.

United now sell an average of one and a half million replica shirts a year globally. It is unknown how much Adidas make, but the industry standard is for the kit provider to receive 85–90 per cent of all revenue from shirt sales after paying the club their licensing fee. The club do earn extra revenue from the printing of the players' names on the shirt, together with the badge. United now earn nearly £100m from retail, merchandising, apparel and products licensing revenue.

As for the club that started the windfall, Braunschweig were relegated and spent 1973/74 in the Second Division. They battled back into the top division, only missing the 1977 title by one point.[18] An attempt in 1983 to rename them as Eintracht Jägermeister was refused by the DFB. In 1984/85, Eintracht Braunschweig were relegated from the Bundesliga again. Despite their difficulties, Jägermeister continued to sponsor the club until 1987.

At the end of the month Pelé turned down £1,500 to guest for Fulham in their showpiece friendly against Benfica. Fulham managed to cope without him to beat Benfica 3-2 in front of a disappointing crowd of 15,000. The friendly had been arranged to celebrate the opening of Fulham's new stand along the river side of the ground, from where fans turned their heads annually to watch The Boat Race. The board had commissioned the stand in 1967 when they were still a top-flight club, but they were now in the Second Division after being promoted the previous season.

The relegations reflected in Fulham's gates, which had halved to around 11,000. Not only would the stand be harder to fill, but its cost of £334,000 would prove harder to repay. Its costs would have huge ramifications for the club that extended well into the 1990s. The stand was named after Eric Miller, who held a controlling stake in the club. In 1976 Miller would receive a knighthood in Prime Minister Harold Wilson's controversial retirement honours list.

Miller's inclusion in the list was heavily criticised, as rumours were already growing that the financial dealings of his companies had not been legitimate. Miller had been involved in the Poulson affair, a corruption case that shook the country in the 70s. John Poulson had built the biggest architectural practice in Europe by bribing MPs, councillors and civil servants to win building contracts. Many towns lost their character with needless ugly facelifts as tower blocks created concrete cities in the sky. Many were purely built for the benefit of Poulson and to better the lifestyles of those on his payroll.

The corruption came to light in June 1972. When Poulson became insolvent, his meticulously maintained accounts would be open to investigators at the bankruptcy hearings. Miller repaid the £250,000 tax bill to stop the hearings, but the genie was out of the bottle. Before long, the scale of corruption was revealed to go as high as the Conservative Home Secretary, Reginald Maudling, a friend of Poulson and Miller. In 1977, a year after being awarded his knighthood, Miller shot himself while under investigation for fraud. The stand at Fulham is now rather less infamously known as the Riverside Stand.

Chelsea recorded their League Cup Final song, *Blue is the Colour*, at a studio in Islington while lubricated by a couple of cases of vodka. The single did well, climbing to number five in the charts, only being topped by the classic singles 'Without You', 'American Pie' and 'Son of My Father', as well as the not-so-classic Eurovision entry, 'Beg Steal or Borrow'. It did, however, outsell Michael Jackson's debut single, 'Got To Be There'.

The squad, fuelled by four bottles of vodka and a couple of crates of lager, would perform their song on *Top of the Pops*. Despite its 12-week stay in the charts, the song only made the players around £300 each.

The Football League announced that all four Home Countries would finally get their players released for international commitments, a luxury previously only enjoyed by England. After years of injustice, Wales, Scotland and Ireland could now field their strongest sides for all competitive matches without fear of club calls on their players.

Only Northern Ireland were in international action during the month, earning a 1-1 draw with Spain at 'home' in Hull. Due to the Troubles, Boothferry Park hosted the rescheduled European Championship qualifier. If that wasn't surreal enough, the game was played on a Wednesday afternoon because of the power crisis.

On Thursday, 10 February, the *Daily Mirror* carried a publicity photo of Bobby Moore in wellington boots at Woolston Hall, for a venture he was fronting with Sean Connery. Moore, like many gifted footballers, was not a talented businessman, and the project to convert the Essex manor house into an exclusive £100-a-year country club drove him to the brink of bankruptcy. As a director, he invested £5,000 and freely gave the use of his name. The project was cursed from the beginning. As the debts mounted, Moore took on increased guarantees at the bank. The club opened for business in August 1972, but within 18 months the owners decided to cut their losses and sell. The outstanding debts amounted to £100,000 and Moore found himself the only partner sued for the sum. It is believed that the costs and legal fees of the subsequent lengthy litigation cost him most of his career earnings. Soon after, a successful leather goods manufacturer he co-owned was unable to operate profitably in Britain because of the three-day week, so Moore moved his factory over to Northern Cyprus. Weeks later, Turkey invaded and that business bit the dust as well.

NOTES FROM ABROAD

On the 23rd, at The Maracanã stadium, where he had experienced so many triumphs, Garrincha made his debut for Olaria.

Second-tier Olaria had lured him out of retirement with a salary of 5,000 cruzeiros a month and a share of the gate money. The increased gates and publicity made it a good commercial move for the club, but what could they expect from the 38-year-old Garrincha, who had been washed up when he left Flamengo back in 1969?

Nearly 50,000 turned up for his debut and saw his pass lead to the opening goal. Although Flamengo equalised, the result was less important to the crowd than the opportunity to see Garrincha play. At the end of the game he was in pain with a swollen knee and realised that he would only be able to play in selected matches. Between February and August, he played ten times, scoring once, before retiring for good.

A testimonial match at The Maracanã in December 1973 gave him the chance to say a proper goodbye to his adoring public. The 1970 Brazil side, with Paulo Cezar and himself replacing Tostão and Gérson, played a FIFA world side. The referee stopped the match so Garrincha could leave the pitch to receive the applause of the 131,000 crowd. The match raised nearly one million cruzeiros[19], which should have given Garrincha a comfortable retirement, but he was already too far down the road to self-destruction. In January 1983, aged just 49, Garrincha died of cirrhosis of the liver, forgotten and destitute. His funeral procession, from the Maracanã to his birthplace, Pau Grande, drew millions of fans, friends and former players to pay their respects.

His epitaph reads: 'Here rests in peace the one who was the Joy of the People – Mané Garrincha.'

MARCH

*'I suppose you could carbon-date the start of
Chelsea's and my own decline from that day
and George Eastham's goal.'*

Peter Osgood

IN THE Cup Winners' Cup, a fine defensive performance earned Rangers a valuable draw in Turin. Rangers opened the scoring through Willie Johnston. After keeping the Rangers goal under siege, Torino equalised after 64 minutes when Paolo Pulici diverted a Giovanni Toschi shot past Peter McCloy. In the return leg Rangers again played tightly, an Alex MacDonald goal in the first minute of the second half being enough to send them through to the semi-final.

Rangers' result against a Torino side that would finish third in Serie A was a good one. The Italian club looked to have finally overcome the tragedies that had plagued them since the war. On 4 May 1949, a plane carrying the entire Torino team home from playing a friendly in Lisbon crashed. At the time, the Grande Torino were chasing their fifth successive title and supplied most of the national side. All but the full-back, Sauro Toma, who missed the trip due to a knee injury, were killed. The club sued the airline company for the damage they had sustained, but after several court cases, the High Court decided that compensation should be paid only for damage to people and property, and not any extra for the 'sporting value' of the players.

Difficult years followed the Superga air disaster. A slow decline led to the club's first relegation in 1959, although they returned to the top flight after one season. In 1963 they appointed Nereo Rocco as manager and by October 1967 the team, inspired by the 24-year-old Gigi Meroni, started challenging for the title again when another tragedy struck. After an evening out, Meroni and team-mate, Fabrizio Poletti, were crossing two lanes of traffic. Meroni took a step back to avoid a fast car to his right, but was struck by a Fiat Coupé that was overtaking at speed. Both men were hit, with Meroni being struck on the leg and thrown to the other side of the road, where an onrushing car hit him and killed him. In an incredible twist to the story, Attilio Romero, the 19-year-old driver of the Fiat, would be appointed as Torino's president in 2000.

Meroni's death marked a significant turning point in Torino's and world football's history, as it was the precedent for insurance payouts to clubs who had lost players through injury or death. Torino again sued the airline in respect of the Superga tragedy and this time their insurance claim was successful, with a final judgement in 1971. Torino were one of the strongest teams in Italy, winning the Scudetto in 1976. Had Meroni not been killed, it might well have been Torino, not their neighbours, Juventus, who dominated Italian football during the 70s.

Celtic travelled to Hungary to play an Ujpest Dosza side that had only played three competitive games since their winter break. Ujpest still seemed to be in hibernation when Celtic got the opening goal in the 20th minute. József Horvath headed Jim Brogan's hopeful long ball past his own keeper. The defender made amends with a vicious rising shot from 35 yards to equalise in the 64th minute. Celtic withstood heavy pressure before snatching a late winner through Lou Macari.

Some of the travelling Celtic supporters returned to the Duna Intercontinental Hotel in Budapest to celebrate the win. Richard Burton, in Budapest filming *Bluebeard*, was staying in the penthouse suite with his wife, Elizabeth Taylor. When they heard they were sharing a hotel with 130 of the Celtic fans, they immediately invited everybody to a party in the hotel lounge. The Hollywood stars left £5,000 behind the bar to pay for champagne and caviar and were happy to pose in Celtic scarves with the fans. Burton delighted the fans by singing 'I Belong to Glasgow' and Taylor was presented with flowers by the star-struck fans. The bash allegedly went on for more than eight hours.

In the second leg at Parkhead, 75,000 saw Lou Macari capitalise on a poor back pass to lob the Ujpest keeper and equalise Antal Dunai's fifth-minute goal. The draw was enough to put Celtic into their third European Cup semi-final in six years.

They were joined by Inter Milan, Benfica and Ajax, who ended English hopes by knocking out Arsenal. The Gunners had got off to a wonderful start in the first leg when Ray Kennedy gave them the lead on 15 minutes after intercepting Piet Keizer's back pass to Heinz Stuy. From then on it was all Ajax. Sjaak Swart hit the bar and Dick Van Dijk hit a post before the Dutch side equalised in the 26th minute. Bob Wilson had Gerrie Muhren's shot covered until it hit Peter Simpson to deflect past him. Arsenal somehow limped into half-time with the scores level, which didn't reflect Ajax's superiority as much as the goal attempts did – 17 to Ajax, two to Arsenal. Arsenal kept on terms until conceding a soft penalty in the 72nd minute. Van Dijk went down rather easily after a soft challenge and Muhren sent Wilson the wrong way from the spot.

The ineligible Alan Ball, who had watched the game from the stands, had his house burgled while he was away. His FA Cup and League Championship medals won at Everton were stolen, but fortunately his World Cup medal was with his parents.

At Highbury, Arsenal only required a 1-0 win to knock out Ajax, but missed a golden opportunity in the third minute. Peter

Marinello, clean through after an error by Ajax, shot into the arms of Stuy. In the 15th minute Ajax got the vital away goal when George Graham headed into his own net while trying to clear. Charlie George had a chance to score a quick equaliser, but he blasted wide with pretty much Arsenal's last chance.

Spurs put one foot in the UEFA Cup semi-finals with a 2-0 win away to UT Arad. In the return leg they seemed to be nursing a hangover from their FA Cup defeat and nearly allowed Arad to become the first team to win a European tie at White Hart Lane. With one of their first attacks, Arad took the lead on the hour, through Domido, before Gilzean saved Tottenham's blushes with an equaliser nine minutes from time.

In the 37th minute, Juventus' £440,000 forward, Anastasi, put the Serie A leaders ahead at home to Wolves. Helmut Haller nearly made it two just before the break. After half-time Danny Hegan, Jim McCalliog and Kenny Hibbitt began to dominate the midfield and in the 66th minute Wolves scored a deserved equaliser. Derek Dougan nodded down Gerry Taylor's cross for McCalliog to slam the ball home.

In the return leg, Juventus showed where their priorities lay by leaving five first-teamers back in Italy to prepare for the following weekend's vital game at Torino. Wolves opened the scoring in the 39th minute when Hegan lobbed the keeper from 25 yards. In the 51st minute Dougan got the vital second from a Ken Wagstaffe corner. Wolves had a late scare when Frank Munro handled a Haller flick, enabling the German to score from the spot, but it proved no more than a consolation.

Back in their hotel, the Juventus players were ordered to bed early in light of the upcoming game against Torino. When manager Čestmír Vycpálek checked the players' rooms he found Helmut Haller missing, eventually tracking him down to a Wolverhampton nightclub. Haller was suspended and missed the Torino game, which Juventus lost 2-1. He returned for the next game against Varese and scored the game's only goal to keep his place for the rest of the season. In the must-win final game of the season, against Vicenza, Haller opened the scoring in a 2-0 win to seal Juventus' first title for five years.

Born in 1939 in Augsburg, Haller joined his hometown club at 18. As German football was still semi-professional, he supplemented his income by working as a lorry driver. He won his first cap for West Germany at 19, and in 1962 helped his country to reach the World Cup quarter-finals. His performances in Chile led to him signing for the Italian side Bologna. In 1964, his dribbling skills and an eye for a telling pass won him the Italian Footballer of the Year award, as he helped Bologna to their first and only post-war league title. Although his move to Italy cost him his place in the national side for four years, he was eventually recalled in time for the 1966 World Cup. His opening goal in the Final was his sixth of the tournament, but Haller saw little more of the ball until the final whistle, when he picked it up and shook hands with the Queen with it tucked under his arm. Despite Geoff Hurst's hat-trick, Haller insisted it was German tradition that the scorer of the first goal kept the match ball. It took 30 years and £80,000 to persuade him to return to England and present the ball to Hurst on the eve of the Euro 96 tournament.

Although hampered by injury in the run-up to the 1970 World Cup, it was Haller's pass that allowed Libuda to score the decisive goal in the 3-2 home win over Scotland. Haller also found time in the dying minutes to help finish Tommy Gemmell's Celtic career.[1]

Qualification sealed, he played his 33rd and last international in the opening match of the World Cup against Morocco. He had moved to Juventus in 1968 and would play a pivotal role in the 1972 title win that kick-started a golden era for the club. He scored 32 goals in 171 appearances for Juventus and was instrumental in sealing back-to-back titles.

His last game for Juventus came against Ajax in the 1973 European Cup Final, before signing to FC Augsburg. He waived a fixed salary and settled for five per cent of the gate receipts. The deal paid dividends in the late summer of 1973 when Augsburg attracted a crowd of more than 90,000 against 1860 Munich, a world record for a non-top-flight match. After his retirement in 1979, he ran a fashion boutique and continued to enjoy the nightlife. In 2003, he married for a third time, to a Cuban woman more than 40 years his junior.

On hearing of Haller's death in 2012, Tommy Gemmell commented: 'If it hadn't been for Haller there is every chance I would never have left Celtic. Although I wanted to kick him over the stand that night, I am sad at his passing.'

The draws for the semi-finals of the European competitions took place. Wolves and Spurs were kept apart in the UEFA Cup while the two Glasgow clubs faced a repeat of their respective 1967 European finals. Rangers would face their 1967 Cup Winners' Cup conquerors Bayern Munich in the same tournament, and Celtic would meet Inter Milan in the European Cup.

Arsenal finally overcame Derby in the second replay of their fifth-round tie. In the fourth minute, John McGovern's 30-yard back pass ricocheted off Colin Todd into the path of Ray Kennedy, who accepted the gift and fired past Colin Boulton. Despite the urging of their supporters, Derby were unable to break Arsenal down. McGovern's mistake ensured that for the next ten years Brian Clough would berate him before every cup tie: 'McGovern, you cost me a cup final once and don't you ever forget it.'

Arsenal's 1-0 win earned them a quarter-final tie away to Orient. They hadn't had a home draw in the last two years of FA Cup competition. Orient gave Arsenal a football lesson in the first half, but after Ball scored within six minutes of the restart Arsenal spent the rest of the second half proving their mastery at protecting a one-goal lead.

First Division Huddersfield's cup hopes took a setback just before half-time when they lost their goalkeeper, Dave Lawson, with concussion after a clash with Birmingham's Bob

Latchford.[2] Latchford added to Malcolm Page's first-half goal before Hatton grabbed a third to make the game safe. Trevor Cherry scored a consolation for Huddersfield.

Don Revie's Leeds side provided pre-match entertainment before their home tie against Tottenham, which more than caught the eye of Eric Todd reporting for *The Guardian*: 'Before the game, Leeds turned out in smart new tracksuits, each bearing the name of its wearer, and under the supervision of Les Cocker, their trainer, gave a display of callisthenics.' The Leeds players lined up in the centre circle to applaud the fans, followed by kicking footballs into the crowd. The pre-match fitness display, together with the tracksuits and numbered stocking tags that each player signed before the match to give to the children in the crowd, were the brainchild of Paul Trevillion, creator of the 'You Are the Ref' column. After Leeds landed the FA Cup, the superstitious Don Revie kept the stocking tags. They remained a part of the kit until the 1976/77 season.

While putting on his new tracksuit top, Jack Charlton forgot to put on his shirt and played the first few minutes of the match in his white vest until his shirt was brought from the dressing room.

With Pat Jennings standing in the way of the home side racking up a cricket score, it was the visitors who opened the scoring. John Pratt curled in a hopeful long ball that beat everyone to fly into the far corner of the net. It was a poor goal to concede and a perfect fit for Gary Sprake's lengthy blooper reel. Justice was served as Leeds drew level a minute before half-time. Jennings saved from Billy Bremner, Terry Cooper's follow-up was blocked and bobbled across the goal, and Allan Clarke forced it in. Leeds took a deserved lead in the 48th minute, through Charlton, who nodded in a Bremner free kick. Magnificent Leeds continued to press strongly, only Jennings stopping them from adding further goals.

The Observer's Hugh McIlvanney described Leeds' football as 'breathtaking in its scope and fluency, alive with dazzling improvisations … In all essences of the game, except courage, Tottenham were outclassed.'

In the other quarter-final, Jimmy Greenhoff gave Stoke the lead on the hour against Manchester United. United had to wait until eight minutes from time for an equaliser, when Willie Morgan crossed for George Best to side-foot home.

The replay at the Victoria Ground was the clubs' sixth meeting of the season. George Best gave United the lead when he glided past a defender and slid the ball past Banks, but just four minutes later Denis Smith headed in George Eastham's corner to level. Stoke settled the tie in extra time when Terry Conroy netted after a goalmouth scramble.

The semi-final draw had kept Leeds and Arsenal apart, to set up a potential final between the defending Double winners and the potential Double winners.

In the league, two headers from Colin Bell were enough to beat West Brom and give Manchester City a four-point lead at the top of the table. Arsenal dropped Ray Kennedy to the substitutes' bench for their match against City, breaking his run of 104 successive first-team starts. Denis Taylor took firm control of the game, booking Mike Summerbee after just 30 seconds. He was the first of six players booked, three for each side. Arsenal more than matched City until Pat Rice handled in the area trying to field an awkward throw from Bob Wilson. For some reason the clear handball led to protests from Wilson and Frank McLintock, with Alan Ball sprinting 50 yards to join in. After Lee dispatched the penalty, Arsenal seemed to give up the ghost. Perhaps they felt Rice had literally handed City the title. Lee made sure of the points with his second goal in the 58th minute.

The following week, Everton's Tommy Wright managed to score an own goal for the second successive Saturday to open the scoring for City. His goal after 32 seconds bettered his own goal in the previous week's Merseyside derby by a second. Freddie Hill, replacing Tommy Booth, got a second before Mick Lyons grabbed a second-half consolation for Everton. With City on top of the table and looking certainties for the title, Malcolm Allison decided to sign Rodney Marsh.

Allison had been on his trail for nearly two years, but Mercer, who thought Marsh was just a fancy back-heeler, strongly advised the board against the purchase. He had thought it a poor deal in the summer at £140,000 and now the price was £180,000. Allison, however, wanted the star quality of Marsh. The home win over West Brom attracted a crowd of just 25,000 in a ground that could hold 55,000. Allison looked enviously at the attendance figures at Old Trafford, frustrated that, although his side was far better than the declining team across town, they didn't have the United celebrity. So he wanted a player who could bring that to City. The board sanctioned the transfer, believing that after City won the Championship the extra revenue from the European Cup would soon cover Marsh's transfer fee and wages.[3] With City desperate to sign Marsh, Jim Gregory managed to push the fee up to a round £200,000.

A crowd of 53,322 turned up to watch Marsh make his debut in the 1-0 win over Chelsea as City stretched their lead at the top to five points. Marsh's first touch of the ball was a gliding effortless dribble that took him with ease past three Chelsea players. Marsh should have added to Tommy Booth's goal, hitting the bar when it looked easier to score. Mercer noticed that whenever Marsh got the ball, he held on to it for too long, forcing the City players to hold their positions to avoid being caught offside.

Marsh retained his place at Newcastle, but provided little, bar a couple of double-shuffles to entertain the crowd. Joe Corrigan missed the 0-0 draw after slipping a disc in training and was ruled out for the rest of the season. Twenty-year-old Ron Healey took his place in goal.[4]

The conventional wisdom over nearly 50 years is that the signing of Marsh cost City the title; Marsh himself seems keen to shoulder the blame. The loss of Corrigan for seven games seems to have been forgotten, even though City lost three of those games. Prior to his absence City had lost only three league games in six months.

As for Marsh, he scored twice in the win over West Ham, and at Old Trafford he won the free kick for the second goal before scoring himself. In City's final match against Derby, he was the man of the match, scoring the first before winning the penalty for the second. If you look at the point dropped at Sheffield United after leading by two goals, and the hammering City received at Anfield, maybe the decline had begun before Marsh even arrived?

Allison could keep a closer eye on his new signing as godfather to a 'benevolent football clan' that had recently been formed. The Clan's members – Marsh, Gordon Banks, Martin Chivers, Geoff Hurst, Francis Lee, Dave Webb, Phil Beal, Martin Buchan and Terry Mancini – attended a photo shoot by Terry O'Neill in Manchester. Only Alan Ball, Alan Hudson and Terry Venables were absent. Allison explained: 'Each member of The Clan will be committed to improving the image of the game and their own knowledge of it. The Clan is not just a gimmick; it can serve a really useful purpose for us all.'

It *was* just a gimmick, but it was an early, if short-lived, attempt by players to enhance their image and earnings inside and outside the game. Terry Venables was The Clan member who best used his profile during the 70s and beyond. 'Footballers have got to become more astute and realise there are a wealth of possibilities out there,' stated the QPR midfielder. Among the many possibilities explored by Venables were novelist, board-game inventor, big-band crooner, nightclub owner and football pundit.

As the decade progressed, so did players' awareness of the off-field riches available. Kevin Keegan led the way, appearing in commercials and TV shows. He also released a single that hit the charts. 'I was always keen to explore different avenues, always wanting to work hard,' said the former Liverpool and Hamburg forward. 'Some of the guys earlier in the 70s had dabbled in it, and my advisers learnt from their mistakes.'

Leeds played some of their greatest football throughout March to keep up the pressure on Manchester City. After ten years Revie had finally taken the shackles off his talented team. At the start of the month we saw, for many, their greatest performance, against Southampton at Elland Road. Leeds had only lost one game since their defeat at Southampton in November. The Saints, on the other hand, had lost their next game 8-0 at Everton. This time, at Elland Road, the TV cameras were in attendance to see them thrashed.

Although Southampton were under siege from the start, it took until the 37th minute for the first goal to arrive. Eddie Gray hurdled a tackle before finding Allan Clarke in the left-hand corner of the area. Clarke took it on a pace and slammed his shot into the opposite corner. Within five minutes, Peter Lorimer doubled their lead by hammering a low shot past Eric Martin.[5] Leeds continued to dominate after the break and, on the hour, Clarke made it 3-0. Four minutes later Lorimer slipped past his marker and fired home from 20 yards before completing his hat-trick in the 68th minute. Both the Leeds centre-halves combined for the sixth five minutes later, Jack Charlton nodding home Norman Hunter's lobbed cross. Twelve minutes from time, Gray sent over a cross that Lorimer nodded back for Mick Jones to sweep the ball over the line, making it seven.

At 7-0, Leeds started to play keep-ball with a wonderful display of arrogance and skill. Barry Davies' commentary for *Match of the Day* is classic stuff: 'To say that Leeds are playing with Southampton is the understatement of the season. Poor old Southampton just don't know what day it is. Every man jack of this Leeds side is now turning it on … It's almost cruel.' According to Peter Lorimer, rather than humiliate Southampton, Revie had instructed his team not to add any more goals and embarrass his friend, Ted Bates, the Southampton manager. Lorimer said: 'As the years went on, they kept showing the 39 passes on programmes and that was what was featured more than the seven goals. But we weren't trying to be cheeky or clever. We were just keeping possession.'

The following week, Jack Charlton marked his 600th League game with the only goal of the game against Coventry. Four days after knocking Tottenham out of the cup, Leeds ran into a committed Leicester side and could count themselves fortunate to pick up an away point. Normal service was resumed when they met Arsenal the following Saturday. Revie's men were magnificent, although all three of their goals could be marked down to defensive errors. Peter Lorimer's cross evaded four defenders before Clarke tapped it home, Mick Jones added a second after indecision between Bob Wilson and Sammy Nelson, and the third saw Lorimer beat Wilson too easily from 30 yards.

Next up for Leeds was a Monday night game against Nottingham Forest. Bottom club Forest faced a Leeds side that had enjoyed eight straight home wins, with a goal record of 25-3. Leeds got the opener when Gray and Mick Jones combined to fashion space for Lorimer to fire past Jim Barron. A complacent Leeds allowed Forest to fluke an equaliser when Alan Buckley's shot deflected off Peter Cormack's shoulder and into the goal. In the 52nd minute, Barron suffered a split lip diving bravely at Clarke's feet. In the four minutes he was off the field to receive treatment, Forest conceded two goals. A Lorimer corner was spilt by stand-in keeper Cormack to allow Gray to fire Leeds ahead, then three minutes later Clarke scored from the edge of the area. Five minutes from the end, Paul Madeley stormed through the middle to feed Lorimer, who fired home between Barron's legs. Clarke and Gray netted two more in added time against a brave Forest side that now had only a faint hope of escaping the drop.

Leeds next travelled to Upton Park and had to claw back a two-goal deficit to snatch a point. Although Leeds were by now favourites for the title, six of their nine remaining games were away from home, where they had accumulated just 14 points from a possible 30.

As spectacular as Leeds were in March, Derby steadily collected 11 points, despite being distracted by one of the most bizarre transfers of all time and their manager courting another club. The Derby supporters became accustomed to seeing the same 11 players week in, week out, so while they entertained Wolves at the Baseball Ground with an unchanged team, Clough did treat his supporters to a new face by parading Ian Storey-Moore before the game.

Nottingham Forest had put the 27-year-old Storey-Moore up for sale and accepted Manchester United's £200,000 bid, but the player failed to agree personal terms. Clough moved quickly, convincing the player that Derby represented a better move than United. Storey-Moore signed the transfer papers, as did Derby's secretary, Stuart Webb. However, Forest secretary Ken Smales refused, meaning that Storey-Moore technically remained a Forest player. Smales warned Sam Longson that there would be trouble if Clough pressed on with the transfer, but Clough reassured his chairman that the player was keen on the deal and not to be concerned.

Just to make sure Storey-Moore remained keen, the night before the Wolves game, Clough took him to meet the Derby squad at the Midland Hotel and booked a room for him to stay the night. Clough, convinced that Storey-Moore was a Derby player, paraded him around the pitch the next day, to Forest's fury, as the paperwork had not yet been completed.

The player watched from the stands as Jim McCalliog's penalty gave Wolves a half-time lead. Five minutes after the interval the referee pointed to the spot for a Derby penalty. Alan Hinton had rattled the bar with an earlier penalty, but made no mistake this time. With 20 minutes remaining, Roy McFarland soared above the Wolves defence to head home Hinton's free kick for the winner.

Unlike the recent efforts of his players, Frank O'Farrell did not know when he was defeated. After getting a heads-up that a deal could be back on, he travelled with Sir Matt Busby the next day to Storey-Moore's home with an enormous bunch of flowers for the player's wife. Following a short conversation, the player signed for Manchester United.[6]

The season's transfers now totalled £4,328,000, compared with the previous season's £2,404,000. Philip Whitehead, the Member of Parliament for Derby, wanted the Government to step in and control this 'flesh market'.

Clough fired off a hectoring telegram to Alan Hardaker, pointing out that Gillies gave him permission to discuss terms with Storey-Moore. Sam Longson, appalled by the tone Clough had taken, sent his own telegram to Hardaker, apologising. Despite Longson's attempt at damage control, Derby were fined £5,000 and Clough was warned 'as to the manner in which any future negotiations regarding the transfer of players are carried out'. Longson and Clough's once-strong relationship was beginning to unravel. At the end of the month it would be tested further.

Storey-Moore hoped his transfer to United would help him back into the England squad after a two-year absence. On 7 February 1970, three weeks after an excellent debut against Holland, Storey-Moore was playing at Manchester City when he was the recipient of a sliding tackle from full-back Arthur Mann. Storey-Moore took the impact on his standing leg, severing the ligaments in his right ankle and putting him out of the next England game and the World Cup squad.

It was small consolation for Storey-Moore that garage group, Esso, still included him in its Mexico World Cup squad. Esso had produced '30 gleaming silvery coins, each bearing the sculptured head of one of England's greatest soccer stars … each coin has a milled edge and is minted in exactly the same way as a coin of the realm'. A bit of an exaggeration, but they were pretty good quality and free with four gallons of petrol. My father had recently been duped into buying a decaying, second-hand Austin Princess that made around 50 yards to a gallon, so I was on a constant supply of medals.

To hit production deadlines, Esso had to guess which players would make the squad, but gave themselves some margin for error by naming 30 players instead of 28. Most of Esso and Ramsey's selections matched, but whereas Esso opted for Paul Madeley, Ian Storey-Moore, Henry Newton, Mick Jones, Alan Oakes and Peter Simpson, Ramsey selected David Sadler, Nobby Stiles, Brian Kidd and Ralph Coates. Esso also promoted Bobby Moore from an OBE to a CBE, something the FA shamefully never arranged.[7]

The skill of a surgeon saved Storey-Moore's career after the Arthur Mann tackle, but it turned out to be a temporary respite. While contesting a ball with David Sadler in training, his weakened ankle ligaments gave way. From January 1973, Storey-Moore only played a further four games before retiring in December 1973 aged just 28.

Terry Hennessey replaced the injured Alan Durban for the trip to Tottenham, Derby's first change since December. The Rams had not won at White Hart Lane since November 1933, but with five minutes to go Mike England attempted a back pass to Pat Jennings. The keeper was too close and, unable to hold the ball, had no alternative but to pull Kevin Hector down after the forward pounced on the mistake. Despite Jennings guessing the right way, Alan Hinton's spot-kick found the corner to record his 15th goal of the season.

John O'Hare, Durban and Hector got the goals in a convincing win over Leicester before Hector's opportunism was enough to give them the two points against Ipswich. Top scorer Alan Hinton limped off after half an hour and was missed when, despite running the legs off a cup-weary Stoke, Derby were unable to get more than a point.

Although Hinton remained on the injury list, the Rams rested John McGovern for their trip to Crystal Palace. Hinton's absence was highlighted when Archie Gemmill missed a penalty, but his replacement, Jim Walker, got the only goal in the 33rd minute.

Coventry's manager, Noel Cantwell, was fired just three days after spending £80,000 on Bobby Graham and Neil Ramsbottom. Although Ronnie Allen, Pat Saward, Bill McGarry and John Bond were all linked with the job, Brian Clough was Coventry's number-one target. After getting Sam Longson's permission, the Coventry Chairman, Derrick Robins, met Clough and outlined his offer. The salary and bonuses would have put Clough on more money than any other manager in the league. Despite his team challenging for the title, Clough was unhappy with the size of Derby's squad and the poor support at recent games. After convincing Peter Taylor, Clough agreed to the move and told Robins they would tell Sam Longson after the Crystal Palace match. Coventry planned to call a press conference the following Wednesday to announce the appointment. After Derby beat Palace, Clough asked if he could have another week or two, which Coventry reluctantly agreed to.

Despite Robins pressing him for a decision, Clough strung him along, hoping to win the title with Derby before departing. He and Taylor finally resigned at the end of April, but Robins, impatient at being given the runaround, had withdrawn the offer. Despite resigning with no job to go to, Clough and Taylor had front, if nothing else, so they went to Sam Longson and promised to stay for more money. The next day Longson discovered he had been duped. Derby secretary, Stuart Webb, who knew nothing of the meeting at Longson's house, told him that he had been informed of the withdrawal of Coventry's offer. Longson was furious, later complaining: 'In the case of Coventry City, I was blackmailed into giving the manager a £5,000 a year rise and the assistant manager £3,000.'

The Storey-Moore debacle had embarrassed Longson and now he had been tricked into giving Clough and Taylor a massive pay rise. Together with Clough's constant courting of the media and controversy, the final rift between him and Longson was only a matter of time. Clough and Taylor would go on to lead Nottingham Forest to a league title and double European Cup success, but it is one of the great what-ifs to imagine what they might have achieved at Highfield Road.

Tommy Wright's own goal gave Liverpool a great start in the Merseyside derby. John McLaughlin added a second in the 66th minute before defenders Chris Lawler and Emlyn Hughes finished the romp.

After a draw at Chelsea, Liverpool hosted Newcastle, who were met by the new 'This is Anfield' sign hanging over the tunnel. By the end of the game they didn't look as if they knew where they were as the Reds ran riot, winning 5-0. Liverpool then racked up their seventh successive clean sheet as John Toshack's header took both points at Southampton. They maintained the pressure on the top three by collecting another two points against Stoke to make it 17 from the last nine games. Gordon Banks was in magnificent form and kept Liverpool at bay as Stoke took an undeserved lead through John Ritchie. Four minutes before half-time Liverpool finally beat Banks, when Ian Callaghan's shot took a wicked deflection. Liverpool started the second half besieging the Stoke goal and scored the winner in the 54th minute through Keegan. Ray Clemence made a flying save from Harry Burrows near the end to prevent Stoke claiming an undeserved draw.

Without a win in six games, Stoke attempted to freshen up their squad by buying the Argentinian, Carlos Babington, for £40,000 from Huracán. Babington, the son of English emigrants, was nicknamed El Inglés. Despite not speaking a word of English, his lineage was impressive; his great-grandfather, the physician William Babington, has a statue in St Paul's Cathedral, and his grandfather, Benjamin Babington, was the famed epidemiologist.

Stoke manager Tony Waddington said: 'There is no question of the player's ability. You have to be good to score goals in

Argentinian football and there is no doubt that he is going to be a tremendous player. But there is nothing settled yet. We have to get official clearance and he needs a British passport.'

Sadly, the transfer was a victim of red tape and fell through. Despite the restrictions on foreign players, Babington would have been waved through if only his grandfather had done his paperwork. Waddington explained: 'The snag was that Babington's grandfather did not register as a British subject when he emigrated to South America ... We had hoped the boy's father could take out a British passport, which would have cleared the way, but this is not possible now.'[8]

A transfer to Inter Milan fell at a similar hurdles, so Babington stayed in Argentina to help Huracán win the 1973 Argentinian title. After starring for Argentina during the 1974 World Cup, he got his European move, staying in Germany to join Wattenscheid 09. In his four years in Germany, the midfielder netted 46 goals in 120 games before a return to Huracán for three seasons.[9] Babington later managed the team and became Club President in 2005.

Despite Stoke running up against the usual bureaucratic problems, foreign players weren't unknown in Britain. Six months earlier, Hamilton Academicals became the first British club to recruit players from Eastern Europe in a deal orchestrated by their Polish chairman, Jan Stepek. Stepek, who owned an electrical wholesale business and a small empire of shops in Hamilton and across Lanarkshire, agreed a deal whereby he would ship washing machines and electrical items to Poland in exchange for footballers. In September 1971, three Polish Internationals – Alfred Olek, Witold Szygula and Roman Strazalkowski – arrived in Hamilton. Although they were approaching the twilights of their careers, they were still highly regarded in their home country. Unfortunately, they were unable to resurrect Hamilton's fortunes and, with the club bottom of the league, they returned to Poland at the end of the season.

On 23 February 1978, the European Community decided

that football associations could not deny access to players on the basis of their nationality. At its summer AGM, the Football League lifted its 47-year ban on foreigners. The ruling hadn't just opened English football to players from Europe; clubs were allowed to sign two players from other parts of the world too. A little more than six years after the aborted transfer of Babington to Stoke, Huracán finally managed to sell a player to an English club. Ironically, while Babington had been refused permission to play in England, he had far more ancestry and connection there than Ossie Ardiles. Fellow Argentinian, Alex Sabella, was uncapped at the time of his arrival at Sheffield United, although at the request of the PFA, the criteria for admitting foreign players was tightened up. Henceforth they would have to be established internationals.

Sabella was a replacement for Sheffield United's original target, Diego Maradona. The Blades' £200,000 deal for the 17-year-old fell through after the Second Division club failed to stump up extra cash on top of the fee. Maradona would recover from his disappointment to have a fairly decent career.

The first foreign footballer had actually arrived in 1892, just four years after the formation of the English league. Walter Bowman, born and raised in Canada, of Swiss heritage, would play for Accrington and Ardwick Association Football Club.[10]

The British game was very insular, as illustrated by the associations not bothering to enter the first three World Cup finals, but by the early 1930s the progress of football overseas persuaded one or two British clubs that the signing of a foreign player might be worth a punt. In attempting to open the game up to foreign talent, Arsenal's forward-thinking manager, Herbert Chapman, would ultimately be responsible for the banning of foreign professionals for nearly half a century. Chapman had previously tried to sign the Austrian goalkeeper, Rudy Hiden, in a deal that included a job as a chef. Sadly, for English football and the culinary world, Hiden never made it past immigration at Dover.

After the Hiden affair, the FA, the PFA, and the Ministry of Labour, made it clear that they were opposed to foreign professionals, but did stop short of legislation. Arsenal and Chapman were unbowed and signed another foreign player, one who was already resident in England. Gerard Keizer, the former Ajax number-two goalkeeper, was playing as an amateur for Margate. Arsenal's only concession to the authorities was to keep him on an amateur contract.

Although Keizer didn't keep a clean sheet in his 12 first-team matches at Arsenal and was dropped by October, he had contributed to Arsenal's first-ever league title in 1931. His signing did motivate the FA to formally change the rules. Now, a player who wasn't British-born had to play for nothing or live in England working at another job for two years before becoming a professional. The change effectively banned foreign players, although colonial footballers could still come to Britain.

A small wave of imports arrived in the aftermath of the Second World War, as British society in general began to open its doors to outsiders. The most famous was goalkeeper Bert Trautmann, who progressed from being a German prisoner of war to making more than 500 appearances for Manchester City.

So, it was the Treaty of Rome – rather than any progressive attitude on the part of football's governing bodies – that finally brought to an end the ban. As usual, British football was forced to adapt rather than initiating changes itself.

In 1989, Arsenal won the last league title to be won without using a foreign player. In 1992 the Premier League started and, although just 13 non-British players appeared on the opening day, with the Sky money flowing into the game, clubs could now match the wages on offer in Spain and Italy. On Boxing Day 1999, Chelsea, under their Italian manager, Gianluca Vialli, became the first club to start a match with 11 foreign players. By the time the Premier League celebrated its silver anniversary, 2,000 foreign players from more than 100 countries had played in the Premier League. Among the powerhouses of world football who had supplied the league were Cape Verde, Grenada, Burkina Faso, Burundi, the Faroe Islands and the Seychelles. In the 2015/16 season, less than a third of all starters were qualified to represent England.

In the Second Division, Norwich's 4-0 defeat at Birmingham knocked them off the top for the first time since mid-September. Fellow promotion chasers QPR visited Birmingham next and escaped with a goalless draw. After another draw at Carlisle, Bob Hatton's last-minute winner against Luton kept Birmingham in the promotion mix. He also scored the only goal at Oxford to register his 16th goal in 22 games since his transfer.

After the hiding at Birmingham, new signing Jim Bone's goal earned Norwich a point at home to Sunderland. Norwich swept back to the top of the table after Alan Foggo scored the winner with two minutes to go against a dogged Hull. A loss at Portsmouth handed the leadership back to Millwall before Norwich returned to form, with a 5-1 thrashing of Blackpool.

With Norwich losing at Birmingham, Millwall's 2-2 home draw with Swindon was enough to top the table. Derek Possee got the goal in the home draw with Cardiff before Millwall dropped another point at Blackpool. They got back to winning ways with a 2-0 win over Oxford, Gordon Bolland scoring the first and crossing for Possee's second to stretch Millwall's unbeaten run to ten games. Possee missed the visit of Portsmouth and although his replacement, Frank Saul, worked hard, he couldn't strike up the same understanding with Barry Bridges that Possee enjoyed. Bridges scored his first goal since Boxing Day to give Millwall a lucky win.

Before their visit to Bristol City, QPR had been level on points with Birmingham, with a better goal average. QPR dominated the first hour but faded after Rodney Marsh limped off with a groin strain in his last game before his transfer to Manchester City. QPR, already missing the influential Terry

Venables, conceded two second-half goals to all but end their promotion hopes.

Fulham's signing of Alan Mullery on a month's loan was labelled an old pal's act by Cardiff Chairman, Fred Dewey. He felt Mullery would give Fulham an unfair advantage over their relegation rivals, who just so happened to include Cardiff. Mullery, out of the Tottenham side since October, was pleased to get the opportunity of first-team football at his old club.

Notts County lost the chance to close on Third Division leaders, Aston Villa, after being beaten 3-0 in their clash at Meadow Lane. Villa took an early second-half lead through Pat McMahon. Ray Graydon stuck out a leg and deflected Bruce Rioch's shot for the second, before McMahon scored his second 12 minutes from time.

After draws at Plymouth and Rotherham, County hosted Chesterfield and lost by a three-goal margin for the second home match in succession. County led after two minutes from Brian Stubbs, but after that it was one-way traffic. The game proved an unhappy end to the Notts County career of Tony Hateley. He was carried off on a stretcher with the score at 1-1 and would miss the remainder of the season with a knee injury.[11] Another draw at home to Rotherham and then a draw at Shrewsbury meant County had taken just four points during March and were now five points adrift from the promotion places.

Villa's Vic Crowe celebrated the win over Notts County by paying a Third Division record fee of £75,000 for Luton centre-half, Chris Nicholl. Over the next four seasons, Nicholl barely missed a game, helping the club to a 1975 double of League Cup glory and promotion to the top flight. His Villa days ended in the summer of 1977, but not before scoring an equaliser in that year's League Cup Final with a swerving, dipping shot from 35 yards in the dramatic 3-2 victory over Everton in the second replay.

Debutant Nicholl was near faultless in the 2-0 triumph over Rotherham, which took Villa's points tally to 32 from the last

36. Although not signed for goals, he opened his account the following week at Shrewsbury with a second-half equaliser to earn his new club a point. A dull goalless draw with Walsall preceded the match everyone in the Third Division wanted to see – Brighton against Aston Villa. The match attracted a crowd of more than 30,000 and the *Match of the Day* cameras. Bruce Rioch equalised Willie Irvine's sixth-minute opener and a draw beckoned before Kit Napier's winner five minutes from time. After losing their previous two games, the win was a vital one for Brighton. They followed their win over Aston Villa with three goals in the last 14 minutes to defeat Torquay. The Seagulls were now a point behind Bournemouth, who they would meet at the start of April.

Ted MacDougall grabbed his 37th goal of the season as Bournemouth beat struggling Bradford. Phil Boyer and MacDougall scored against Bristol Rovers to give Bournemouth their third consecutive victory before Boyer and Bill Kitchener made it four wins on the trot at Swansea. MacDougall's goal earned them a point at Walsall, but his strike against Bolton was trumped by veteran Roger Hunt's last goals in professional football in a shock home defeat. They followed by losing to Oldham to give them back-to-back defeats for the first time during the league campaign. Bournemouth's poor month was completed by dropping another point to Rochdale.

Villa bounced back from the Brighton loss with a comfortable victory at Wrexham.

At the end of February, Lincoln were third in the Fourth Division. David Herd had revitalised the club, which had applied for re-election the previous season. In January, he had become the first Imps manager to win a manager of the month award after victories over Workington, Brentford and Doncaster and a 2-2 draw at Grimsby. Their month was only spoilt when club captain, Graham Taylor, limped off in the 2-1 win over Southport at the start of the month. Taylor had moved to Lincoln from Grimsby in the summer of 1968, scoring on his debut on the opening day of the season.[12]

As one of a number of players who were openly critical of Herd, Taylor had been promoted to player-coach to try to placate the growing rift between squad and manager. Although the 1-0 win on 18 March, over leaders Scunthorpe, lifted Lincoln into second place, just three wins from their last 11 games would leave them a point short of promotion. The following season Lincoln struggled and the acrimony between the manager and players worsened. In December 1972, Chairman Dennis Bocock invited Herd to resign and replaced him with Graham Taylor on a weekly salary of £50.[13]

Brentford recovered from a home loss to Colchester to beat Lincoln 2-0. John O'Mara, back from suspension, headed the opener for his 23rd of the season. The Bees had only picked up two points without him and his goal was their first in 325 minutes of play. Terry Scales got their second to condemn Lincoln to their first defeat of the year. It was the first of five successive wins, including a win over Grimsby, to put Brentford's promotion hopes back on track.

Southend started the month with a draw at Exeter before rattling off six wins. Bill Garner's hat-trick in their 4-2 win over Chester fired them into fourth. Wins over Crewe and Darlington followed before it was Billy Best's turn to score a hat-trick in the 4-1 win at Reading. Gary Moore's goal against Aldershot edged them into second place before Garner and Best saw off Doncaster in front of their biggest home crowd of the season.

The season's first domestic cup final took place when Chelsea and Stoke met in the League Cup Final at Wembley. In the hour before the game, the 100,000 crowd, giving receipts of £132,000, was entertained by the final of ITV's *Penalty Prize* competition, compèred by Jimmy Hill. Youngsters had been taking penalties against professional keepers up and down the country throughout the season to reach the final, where they now got the opportunity to challenge the finalists' reserve keepers, John Phillips and John Farmer.

Stoke were led out by Tony Waddington, who had arrived 12 years earlier when Stoke were averaging crowds of less than 10,000 and struggling to remain in Division Two. With a decent youth policy and some astute signings, he had built a formidable side. One of his key signings was the £35,000 he paid Arsenal for George Eastham in 1966. Eastham had begun his career in 1953 at Ards in Northern Ireland, where his father was the player-manager.[14] Whereas George senior was only capped once for England, George junior would win 19 caps, making the squads for the 1962 and 1966 World Cups.[15] Father and son played together until George junior transferred to Newcastle United in 1956. Eastham soon fell out with Newcastle over the house they provided him with. The club argued that the crumbling property had been good enough for the great Jackie Milburn. Eastham asked for a transfer and, when his request was turned down, went on strike, eventually forcing Newcastle to cut their losses and sell him to Arsenal for £47,000. Eastham first heard about the transfer on the radio and, with the assistance of the PFA, took the club to court to claim his unpaid wages and bonuses.

The PFA used Eastham as a test case to try to overturn the Football League's retain and transfer rules. In the 1964 'Eastham versus Newcastle United' case, the retain and transfer system was ruled an unreasonable restraint by the High Court. Players could now leave their club when their contract ended. For a while, it looked as if the court case would be Eastham's sole legacy to the game. After his troubles at a declining Newcastle, his stint at Arsenal came in the middle of the club's 17-year barren spell.

When the captains met for the coin toss at the League Cup Final, Ron Harris gave Peter Dobing a blue Chelsea pennant and in return received a beautiful framed china plate from Stoke, the home of the Wedgwood Bone China Company. Harris had the good grace to look embarrassed at the exchange, but his team quickly repaid the generosity with some inept defending to gift Stoke the opening goal. Dobing's fifth-minute long throw caused havoc inside Chelsea's six-yard box. Peter Bonetti only managed to punch weakly away to Eastham, who returned the ball into the mix. After a goalmouth scramble, Terry Conroy nodded in the loose ball.

Chelsea immediately pressed for an equaliser. Charlie Cooke had a 20-yard shot well saved by Banks, and Chris Garland was hacked down by Alan Bloor on the edge of the area when clear. After Norman Burtenshaw booked Bloor, John Hollins fired the free kick just wide. Soon after, Garland was clean through again. This time it was Mike Pejic's turn to scythe him down and join Bloor in the referee's notebook. The petulant Peter Osgood, who had finally earned a booking for shoving Denis Smith, equalised for Chelsea in the last seconds of the first half by hooking the ball home while prostrate on the pitch.

Chelsea were forced to shuffle their side at half-time to replace the injured Paddy Mulligan with Tommy Baldwin. Osgood dropped back to midfield, Hollins moved into central defence and Dave Webb over to right-back. Manager Dave Sexton obviously hadn't learnt his lesson from the 1970 FA Cup Final, when Eddie Gray had shown that Webb wasn't a full-back. Terry Conroy would confirm this in the second half.

The veteran George Eastham hadn't had a great game. He had been regularly caught in possession and the speed of the game seemed to pass him by. With just over 15 minutes remaining, Conroy beat Webb down the left and crossed from the edge of the area. John Ritchie headed down for Jimmy Greenhoff to swivel and volley. Bonetti made a good save, but Eastham pounced on the rebound, poking the ball home.

Chelsea threw everything at Stoke in search of an equaliser, but the Potters defended grimly. Osgood, Webb, Garland, Baldwin and Alan Hudson were all thwarted by sharp saves, tackles and blocks from the Stoke back 11. Chelsea's best opportunity came from a dreadful Mike Bernard back pass in the dying seconds. The 'best through ball of the game', according to Eastham, put Garland clear again, but Banks came out to the edge of his area and blocked the shot with his knee. Banks was fouled as the Chelsea corner flew in and, as he took the free kick, the final whistle blew. The League Cup's very own Matthews Moment had won the world's second-oldest club its first silverware.

Peter Osgood would write in his autobiography: 'I suppose you could carbon-date the start of Chelsea's and my own decline from that day and George Eastham's goal.' Dave Webb believed the sale of Keith Weller at the start of the season was the key event, but whenever the Chelsea decline began, most will agree its origins were during the 1971/72 season. Hudson and Osgood were beginning to look stale and unmotivated. Osgood was unhappy about being transfer-listed after the 3-2 loss to United back in August, and Hudson was upset after being repositioned to the right side of midfield to accommodate Steve Kember.

At the end of the season, chairman Brian Mears announced plans for the total redevelopment of the ground. His hand had been forced by the local authorities, who told the club that the East Stand would not get another safety certificate for the 1972/73 season. Mears' vision was to create a new 60,000 capacity stadium by the end of the 70s at a cost of more than £5m. The first stage of the redevelopment would see a massive three-tier, 12,000-capacity stand built in place of the existing East Stand.

Chelsea kicked off the next season with a gaping hole where the East Stand once stood. The average attendance dropped by 10,000, while building costs for the new stand rocketed. Due to the spiralling costs, Chelsea didn't buy a single player between August 1974 and June 1978. The 1972/73 season kicked off with a 4-0 win over Leeds and the club were fourth by December but, after losing to Norwich in the League Cup semi-final, Chelsea's season fizzled out.

They won just five of their last 21 league games to finish 12th. The following season, the feud between Sexton, Osgood and Hudson reached boiling point after a home defeat to West Ham on Boxing Day and both were sold within months. A disillusioned Dave Webb asked for a transfer and left for QPR as Chelsea finished the season in 17th place. Although Sexton was sacked after a poor start to the 1974/75 season, his successor, Ron Suart, was unable to stop the club's relegation. Just four years after lifting the Cup Winners' Cup, Chelsea were in the Second Division with just Bonetti, Harris, Cooke and John Dempsey remaining from their great 70s side. By 1977, the costs for the East Stand had escalated out of control and the club's debts stood at £4m.

Chelsea became a yo-yo team. Between 1975 and 1989 they would spend a total of eight years in the Second Division. In 1983, they avoided relegation to the third tier by just two points. Mears resigned as chairman in 1981 and, a year later, Chelsea – heavily in debt and losing £12,000 a week – were acquired by Ken Bates for £1. The sale ended the Mears family's 76-year association with the club. Bates would describe what he took over as 'a social club with a little football played on a Saturday'. Bates eventually got the club on a stable financial footing and in 1997, a quarter of a century after the League Cup loss to Stoke, they won the FA Cup. They were back to exactly where they were in 1972 – a good cup side and a solid league team. It took Roman Abramovich's purchase of the club for £140m in 2003 to turn them into one of the Premier League's leading sides.

Former Chelsea boss, Tommy Docherty, announced his Scotland squad for the Independence Tournament in Brazil. The 20-strong party included 12 Anglos and welcomed back Denis Law after a three-year absence.

At Ashton Gate, England lost their first Under-23 international on home soil for 13 years, to East Germany. West Brom's Gordon Nisbet made his international debut after just 12 games in the number-two shirt.[16] An unimpressive England had no reply to Jürgen Sparwasser's first-half goal. Sparwasser was one of three full internationals in the East German side and would star for the East German Olympic team in the summer. He played in all seven matches, scoring five goals, as his country shared the bronze medal.

He leapt to international fame at the 1974 World Cup in Germany, by scoring the winning goal for East Germany against West Germany. While his goal was exploited politically, Sparwasser did not profit from it. 'Rumour had it I was richly rewarded for the goal, with a car, a house, and a cash premium. But that is not true.' In 1988, Sparwasser defected to West Germany while taking part in a veterans' tournament there.

All eyes were turning towards the following month's Wembley clash between England and West Germany. Though the Germans won in Hungary at the end of the month, they looked a team in crisis. Injuries had robbed them of Berti Vogts, Wolfgang Overath and Jürgen Grabowski, and the ongoing bribery scandal in the Bundesliga meant they were also without Reinhard Libuda and Klaus Fichtel.[17]

England seemed more concerned with the row over the live televising of the quarter-final clash than the actual game. Alan Hardaker reported that there was a state of open war between the Football League and the Football Association over the FA's decision to accept £60,000 for the live television rights.

A match between the Football League and the Scottish League gave a run-out to players hoping to force their way into Alf Ramsey's plans. Tony Currie was the star of the show with two goals and an assist for Mike Doyle after beating three players on the byline. Denis McQuade and Colin Stein got Scotland's goals. Many of the 20,000 crowd struggled to see the game clearly because of the glare from the extra floodlighting used to assist the television cameras. Desmond Hackett wrote: 'It is fine for audiences to watch soccer on their colour TV screens in the comfort of their homes, but if the paying public become absentees, soccer will go out of business.'

Bobby Moore and Geoff Hurst were the only regular England starters in the Football League side. The pair would make a more important appearance on 22 March, this time against the taxman at a High Court in Stratford.

England's 1966 World Cup victory hadn't made the players rich; they received a suit, a raincoat and £1,000 each. Originally, England's £22,000 pool was to be allocated in respect of appearances, but the first 11 felt the victory was a squad effort and that the money should be shared equally. In comparison, the German players received £10,000 each and a Volkswagen car just for reaching the Final.

To add insult to injury, the Inland Revenue wanted to tax the England players £300 on their bonus. HMRC inspector, William Griffiths, contended the money was taxable, as were the other bonuses some players received. Moore had received an extra £500 from Radox Bath Salts for being voted the best player in the tournament, and £250 for being the star of the England team. Hurst collected £250 from Radox for being England's top scorer. At the time, Moore earned a basic £140 a week; his income for the 1966/67 season had been assessed at £12,125, which included the £1,000 bonus, but not the other bonuses.

Moore and Hurst's counsel, Hilda Wilson, argued that the bonuses were a special tribute for their footballing qualities and not part of their earnings. The judge, his finger on the pulse of popular culture, asked how often the World Cup was held, and was told that it took place once every four years. Mrs Wilson, obviously more attuned to our national game, advised him that: 'England does not expect to win every four years.'

Justice Brightman reversed the tax commissioner's decision and ruled that the £1,000 bonuses were 'an applause for victory' and not professional earnings. Brightman also ruled against the taxman on Moore and Hurst's individual bonuses. Brightman's decision in Moore versus Griffiths (Inspector of Taxes) is still cited in tax cases. In 2012, Moore and Hurst's old team-mate,

Harry Redknapp, tried to introduce a precedent from the case in his tax evasion trial.

England's World Cup win never set the players up financially; all but Roger Hunt and the Charlton brothers had to sell their winner's medal to provide for themselves or their families. George Cohen was the first to sell his medal, to Fulham, for £80,000. Full-back partner, Ray Wilson, also received £80,000 from a private collector, who subsequently resold it in 2014 for £136,000. In 2000, Bobby Moore's widow sold his medal, together with other memorabilia, to West Ham. The medal was valued at £150,000. The following year, Hurst and Martin Peters sold theirs to the club for the same price. The same year, Gordon Banks received less than £125,000 for his medal.[18] In 2005, Alan Ball got £140,000 for his, the record until a tearful Nobby Stiles sold his for £160,000 in 2010. In total, the medals managed to raise a little more than £1m – or a little over three weeks' salary for Manchester City's Kevin de Bruyne.

NOTES FROM ABROAD

On 6 March 1971, Vic Buckingham, the former manager of Ajax, was appointed manager of Seville with the near impossible task of trying to save the Spanish club from relegation with just ten games to go. In his first tenure at Ajax, Buckingham won the Eredivisie title and Dutch Cup as well as unearthing a prodigiously talented 12-year-old Johan Cruyff. Buckingham would hand the 17-year-old Cruyff his debut during his second period at the club.

As much as Buckingham would downplay his contribution to the emergence of Ajax, there are many who call him the father of Total Football. After his unsuccessful second tenure at Ajax, Buckingham endured three years of struggle at Fulham before heading to Greece to coach Ethnikos Piraeus. After a year there he unexpectedly moved to Barcelona, who were near the bottom of La Liga. Buckingham steadied the ship to take them to a fourth-place finish and European qualification. The following season saw Barcelona win the cup and come within a point of a domestic double. After just a season and a half in charge, the need for surgery on a persistent back problem forced Buckingham to step down as coach, to be replaced by Rinus Michels.

After months of recuperation following his surgery, Buckingham was preparing to return to management in Greece when he got the call from Seville. Despite three draws and a win in his first four games, it was a mission beyond even his powers of motivation. Seville lost five of their last six games to go down and end Buckingham's spell in Spain.

One more high-profile job fell Buckingham's way in the summer of 1975, at Greek giants Olympiacos, but he was sacked six months later amid the riots that surrounded a 4-0 home loss to PAOK.

Buckingham died in 1995, mourned by the fans of Ajax and Barcelona, but widely unheralded in his own country.

APRIL

'Although I didn't set out to blaze a trail
for other black players to follow, it was
always at the back of my mind that I was
representing the guy driving the train, the
guy cleaning the toilets.'

Clyde Best

AS THE First Division title race entered the home stretch, Manchester City held a one-point lead over Leeds and Derby, with Liverpool three points further back. At the bottom, Nottingham Forest were four points from safety with just six games remaining. Huddersfield joined them in the relegation places, but were breathing down the necks of Southampton and Crystal Palace.

Manchester City started the month with a home game against Stoke, while Derby and Leeds faced off at the Baseball Ground. Since securing their League Cup Final place, Stoke had only picked up three points from six games. Relatively safe in the league, their main focus was on the upcoming Cup semi-final with Arsenal. Although the muddy Maine Road pitch did much to neutralise the Manchester City side, they still dominated the game only to be kept at bay by an inspired Gordon Banks. Many at the game thought his double save from Lee in the second half was at least the equal of his 'save of the century' from Pelé. Despite Lee equalling Derek Kevan's club record of 30 goals in a season, a Doyle own goal and a John Ritchie strike gave Stoke the win and put a large hole in City's title aspirations.

With City losing, Leeds United's visit to Derby County gave the winner the opportunity to overtake City. Derby drew first blood after 16 minutes when John O'Hare headed home Alan Durban's cross. After the break, O'Hare had an opportunity to get his second, but instead Gary Sprake parried his shot straight at Norman Hunter and the ball rebounded into the net for an unfortunate own goal.

The same day at White Hart Lane, a little bit of history took place as West Ham fielded three black players – Clyde Best, Clive Charles and Ade Coker – for the first time in British football. West Ham won comfortably, with Brooking scoring the first goal and Coker side-footing the second in the last minute.

The first black player in British football was Andrew Watson, about whom little is known other than he was an outfield player who played for Scotland in the 1870s. Tottenham's Walter Tull became the first black outfield player in Division One and also the first black combat officer in the First World War, dying in the Spring Offensive of 1918. Jack Leslie, a London-born Anglo-African, was the first black player to enjoy genuine longevity in the British game, playing more than 400 games for Plymouth in the 20s and 30s. He was the victim of one of the most shameful incidents in English football when, after being selected to play for England, he was later omitted because the FA officials had not realised 'he was a man of colour'.

Other notable players included Jamaican-born Lloyd 'Lindy' Delapenha, who played for Middlesbrough from 1950 to 1957, scoring 90 goals in 260 appearances. Charlie Williams made 158 appearances for Doncaster Rovers over ten years in the 1950s. Tony Collins lasted even longer, playing for 15 years before becoming the first black manager in British football at

Rochdale in 1960. Leeds United's Albert Johanneson became the first black player to play in an FA Cup Final in 1965. After his early retirement in 1970, Johanneson struggled with alcoholism. In 1995 he would be found dead in his council flat at the age of 55.

In the 60s and 70s, Johanneson and Clyde Best faced much more hostility than Williams or Delapenha had in the 40s and 50s. Britain's BAME population grew from the low tens of thousands in the late 1940s to over one and a half million by 1975. To appease public opinion the government had passed an Immigration Act in October 1971; now only those with a parent or grandparent born in the UK had the right to settle in Britain, and all others had to apply for work permits. This legislation favoured whites, Home Secretary Reginald Maudling feeling that immigration ought to be limited to people from a 'cultural background fairly akin to our own'.

After Enoch Powell was sacked from the shadow cabinet for his Rivers of Blood speech in 1968, dock workers marched through the East End of London in his support. A year later, Clyde Best made his debut for West Ham, the club supported by fictional icon and Powell supporter, Alf Garnett. Best, and the black players who followed immediately after, like the rest of their community, had to contend with the aftermath of Powell. One can only admire Clyde Best's view of the abuse he received. 'Some grounds were worse than others, but you had to put it out of your mind. You also had to be careful not to react to provocation from opponents. You had to think of the people watching, the children. You had to think of your team-mates too. You couldn't be selfish and retaliate because the people provoking you were only trying to get you sent off. I was never sent off. Although I didn't set out to blaze a trail for other black players to follow, it was always at the back of my mind that I was representing the guy driving the train, the guy cleaning the toilets. Even at 18 I felt a responsibility to act in a certain way.'

Best demonstrated that the stereotypes of black players being unable to cope with the weather or the physicality of the English game were nonsense as he inspired the next generation of Afro-Caribbean players. The 70s saw the far-right National Front begin to mobilise anti-immigrant sentiments and make its presence felt in and around English football stadiums. Its membership would number around 14,000 by 1973. Although it was an insignificant proportion of the population, it was more than half of what the membership of the Nazi party had been in 1923, just ten years before they gained power in Germany.

To illustrate that it was one step forward and two steps back for race relations at the time, 12 days after Best, Coker and Charles played at White Hart Lane, *Love Thy Neighbour* debuted on television. The series would last for seven series and at one time was the most popular sitcom on British television. The 1973 spin-off film was Britain's 15th most popular film. While it wasn't a vintage year for movies, to imagine this drivel battling it out at the box office with *American Graffiti* and *Mean Streets* was wrong on so many levels.

As well as playing in a stronghold of Powellism, Clyde Best was playing in a country where Enoch Powell was its most popular politician. In 1972, Powell would be voted Man of The Year in a BBC poll for the second consecutive year. In defence of that generation, Powell's award can only be put into its naïve context by pointing out that in December 1971 Jimmy Savile was voted the Variety Club's showbusiness personality of the year and Rolf Harris appeared on *This is Your Life*.

By the mid-70s, the number of professional black players had risen into double figures and was growing fast. In the early 1980s, the Commission for Racial Equality and the FA agreed that the problem of racism in football was too small to be worried about. Consequently, the players had to make the journey for acceptance by themselves and in the face of relentless provocation. Despite the occasional lapse, they did so with great dignity and more than a little panache. By the mid-80s there were more than 100 professional black players, leading Hasbro – makers of Subbuteo – to reflect the new diversity in our game by including three black players in each of their teams from 1987.

By 1993 there were 244 black players in English professional football. Occupying 15 to 20 per cent of the professional labour pool through the 1990s from perhaps two to three per cent of the population is an overachievement by anyone's measure.

Although football shouldn't rest on its laurels, it's hard to justify the massive gap where the 20 per cent of our black players produce, at best, four per cent of our managers. Most disappointing is the lack of black faces on the terraces. It is still common to find football grounds across the country where there are more black people on the pitch than there are in the stands. Clubs in London, the West Midlands and Lancashire are located in areas with large, ethnically diverse communities, but generally fail to attract many of that demographic to games.

As for the shameful abuse that Best and his successors endured, my view is that on the terraces, as in life, there were and still are a few bigots. I believe that for most, the reason for the racial abuse was as simple and simple-minded as trying to put off an opposition player. Very often their best player. Clyde Best quoted the example of his team captain, Bobby Moore. 'Bobby took abuse wherever he went, not because of the colour of his skin but because of how good he was. From him I learnt that it doesn't make sense hiding, you have a job to do.'

Much has changed about England since Clyde Best first arrived from Bermuda more than 50 years ago, and a lot for the better. Although Best came not as a campaigner but as an outstanding 17-year-old footballer, his success helped to pave the way for the black players that followed.

At Ipswich, Chelsea's Dave Webb scored two goals to make it four in a week in his temporary position up front. Ipswich must have been heartily sick of Webb, given his performance in goal against them at Christmas.

Derby's win over Leeds put them top, and Liverpool had closed to within a point of Leeds with a win over West Brom. Derby, Manchester City and Leeds were all 2/1 for the title, with Liverpool at 10/1.

Two days after the Leeds game, Derby undid all their good work by losing to Newcastle. On the same night, Liverpool won 3-0 at Old Trafford to continue the run that had brought them 22 points from their last 12 games. Chris Lawler's sixth goal in 11 games opened the scoring, with John Toshack and Emlyn Hughes grabbing the others. Future Anfield legend Phil Thompson made his debut, coming on as a substitute for Toshack.

The following day, Manchester City attempted to regain the top spot at Southampton. Unlike Stoke, relegation-threatened Southampton did have something to play for. Ron Davies headed the opening goal in the 17th minute and proved he also had talent on the deck by firing home a second from 15 yards on the hour. A desperate City switched to a nine-man attack for the last half an hour. Francis Lee hitting the underside of the bar from five yards summed up their day.

Leeds welcomed back Mick Jones for their home game against Huddersfield, and it was he who opened the scoring in the 20th minute. Huddersfield matched Leeds for much of the match and equalised in the 56th minute through Steve Smith, before Leeds put their foot on the gas and scored through Peter Lorimer and Eddie Gray. Huddersfield's position had been fairly hopeless coming into April, but the defeat to Leeds would be the first of five successive losses to seal their fate.

The following Saturday, Manchester City got back to winning ways against West Ham. Rodney Marsh got the opener before crossing for Colin Bell to add the second. For the third, a scuffed shot from Wyn Davies turned into a defence-splitting pass, which Marsh slid home. Geoff Hurst got a late consolation for the London side.

Despite his two goals, Marsh was dropped to the bench for the Manchester derby. After a dull first half, Martin Buchan put United ahead after a mistake from Tommy Booth. Two minutes later, Francis Lee equalised with a back header that baffled United's stand-in goalkeeper, John Connaughton.[1] Four minutes after City brought on Rodney Marsh for Mike Doyle, Lee broke the Manchester City post-war individual scoring record to put City back into the title mix. Marsh made sure of the points five minutes from time, sliding Bell's pass home.

After Tony Towers gave his side the lead at relegation-threatened Coventry, Malcolm Allison inexplicably pulled Mike Summerbee back into midfield. This left Lee and Davies without support, resulting in his side defending too deeply. Coventry equalised ten minutes from time to take another vital point from Allison's men. After the game, Joe Mercer fell into conversation with the Coventry chairman, Derrick Robins. By now Robins was giving up on the idea that Brian Clough would be joining them. Knowing Mercer was unhappy at City, Robins sounded him out about taking over.

Portman Road had never been a happy hunting ground for City. They had not won there since their first visit in 1961, but now their visit to Ipswich was a must-win game.[2] After a poor season Ipswich were running into form, having won three of their last four games. Trevor Whymark fired Ipswich ahead in the 32nd minute, beating Ron Healey with a spectacular overhead kick. Summerbee got the equaliser in the 55th minute before the game's turning point five minutes later. Everyone in the ground, bar the referee, saw Bell's goal-bound shot palmed on to the bar by Ipswich full-back Colin Harper. Inevitably, it was Harper who headed home the winning goal to end City's title challenge.

After their disappointing loss at home to Newcastle, a jaded Derby travelled to West Brom and seemed as happy as the home side with the goalless draw. Derby's lack of goals – just five in their last six matches – was becoming a concern. Just when it seemed that they, too, were doomed to fade on the run-in, they rediscovered their form to hammer Sheffield United. Keeper John Hope lost the ball for Archie Gemmill's opener and failed to gather Alan Hinton's corner, enabling Alan Durban to force the ball home for the third. Hope's errors sandwiched a neat finish from Kevin Hector and it was left to John O'Hare to apply the coup de grâce. Whereas Manchester City had run into Gordon Banks having one of his greatest games, Derby met an out-of-form John Hope. On such small margins a 42-game season can be decided.

Derby next took revenge against Huddersfield, who had beaten them back in November, with goals from Roy McFarland, Hector and O'Hare. Derby took time off from the title race to pick up the Texaco Cup in front of a 25,000 crowd. Debutant Roger Davies scored the vital second goal in the 2-1 win over Airdrie.

David Harvey replaced the injured Gary Sprake in the Leeds goal for the visit to Stoke. The Potters, who had done so much to derail Manchester City's title bid, played well until the heavy pitch and the relentless power of Leeds told. Mick Jones scored two goals and Peter Lorimer the other, but their celebrations were spoilt by Terry Cooper breaking his leg. In a bizarre coincidence, Cooper's natural replacement, Nigel Davey, suffered a double fracture of his right leg in a reserve game against West Brom the same afternoon.

Two days later, with an eye on their upcoming semi-final against Arsenal, Stoke City fielded nine reserves in a 2-0 home loss to Nottingham Forest. Forest's win, their second in three days, pushed them to within two points of possible safety. Football League secretary Alan Hardaker said the Stoke team sheet would be examined and that there might be an enquiry.[3]

Although they didn't slip up to Stoke, as Manchester City had, Leeds also fell to Derby's conquerors, Newcastle. Malcolm Macdonald's goal, nine minutes from time, meant you could get 3/1 on Leeds to win the title, with Derby now 5/4 favourites and Liverpool second favourites at 7/4.

Liverpool continued their run with a 3-1 home win over Coventry. Kevin Keegan gave them a first-half lead, which Tommy Smith doubled from the penalty spot. John Toshack added the third. At West Ham they took advantage of a couple of defensive errors. In the tenth minute Bobby Ferguson watched his clearance cannon into the net off Toshack's chest. Their second, a minute after half-time, was the result of Bobby Moore losing possession to Steve Heighway, who finished with ease. Liverpool finished the month with their eighth successive win, a couple of goals from John Toshack beating an uncompromising Ipswich team.

On the same day, Leeds visited West Brom and Derby travelled to Maine Road. Whereas a controversial goal at West Brom had cost Leeds the previous season's title, it looked as if a controversial penalty might have handed them this season's title. Mick Jones appeared to fall very easily as Ray Wilson and Alistair Robertson came in to challenge. Johnny Giles tucked the penalty away to give Leeds the points.

Any second thoughts Joe Mercer was having about Coventry's offer must have vanished when he turned up for the last game of the season at Maine Road to find Malcolm Allison's car parked in his traditional space. In June, Mercer would resign to become manager of Coventry. As he had with Allison, he took a young protégé with him. This time, Gordon Milne, the manager of non-league Wigan, would assist him.[4]

In a match that was now an irrelevance for them, City took Derby County apart. Man of the Match, Rodney Marsh, displayed his full repertoire of flicks and tricks. In the first half he picked up a long ball on the right touchline, cut inside two defenders and drilled home a low right-foot shot. Four minutes before the interval, Derby's Ron Webster had to go off with a knee injury, to be replaced by Terry Hennessey. It was Hennessey who upended Marsh in the box to enable Francis Lee to dispatch his record-breaking 15th penalty of the season.

Although Joe Corrigan, back after a seven-game absence, had been a spectator for much of the game, he made a couple of excellent saves from John Robson and Alan Hinton when called on. City had finished their campaign and now led a league championship they couldn't win. Liverpool and Derby were due to play each other on May Day and both were a point behind City with a better goal average. Any result would knock City from the top.

Ron Davies, after a season beset by injury and poor form, finally rallied to drag Southampton to safety. After his two goals against Manchester City, his header against Leicester snatched another win. Although he would grab another brace against Manchester United, who always struggled to contain him, United were already three up by then.[5] He ended a disappointing season on a high, scoring two goals in the home draw against Chelsea to give him seven goals in five games.

Crystal Palace played their best football of the season to draw 2-2 with Arsenal, and the 2-0 win over Stoke ensured their First Division status for another season. They finished their season with a dreary 0-0 draw at home to Huddersfield. On the evidence of the game, there was no mystery as to why Huddersfield were relegated, only surprise that Palace weren't joining them.

Nottingham Forest's 3-1 defeat to Wolves ensured they would be joining Huddersfield. Tommy Gemmell's fifth goal in nine games was only a consolation as goals from Danny Hegan, John Richards and Kenny Hibbitt sent them to the Second Division.

Newcastle, who had done so much to shake up the title race with their wins over Derby and Leeds, played out a thrilling 3-3 draw at Stamford Bridge. Chelsea's Tommy Baldwin hit a brace for the second consecutive game to add to Kember's first goal of 1972. Macdonald hit his 24th goal of the season, but was outscored by strike partner John Tudor. Although it was the most exciting game of the day, the television cameras didn't cover it, which was probably just as well. The previous season's corresponding fixture had been broadcast on *Match of the Day*. Alan Hardaker, feeling David Coleman's criticisms of the referee were unfair, responded in the press somewhat forcefully. The affair would rumble on until January 1973, when Coleman served Hardaker and the newspaper with a writ for libel.[6]

Manchester United finished a season that had promised so much with a 3-0 win over a Stoke side shorn of Gordon Banks and four other regulars. Bobby Charlton opened the scoring before Ian Storey-Moore scored his fifth goal in 11 games. George Best's penalty gave him 26 for the season.

Birmingham petitioned, unsuccessfully, to move their FA Cup semi-final away from Hillsborough. They complained that the stadium was 77 miles from Birmingham, but only 33 from Leeds, and that Hillsborough had been used as a home ground by Leeds at the start of the season. In addition to the dispute over the venue, there were also issues with the two teams' kits. Leeds' all-white kit apparently clashed with Birmingham's blue 'pelican' strip. In the end, Leeds opted to play in yellow, while Birmingham wore a kit that substituted red for the blue. How different the change would be for the majority of television viewers still watching in black and white is a mystery. Mick Jones scored two and Lorimer the other as Leeds won their fifth semi-final in seven years at a canter.

The Arsenal and Stoke match at Villa Park proved just as dramatic as their semi-final the previous season. Arsenal opened the scoring when George Armstrong smashed the ball past Gordon Banks. With just over 20 minutes remaining, Arsenal goalkeeper Bob Wilson tore a cartilage in his knee. Bertie Mee's decision to keep the hobbling Wilson on the field backfired when a Terry Conroy cross, which would ordinarily have been easily collected by the keeper, was headed into his own net by Peter Simpson. Arsenal immediately changed things. Ray Kennedy came on for Wilson, who was replaced in goal by John Radford. Stoke piled the pressure on the stand-in keeper for the last quarter of an hour, but Radford heroically kept them at bay.

Two days before the replay, Gordon Banks became only the second goalkeeper after Bert Trautmann to win the Football Writers' Player of The Year.

Geoff Barnett replaced Bob Wilson for the replay at Goodison Park, his old home ground. The highlight of Barnett's Everton career had been his part in their 1965 FA Youth Cup Final win over Arsenal. He made just ten league appearances in seven seasons before being hurriedly signed by Arsenal after Bob Wilson broke his arm in 1969. Barnett made 11 league appearances while Wilson recovered, but hadn't played for the Arsenal first team since.

For the second successive year, Stoke lost to Arsenal in a semi-final replay and could feel more than a little aggrieved. In the fifth minute, Denis Smith's header looked well over the line before it was cleared by Bob McNab's scissor kick. In the 19th minute, Jimmy Greenhoff was sent clear by John Ritchie, only to be hauled down by Barnett. Greenhoff took the penalty himself to put Stoke ahead.[7] Stoke had chances to add to their lead. George Eastham laid on a chance for Peter Dobing, who delayed his shot too long. Immediately afterwards, man of the match, Eastham, crossed for Ritchie who headed wide of an open goal.

Although Arsenal improved in the second half, it took a soft penalty to get them back into the game. To the astonishment of everyone, referee Walker gave a penalty after Dobing collided with George Armstrong. Charlie George coolly sent Banks the wrong way from the spot.

Arsenal's winner 15 minutes from time was one of the most controversial incidents in any FA Cup semi-final. Linesman Bob Mathewson mistook one of Everton's white-coated programme sellers on the far side of the ground for the white change kit of a Stoke defender and kept his flag down as the offside Radford raced clear to plant the winner past Banks.

As exciting a cup tie as it was, I was bemused when two of the goals from the tie made it into the selection for the *Daily Mirror's Goal Action Replay* booklets – or flicker books, as they were better known. For those who know what these were, I have no need to explain how wonderful they were. For those of a younger generation, I will attempt to describe them. From August 1972, the paper printed a token every day. Once three tokens had been collected (or stamps, as they were named), you could send away for a flicker book. So that was three tokens, a stamped addressed envelope and a 10p Postal Order. Debit cards and PayPal were long in the future, so yes, this was as much of a pain as it seems.

There were six flicker books, each having two 'action replays'. Basically, they were individual frames of a goal in black and white which, when flicked, recreated the goal as seen on television. Careful thumb control even produced a slow-motion replay. You have to remember that we had no YouTube, DVD or video, so if there was a piece of action you wanted to see again, you had to hope that *On The Ball*, *Football Focus*, *Match of the Day* or *The Big Match* replayed it. Obviously, they would come up randomly or you could request a piece of action to be shown on *The Big Match*. This did carry the risk of Brian Moore reading out your full home address as he read out your letter. No Data Protection – or indeed common sense – back then either.

Twelve pieces of action were lovingly preserved across the six flicker books. It was, as ever, an eclectic choice. There were two of the dullest ever Pelé and Cruyff goals, to give it an international flavour. Also included were the Bobby Charlton thunderbolt versus Mexico, from the 1966 World Cup, and Geoff Hurst's second from the tournament's Final which, no matter how slowly you flicked, even down to examining individual frames, came no nearer to determining if it crossed the line. Also featured from the 1966 tournament was Eusebio hitting Portugal's third goal to knock out Brazil. After a couple of decidedly average Francis Lee and Martin Chivers goals,

George Best's goal against Benfica in the 1968 European Cup Final – the highlight of the collection for me – finished things off, along with four goals from the 1971/72 season. Ronnie Radford's goal against Newcastle was a welcome addition, as was Allan Clarke's diving header in the Cup Final, but Armstrong's semi-final goal against Stoke and Charlie George's penalty in the replay can only have been selected by an ardent Arsenal fan. Where was Banks' penalty save against Hurst? Or Best's goal against Sheffield United? If they had to include Arsenal, then surely Charlie George's diving header against Derby? I still have all of the flicker books and will still flick and replay Ronnie Radford, George Best, Allan Clarke, Bobby Charlton and Eusebio, feeling that it recaptures a bygone age far better than YouTube ever can. I confess the other clips have not been flicked in 48 years and counting.

The semi-finals of the European competitions took place, with Britain still represented in all three competitions. Tottenham cancelled Alan Mullery's loan at Fulham and dramatically recalled him for their UEFA Cup semi-final against AC Milan. Nereo Rocco, the Italian team's manager, lodged a protest to little avail.

Tottenham, playing their sixth match in 12 days, had Steve Perryman to thank for the slender lead they would take to Italy. Milan took the lead in the 25th minute when Terry Naylor's headed clearance was returned with interest by Romeo Benetti. Spurs equalised eight minutes later when Perryman hammered home a rising drive.

The match was scarred by 60 free kicks as the Milan side resorted to fouling and time-wasting in their quest for a draw. Riccardo Sogliano was sent off after an hour for stubbornly refusing to retreat ten yards for a free kick.

If Perryman's first goal was rare, his winner from 25 yards in the 64th minute was a true collector's item.

Alan Mullery silenced the San Siro crowd of 80,000 by firing home from the edge of the area in the sixth minute of the second leg. Spurs lived on their nerves in a frantic last 20 minutes, after Gianni Rivera levelled the game from the penalty spot, but held on to get to the Final.

Wolves took an 18th-minute lead at Ferencváros through John Richards, then nearly threw the game away in two minutes. Bernard Shaw handled in the 13th minute to enable István Szőke to slot home a penalty. Shortly afterwards, Szőke crossed low for Florian Albert to give Ferencváros the lead. Sixteen minutes from time, Phil Parkes saved another penalty from Szőke before Frank Munro gave Wolves a vital away draw with a header from a Ken Wagstaffe corner.

In the return leg, 18-year-old Steve Daley got Wolves off to the best possible start with a goal in the first minute. Ferencváros equalised just after half-time, but Frank Munro got a late goal to seal the tie. Phil Parkes repeated his heroics by saving another second-half penalty from Szőke to give us an all-English European final for the first time.

In the Cup Winners' Cup, Glasgow Rangers returned with a deserved draw from Germany. Paul Breitner opened the scoring in the 23rd minute, but a Rainer Zobel own goal in the 48th minute got Rangers back in the game and seemed to deflate Bayern Munich. Rangers finished off the job at Ibrox with two goals in the first 23 minutes. The first came from Sandy Jardine after Franz Beckenbauer uncharacteristically gave the ball away. Rangers doubled their lead through Derek Parlane, a last-minute replacement for the injured John Greig.

In the European Cup, Celtic gave a disciplined performance to snatch a goalless draw in Italy. Jimmy Johnstone's roving role caused Inter Milan problems throughout the game.

On the 19th, Glasgow was the centre of the football world as both of the Auld Firm were at home in European semi-finals. Kicking off slightly later than Rangers, Celtic couldn't break down Inter Milan, who suffocated the life out of the game beyond 90 minutes and right through extra time to bring Celtic Park its first-ever penalty shoot-out.

Sandro Mazzola, who'd dispatched the Inter penalty in the Final five years earlier, got the Italians off to a good start before John 'Dixie' Deans strode forward for Celtic. At the last second, Deans seemed to change his mind and fired the ball over the bar. With no other penalties missed, Inter had taken revenge for Lisbon and were through to the European Cup Final. Deans was inconsolable, but would get the chance to make amends in the Scottish Cup Final.

In the other semi-final, holders Ajax beat Benfica with a goal from the veteran Sjaak Swart. A goalless draw in the second leg in Lisbon was enough to take the Dutch side back to the Final as the Béla Guttmann curse held fast.

After being turned down by the board for a pay rise, Béla Guttmann had resigned as the Benfica manager in 1962. He allegedly cursed the club, declaring, 'Not in a hundred years from now will Benfica ever be European champions.' Benfica have since gone on to lose all eight of their European finals – five European Cup finals and three UEFA/Europa League finals.

In the Second Division, the promotion places still looked to be Norwich and Millwall's to lose. Although they had taken 17 points from the last 20, Birmingham remained three points behind Norwich, who were two points behind Millwall with a game in hand.

While QPR appeared to be out of it, they would play six of their last eight games at Loftus Road and could make a late run if the top three faltered.

Norwich wrestled the lead back from Millwall with a 2-0 win over Charlton. David Cross headed the first and new signing Jim Bone scored a superb individual second. They then had a tricky visit to QPR, but a tough-tackling performance got them a valuable point. Another difficult away game against Bristol City brought another draw, Cross and Bone getting the goals again. Norwich were picking up much-needed points without frills and extras, so it was apt that Duncan Forbes earned a win over Sheffield Wednesday with his first goal of the season.

Norwich would remain top despite a loss at Middlesbrough, as Millwall and Birmingham dropped points. Duncan Forbes got the only goal for the second home game in succession to give Norwich a win at home to Swindon. Thousands of supporters invaded the pitch at the end to proclaim that they were the champions, but they still needed a point to ensure promotion and three to make sure of the title.

Two days later, a win at Orient clinched promotion to the First Division for the first time in Norwich's 67-year history. They finished their season with a 1-1 draw at bottom club Watford to go up as Champions.

Millwall, so strong at home, had five of their last seven games away. They started the month by faltering at Craven Cottage, where Mullery masterminded Fulham's win. Millwall could now feel as aggrieved as the relegation-threatened clubs about his controversial loan. They then spurned the opportunity to join Norwich on 50 points with a 3-3 draw at Carlisle.

Their third away game in succession saw them travel to Birmingham, where their ambition was illustrated by keeper Bryan King's warning for time-wasting in the first few minutes. Bob Latchford got the breakthrough in the 76th minute with his 26th goal of the season. Birmingham still had Paul Cooper to thank for a superb save from Gordon Bolland in the last ten minutes to ensure they held on to both points. Birmingham were now breathing down the necks of the Lions.

Barry Bridges and Derek Possee earned Millwall a win over Hull to ease their nerves, but their promotion hopes faded after a comprehensive defeat at Burnley. They then made the short trip to Charlton and put one foot in the First Division with two goals in the last quarter of an hour. Bolland calmed Millwall nerves in the 75th minute and Possee hit the second in injury time.

Believing that Birmingham had lost at Sheffield Wednesday, the Lions celebrated promotion after beating Preston 2-0, before the hoax became apparent. Although Millwall had finished their season a point above Birmingham, they still needed to rely on Orient defeating Birmingham the following Tuesday, due to Birmingham's superior goal average.

Birmingham had begun the month with a visit to Cardiff. With the teams at opposite ends of the table, both desperately needed the two points on offer. A crowd of nearly 24,000 witnessed a 0-0 draw, which suited neither. Birmingham's biggest crowd of the season saw them warm up for the visit of Millwall with a 2-1 win over Blackpool. After the win over Millwall, the Blues had to play a Fulham team that had done them a huge service by defeating Millwall in their previous home game. Birmingham's 17th clean sheet of the season secured a 0-0 draw and another valuable away point. Middlesbrough, who had been promotion contenders for most of the season, equalised a first-half goal from Trevor Francis to snatch a draw.

At this point, Millwall and QPR could only get a maximum of 55 points, whereas Birmingham could finish the season with 56 if they won their remaining three games. However, two of the matches were away. Alan Campbell opened the scoring against Hull from the penalty spot before Trevor Francis scored the goal of the night, deceiving three defenders before firing home. At Sheffield Wednesday, Francis's fourth goal in six games was enough to leave Birmingham needing just a draw at Orient at the start of May to take them up.

QPR's faint hopes of a promotion slot had faded with the draw against Norwich, and the 0-0 draw with Fulham ensured that both the London clubs would reside in the Second Division next season. Their comprehensive 3-0 home win over Carlisle was too little too late. Having an unusually quiet game for Carlisle was Stan Bowles. The following season, it would be his signing that would transform the West London club.

Watford's mathematical chance of retaining their Second Division status ended with their draw against Oxford, leaving Charlton and Fulham to battle it out to ensure they wouldn't join them. Their face-off at the Valley ended in a 2-2 draw.

Both had tricky run-ins, but Fulham beat Millwall and drew against Birmingham and QPR to preserve their Second Division status. Despite surviving, Fulham would replace Bill Dodgin Jnr with Alec Stock in June. Stock had resigned as manager of Luton at the end of April, unable to cope with the 120-mile daily round-trip from his home in Epsom. He would stabilise Fulham's league position with four seasons of mid-table consistency, and taking them to the 1975 FA Cup Final would guarantee him legendary status at Craven Cottage.

Despite last month's defeat at Brighton, Aston Villa were still the favourites for promotion from the Third. Second-placed Bournemouth had only taken one point from their last three games and had to play Brighton in a must-win game. Early pacemakers, Notts County, were now five points behind Bournemouth, although they did have three games in hand.

Aston Villa rattled off four successive victories, virtually guaranteeing them a place in next season's Second Division. Their seven-point cushion meant they could afford to lose 2-1 at Torquay. They all but clinched promotion with three games to spare, when an eighth-minute goal from long-serving full-back Charlie Aitken gave them the points at Bradford. Geoff Vowden's goal looked to have sealed the title for Villa, but Mansfield's injury-time equaliser kept the champagne on ice. However, the point did make Vic Crowe's team mathematically sure of promotion.

The day after Villa guaranteed promotion, their youth team defeated Liverpool in the second leg of the FA Youth Cup Final. The Villa youngsters had reached the Final for the first time with a Bobby McDonald goal against Arsenal.

In the first leg of the Final, a John Gidman penalty had given Villa a narrow 1-0 win over Liverpool at home, but few expected that to be enough at Anfield. The Villa youngsters showed no fear, however, beating Liverpool's young hopefuls 4-2 to complete an aggregate win. Although Phil Thompson had equalised in the last minute of ordinary time, the visitors overwhelmed Liverpool in extra time, despite McDonald's dismissal.

For Gidman, who had been discarded by Liverpool, victory was particularly sweet. Together with Brian Little he would go on to become an Aston Villa legend as both won international honours at the club. McDonald also broke into the first team, but would enjoy greater success at Coventry and Manchester City.

Villa earned the point they needed for the Third Division title by beating Torquay. Although Vowden scored twice and Andy Lochhead hit his 25th goal of the season, it was the teenage Little who stole the show. He had joined the rest of the youth team to parade the FA Youth Cup before making his first senior start. In a dazzling performance, he made two goals and scored another in the first half-hour. Cliff Jackson completed the scoring for Villa by putting into his own net.

Brighton's 1-1 draw at Bournemouth made them favourites for the other promotion spot. Ted MacDougall put Bournemouth ahead with a goal that should have been disallowed for handball, but Brighton stuck to their task, earning a point with Bertie Lutton's late equaliser. Although Bournemouth dropped another point at Chesterfield four days later, it was the 2-1 defeat at Blackburn that ended their promotion hopes. MacDougall's 46th goal of the season gave Bournemouth the lead, but Blackburn levelled through a twice-taken penalty by Tony Field, before David Bradford hit the winner in the 75th minute.

Barnsley gave Brighton all manner of problems before an 86th-minute winner from John Templeman took the points. After that, Brighton efficiently took 12 points from their next seven games and left Bournemouth and Notts County to make the mistakes. Notts County had looked well placed to take the second spot until back-to-back defeats at Halifax and Barnsley ended their hopes.

Ken Beamish, Brighton's £25,000 signing from Tranmere, scored a vital five goals during the run-in. His old club's hopes of avoiding relegation were improved by Ron Yeats' second-half winner at Port Vale.

At the start of April, it was a matter of perming four from five for promotion from the Fourth Division. Leaders Scunthorpe had a two-point cushion over the chasing pack, and Lincoln were just a point behind fourth-placed Brentford, with a game in hand.

Scunthorpe fell to a Ron Young goal at Hartlepool, allowing Grimsby to leapfrog them to the top with a 2-1 home win over Cambridge. Lawrie McMenemy's Grimsby side would handle the pressure better than their rivals to take 14 points from their last nine games and go up as champions.

Southend went into the game at Lincoln looking for their seventh successive victory. The Imps missed the opportunity to put pressure on Southend for the fourth promotion place with a 0-0 draw. After dropping another home point to Cambridge, Lincoln threw away their promotion chances with losses against Hartlepool and Darlington. Although Scunthorpe only took seven points from their last ten outings, it was enough to take the last promotion spot by a point from Lincoln.

Despite Scunthorpe and Lincoln fading, Tommy Spratt's four goals in the last five games weren't enough to fire Workington into the promotion spots. When just 16, Spratt, an England schools and youth international, had scored 14 goals on his fifth-team debut for Manchester United in 1957/58.

Joining Grimsby and Scunthorpe in next year's Third Division were Southend and Brentford. At the bottom, Crewe were doomed, and it looked as if three from Hartlepool, Newport, Darlington and Stockport would join them in seeking re-election.

Hartlepool won eight of their last 11 games to steer themselves out of trouble, and Darlington also dragged themselves to safety with four wins. Rod Jones scored five goals in five games to ensure Newport would preserve their status for another year. So it would be Barrow and Northampton who would join Crewe and Stockport in seeking re-election.

Barrow had looked to be safe after two wins at the end of March, and a further two at the start of April took them out of the bottom places, but six losses in their last seven doomed them to the re-election places. Utility man Bobby Knox tried harder than most to ensure their safety, even donning the keeper's gloves against Cambridge and Darlington.[8] Sadly, it was Knox's own goal that levelled the scores at half-time in Barrow's last match against Exeter, before a second-half collapse led to them being thrashed 7-1.

Northampton, a club that had been in the First Division just six years earlier, would have to seek re-election for the first time. The 6-1 defeat of Gillingham on April 1 would be their only win in their last 15 games.

Wigan, one of the candidates looking to be elected to the Football League in place of one of the bottom clubs, decided to take the unusual step of applying for a place in next season's Scottish Second Division. After staging the previous month's amateur international between England and Scotland, they had been encouraged by the positive feedback from the Scottish officials for the facilities at Springfield Park. The previous season, their experience when applying for election to the Football League for the 33rd time had soured them to the process. They had felt that a northern club was due to be elected to the Football League and, as Northern Premier League champions – in addition to narrowly losing at Manchester City in the third round of the FA Cup – they believed their time had come.

However, before the vote in June 1971, Wigan chairman, Ken Cowap, made a terrible mistake. His gift of a Parker pen to each of the club chairmen was viewed as a bribe and Wigan won just 14 votes, four fewer than the year before. The league clubs were comfortably re-elected, with Cowap inevitably becoming known as Ken the Pen.

Wigan's bid to join the Scottish League was not as crazy as it seemed. They believed they would comfortably have the biggest gates in the Scottish Second Division and could win immediate promotion. The problem remained, however, that Wigan, unlike Berwick Rangers – the other English club playing in Scotland – was more than 100 miles from Scotland, and the Scottish League's record on admitting clubs was even worse than England's.

Since 1931, only Clydebank had been given a league place. Inevitably, Wigan's bid was rejected and they remained in the NPL. Six years after being turned down, they would be the last team elected to the Football League when they replaced Southport in 1978.

In May, Wigan's fellow Northern Premier League side, Stafford Rangers, would clinch the non-league double by pipping Boston United to the title and comfortably beating Barnet in the FA Trophy Final at Wembley with a three-goal burst late in the second half.

In goal for Stafford was Milija Aleksic, who had started his career at Port Vale before being released and drifting into non-league football. His displays during Stafford's success brought him to the attention of several league clubs and, in March 1973, a £3,000 fee took him to Plymouth Argyle. Almost his first touch at Home Park was to retrieve a Pelé penalty from the net in a friendly against Santos.

Aleksic struggled to claim the number-one spot at Argyle and, after loan spells at Ipswich and Oxford, he moved to Luton Town in 1976. His form at Luton would lead to the Spurs manager, Keith Burkinshaw, paying £100,000 to take him to White Hart Lane in December 1978.

Aleksic was in goal as Spurs lifted the 1981 FA Cup and narrowly beat John Radford to become the first player to win both the FA Trophy and the FA Cup. An FA Cup winner in 1971, Radford would win the FA Trophy with Bishop's Stortford two days after Spurs' FA Cup win.

The following summer, Aleksic lost his first-team place to Ray Clemence and, despite being an FA Cup winner just a year previously, dropped back into non-league football.

Scotland manager Tommy Docherty brought Denis Law back from the international wilderness and named him as captain for the friendly against Peru. The South American side included Teófilo Cubillas, Hugo Sotil, Juan Muñante, Rodolfo Manzo, José Velásquez and Percy Rojas, all of whom would play in the World Cup win over Scotland six years later.

John O'Hare put Scotland ahead shortly after half-time from Willie Morgan's free kick. Denis Law celebrated his return by blasting the ball into the roof of the net for the second after 65 minutes.

In December 1969, Roger Hunt had left for Bolton after ten seasons at Liverpool. Club rules at the time stipulated that a player could not have a testimonial until they had retired from playing. Kopites never forget a hero and, despite the torrential rain, the gates were locked half an hour before kick-off, with an estimated 10,000 still outside. The official attendance of 55,214 was the largest ever recorded for a testimonial in England.

The crowd saw Hunt hit a hat-trick as Liverpool's 1965 FA Cup-winning team beat an England select, 8-6. The England XI included George Cohen, Bobby Moore, Martin Peters, Nobby Stiles and Geoff Hurst from the World Cup-winning side. A.N. Other, looking suspiciously like the still-banned Tony Kay, came on as substitute and was the choice of many as man of the match.

To assist England's upcoming visit of West Germany, Ron Greenwood rested Bobby Moore and Geoff Hurst for West Ham's league game against Arsenal. The Gunners followed suit by resting Alan Ball and Peter Storey from their midweek game against Manchester United. Brian Clough, however, announced that Roy McFarland and Colin Todd would be out injured for the international. McFarland was Alf Ramsey's preferred choice to partner Bobby Moore in central defence and would be a huge loss.

To replace McFarland, Ramsey decided to play Norman Hunter, with Bobby Moore taking the number-five shirt. On the odd occasions Ramsey had tried the combination before, it had not been a success; against the Germans it would be a disaster. Much to Ramsey's fury, both McFarland and Todd played against Liverpool two days after the international.

All the indications from the West German camp were that they intended to play a tight defensive game and would be happy to settle for a draw or narrow defeat. As England were at home, West Germany would play in their change kit of green shirts, which many still believe is worn as a tribute to Ireland. Apparently, as Ireland were the first country to play Germany after the Second World War, the Germans were so grateful to the Irish for bringing them back into the international fold that they chose green as their away strip to honour them. A twist on the story has the teams swapping shirts after the match and, as the Germans were so poor, they used the Irish shirts, with the crest replaced, for their next away match, so beginning the tradition of playing in green as a change strip.

Sadly, both versions are nonsense. In October 1951, Ireland were in fact the fifth team to play the Germans after the war. As regards Germany's change colours, red actually predates the green, but because red had been heavily associated with the Nazi Reich, it was now a no-no. Therefore, after the war the colours of the Reich were changed to the less symbolically charged green part of the traditional heraldic colours of the Rhineland.

In June 1951, four months before their match against Ireland, West Germany played Turkey in Berlin, wearing green shirts and shorts.

Despite the World Cup quarter-final defeat to West Germany two years earlier, England were still regarded as one of the best international sides in the world and were considered favourites against the young and relatively inexperienced German side. The average age of Germany's starting XI was

23, four years younger than that of England, who featured five players from their World Cup-winning side of 1966.

The match would signal the beginning of the end, not only for some of the heroes of 66, but also for Alf Ramsey. England did not know what hit them, as they were swamped from the kick-off by quick combination play and wave after wave of attacks as West Germany, and in particular Günter Netzer, took the game by the scruff of the neck.

In the 26th minute, the constant German pressure led to Bobby Moore making a mistake. A cross from Held was controlled by the England captain, who seemed to have mopped up the danger. He turned into Herbert Wimmer and, although he evaded the German's challenge, he gave the ball away to Müller who slipped it to Held. Held rolled the ball to Uli Hoeness whose shot passed the wrong-footed Gordon Banks at a comfortable height.[9] Although Hoeness had made his international debut a couple of months earlier, he was retaining his amateur status to take part in the Olympic Games later in the year.

The Germans continued to dominate the first half, but a second goal refused to come. England's only tactic in the first half was to pump long, high balls into the box for Chivers and Hurst.

England came into the game a bit more in the second half and nearly equalised when Emlyn Hughes clipped the bar with a half-volley. Hurst looked increasingly out of touch and was replaced by Rodney Marsh on the hour. It would be Hurst's last appearance for England.

With 12 minutes to go, Colin Bell played a one-two with Peters before shooting. Sepp Maier parried the shot to Francis Lee, who tapped in from two yards. Despite having the draw they came for, the Germans kept pressing for a winner. In the 84th minute England gave away possession and, as Held strode forward, Moore brought him down just inside the box. Banks got both hands to Netzer's penalty, but could only push it on to a post and in. Might the Banks of two years earlier have done better?

Banks was certainly culpable for the decisive third goal, when he threw the ball to Hughes in stoppage time, putting him under pressure. The Liverpool man was robbed by Held, who fed Hoeness. He slipped the ball to Müller, who swivelled and hooked a low shot past the right hand of Banks.[10] The 3-1 scoreline was a fair reflection, even if the second and third goals hadn't come at a time of German supremacy.

Although the game had been a disaster for the England team, it was a financial success for the FA, raising £187,000 in gate receipts, in addition to the £64,000 for the TV rights. The undoubted star of the night was Günter Netzer, although had Wolfgang Overath been fit it is doubtful Netzer would have even played.

Netzer made his international debut in October 1965. Despite winning three caps by the time of the 1966 World Cup, he didn't make the squad. The German manager, Helmut Schön, tried on a couple of occasions to play Overath and Netzer together, but the disastrous draw in Albania in 1967 showed the difficulty in accommodating both of them. Leading up to the 1970 World Cup, both players were in magnificent form, but Overath remained first choice for the national side. Netzer would again miss out on the squad, this time from injuries sustained when he crashed his Ferrari.

Although Overath succeeded Uwe Seeler as captain of the German national team after the Mexico tournament, Schön was finding it hard to ignore the claims of Netzer. Schön had two outstanding playmakers available, one who had already proven his worth in two World Cups and the other who was the star of the Bundesliga champions. Schön kept trying to accommodate them both, with little success.

During the 1971/72 season, Overath helped make up his mind with a series of minor injuries, which culminated in a severe groin injury in March 1972. Needing an operation,

Overath would be out of action for months and miss the 1972 European Championship. After playing a major role in winning the European Championship, it looked as though Netzer would remain Germany's number 10, but now it was his turn to be troubled by nagging injuries. He would play in only one of the ten internationals in 1973, forcing Schön to recall Overath.

Netzer struggled to adapt after his move to Madrid, and in the German training camp before the World Cup it was clear he wasn't in good physical shape. Schön decided to start with Overath for the third successive World Cup.

Overath played well, apart from the game against East Germany when he was substituted for Netzer after 70 minutes. Overath kept his place in the starting 11 for the next game against Yugoslavia, and retained it through to the Final. After Germany won the tournament, Overath quit the national side, having won 81 caps over 11 years. Netzer would eventually settle at Madrid, winning two titles, but his international career all but ended at the 1974 World Cup.[11] Although he became the first player to receive a winner's medal while playing abroad, those 20 minutes against East Germany would be his only action in a World Cup.

Overath enjoyed the greater international success, but Netzer could content himself with a performance at Wembley on a wet April evening that would forever be bracketed with that of Puskas in 1953 and Cruyff in 1977.

MAY

*'Give us a penalty, wee man, and
I will give you a grand.'*

Billy Bremner

ON 1 May, Derby hosted a Liverpool side unbeaten in the
league since early January. Brian Clough was expected to replace
the injured Ron Webster with Terry Hennessey, but instead
selected 16-year-old Steve Powell for only his second league
game. Powell had made his debut in a Texaco Cup tie against
Stoke the previous October, aged just 16 years and 30 days, to
become Derby's youngest ever player.[1] His father, Tommy, had
also made his debut for Derby as a 16-year-old, on Christmas
Day 1941.

In front of a capacity crowd of 40,000, the match – with
so much at stake – was never likely to be a classic. Although
Kevin Hector hit the bar in the 14th minute, it was Liverpool
who made the early running. Tommy Smith brought a fine save
from Colin Boulton, and Toshack missed a great opportunity
after good work from Keegan.

Liverpool had kept a clean sheet in their last six away games,
and conceded only three goals in their last 16 league matches.
With the quality of the defenders on both sides, the game was
always likely to be decided by a single goal. It was the Derby
captain, John McGovern, who got the breakthrough in the
62nd minute. Hector's quick throw found Archie Gemmill on

the edge of the Liverpool area. He wrong-footed the Liverpool defence before sweeping the ball across the face of goal. After Alan Durban stepped over it, the ball ran on to McGovern to score his third goal of the season while falling backwards. With their season finished, all Derby could do now was wait and see if 58 points would be enough to take the title.

After Brian Clough inherited him at Hartlepool, John McGovern would play for Clough at another three of his clubs. By the time he was 19, he had played in all four divisions. 'He couldn't run and often looked ungainly,' said Clough. 'But he would always stand up straight, he always strived to get and to pass the ball, and he would do that whether the team was losing 3-0 on a filthy night at Walsall or winning 4-0 on a sunny afternoon at Wembley.' McGovern was a playbreaker and a playmaker, the type of player whose value has only become truly apparent in modern times.

While Derby were beating Liverpool, Leeds beat Chelsea 2-0 in a game littered with fouls, as was the case whenever these two teams met. Their game in December had been shown on *Match of the Day* and was called, 'One of the most cold-bloodedly violent games ever shown on television.'

After the games, the bookies had Leeds at 3/1 on for the title. Derby were 5/1 and Liverpool 7/1. Off the pitch, Leeds utility man Paul Madeley's father married Paul's mother-in-law over the weekend. Paul and his wife were now also stepbrother and sister, and technically uncle and aunt to their 18-month-old son.

Francis Lee was taken ill after returning home from a business trip in Liverpool. His wife drove him to Bolton Royal Infirmary where he was discovered to be suffering from physical and mental exhaustion. As managing director of FH Lee (Paper Converters) Ltd, he had been leading a busy life.[2] For the last five years, his working life stretched to 18-hour days, seven days a week.

After a demanding season, in which he had been an ever-present, Lee was preparing to play in a testimonial for team-mate, Alan Oakes, his fourth match in five days, when he fell ill. Lee's toilet roll manufacturing business would make him a multi-millionaire and give him the money to oust Peter Swales as chairman of Manchester City in 1994. Originally welcomed as a hero by supporters, his appointment of friend and ex-England team-mate, Alan Ball, as manager was a disaster. By the time Lee stepped down as chairman in 1998, he was on his sixth manager and the club was on the brink of relegation to the third tier of English football.

Although his chairmanship was unsuccessful, Lee's negotiations with the city council helped the club secure what would become the Etihad Stadium. The stadium, which had been constructed for the Commonwealth Games of 2002, would be a major factor in Sheikh Mansour's decision to buy the club.

A sad consequence of Lee's time as chairman was the rift that developed between him and ex-team-mate Colin Bell. Bell had rejoined Maine Road in 1990 as youth development officer, but problems developed after Neil McNab joined the coaching staff. Bell and McNab frequently clashed and in May 1997 the club gave up mediating and sacked both of them. Bell took the club to an employment tribunal, where the two parties settled out of court as per the tribunal's suggestion. Bell would eventually make up with the club, but sadly not with Lee.

In the build-up to the Cup Final, Esso ran a promotion similar to its Mexico 70 extravaganza. This time the giveaway was silver alloy coins featuring the club badge of a previous FA Cup winner. By now my father had upgraded his car to a Riley, which burnt more oil than petrol, so completing the collection proved little problem.

The official crowd receipts for the Final would be a record £192,917. Seats priced at £5 were selling for up to £200 on the black market, quite a contrast to the 4,554 spectators who turned up to watch the league match between Arsenal and Leeds on 5 May 1966.[3] Whereas just George Armstrong and

Peter Storey remained of the Arsenal side, should Leeds select Gary Sprake they would line up with seven of the same team. Terry Cooper, who would miss the Final with a broken leg, had been their substitute six years earlier.

In the press, Norman Giller predicted that Arsenal would win the Cup, but Leeds would win the title.

FA Cup Final day was when broadcasters made up for the dearth of live football on the television with more than ten hours of coverage. In the 1970s, as far as live football was concerned, we were rationed to the FA Cup Final, the European Cup Final, the England versus Scotland Home International and maybe the occasional England international. BBC and ITV both showed the Cup Final live and battled to grab your attention early, with their pre-match build-ups starting four hours before the match.

Amongst the fare would be rehashes of the highlights of the televised cup games during the competition, the summariser desperately trying to convince you of the relevance to the Final of the Wolves–Leicester third-round tie. During the *Grandstand* Cup Final special, Ronnie Radford's goal against Newcastle was announced as the winner of their second Goal of the Season competition. ITV – trying to top the BBC – carried a Goals of the Century segment. Both sides would show goals from previous finals as well as interviews with the players and managers from this year's Final. This year we also had a 'My Dad's at Wembley' feature, in which the players' children were interviewed. It was a shame Paul Madeley's son was a little young to take part; it would have been fascinating to hear how the utility man filled the dual roles of father and uncle.

As there were only a couple of hours' televised highlights each week, the broadcasters struggled to fill the eight hours spread over the two programmes with football clips, so they had to get creative. Although *World of Sport* showed their usual wrestling and some international athletics from Crystal Palace, *Grandstand* would retaliate with Cup Final *It's a Knockout*, for me the highlight of the build-up.

The programme had begun the previous year and by now Stuart Hall had taken over hosting duties from David Vine. To try to inject an air of gravitas, Arthur Ellis refereed the games. Twenty years earlier, Ellis had refereed Arsenal's Cup Final loss to Newcastle. The Cup Final-themed competition was between supporters of the two finalists. Leeds' midfield duo, Billy Bremner and Johnny Giles, turned up to support their team, but bizarrely, Stoke players Gordon Banks and George Eastham joined disc jockey Peter Murray to cheer on Arsenal. I can only assume they'd been booked before the semi-final replay by someone who fancied Stoke to win through.

World of Sport added a celebrity element to the proceedings with their Wembley Starspot segment as Dickie Davies talked to some of the stars and personalities at the game. The passage of time blurs the participants, but I'm guessing that Kenny Lynch numbered among them. ITV also featured some of the acts from *The Comedians* television show. The hit show had been running for just over a year and made household names of Bernard Manning, Frank Carson and Jim Bowen, amongst others. One of the roster, Charlie Williams, had played for Doncaster Rovers during the 1950s. Williams was quite the trailblazer. As few black footballers as there were in that decade, there were even fewer black comedians in the early 70s.

As kick-off approached, both channels interviewed the players on the pitch, which gave us the opportunity to see how awful their suits were. Players' Cup Final suits have a proud tradition of being dreadful but, given that the early 70s were the era that fashion forgot, I'm imagining huge collars and flares in beige and cream polyester.

After a quick ten minutes from the band of the Royal Marines, we had the Centenary Cup Final Parade featuring all 37 previous winners.[4] Club flags were carried, followed by kitted-out representatives of previous winners, with the number of representatives signifying how many times each club had won the Cup. Of the finalists, Leeds weren't part of the parade, whereas Arsenal's four wins were represented by apprentices in full kit carrying signs with the name of their club. They were led by 16-year-old Liam Brady, who had been at the club less than a year. The next time Arsenal appeared at Wembley – in the 1978 FA Cup Final – he would be the star of their team.

By now I was joined in front of the telly by my father, just in time for the singing of *Abide with Me*, led by Tommy Steele.[5] The hymn had first been sung before the 1927 FA Cup Final. My father would insist I make him a cup of tea, which was just an excuse to get me out of the room as he watched with tears welling. After I hit my forties, I too would get emotional during *Abide with Me*. I assume it's an age thing, or perhaps something hormonal.

Both sides had panels to lend their expertise. ITV featured Malcolm Allison, Derek Dougan and Pat Crerand. Bob McNab, the other member of their Mexico 70 panel, was unavoidably detained playing in the match. Over on the BBC, Brian Clough and Bobby Charlton were joined by Bob Wilson and Terry Cooper, both of whom, but for injuries, would have joined McNab on the pitch. Cooper's injury would also keep him out of the following year's Cup Final against Sunderland.

Half an hour before the game, Leeds manager Don Revie revealed that David Harvey would retain the goalkeeper's jersey in place of Gary Sprake.

Leeds and Arsenal had previously met in the 1968 League Cup Final at Wembley. Everyone hoped that this game would be more interesting.

The preamble complete, the two teams were led out on to the pitch by their managers. The captains – Scotland team-mates, Bremner and McLintock – chatted all the way. Billy Bremner was given the Leeds captaincy over the older, more experienced Jack Charlton because Charlton used to insist on being the last player out of the tunnel. Although the Queen was in attendance for the first time since 1965, she left the presentation of the teams to her husband.

Finally, at three o'clock, the game kicked off. Brian Moore was commentating for ITV, while David Coleman covered his first FA Cup Final for the BBC. After flicking between the channels during the build-up, we – like many others – always watched the match on BBC. Moore was too much of a screamer for my taste, although he did calm down in later years.

Immediately after the kick-off, Alan Ball took the ball into the Leeds half and was fouled by Allan Clarke. Two seconds in and the first free kick was given. Within a minute, we had our first booking. Peter Lorimer picked up the ball on the right-hand touchline and was caught by Bob McNab, whose name was taken by referee David Smith.

After just four minutes there had been five free kicks, with as many robust challenges going unpunished. Between the fouling, the odd chance was carved out. Clarke hammered an inviting low ball across the goalmouth, but Mick Jones couldn't reach it. Frank McLintock's low drive changed direction off the turf, the ball stuck between Harvey's chin and shoulder, and Ball had a volley blocked on the line by Paul Reaney.

Leeds soon began to dominate. Lorimer's shot was fumbled past the post by a relieved Geoff Barnett, and Clarke had a header drop off the face of the Arsenal crossbar. The game's most telling statistic was the 24 fouls in the first 36 minutes, as Norman Hunter and Bremner joined McNab in the referee's notebook.

The second half began in the same fashion, with Charlie George becoming the fourth player to be booked after lunging at Bremner. Typically, the caution was for a throwaway comment rather than the foul itself. The FA Cup Final hadn't seen any cautions in its first 100 years. Now we had four.

By midway through the second half, every outfield player had been penalised at least once. In the 54th minute, Leeds finally broke the deadlock with a goal worthy of winning any contest. Charlton dispossessed George and fed Paul Madeley, who carried the ball into the Arsenal half. He passed to Lorimer, who sent Jones free down the right wing. The centre-forward sent an inviting centre beyond the penalty spot to where Clarke was lurking. Clarke threw himself forward, heading the ball past Barnett into the bottom corner.

After the brief interlude for football, the game reverted back to type. In the 63rd minute, Ball hacked Bremner's legs from under him, then angrily tried to lift the Leeds captain to his feet. Only Bremner's sporting intervention saved the Arsenal man from being the fifth player booked.

Arsenal almost snatched an undeserved equaliser in the 69th minute. Ball's 20-yard shot deflected off Bremner's heel, falling nicely for George, who crashed the ball powerfully against the bar. Peter Simpson, following up, could only smash the ball high and wide.

Leeds hit the woodwork again themselves, through Lorimer. With seconds remaining, Hunter sent Jones clear down the right. After slipping past McLintock he bore down on goal. Barnett dived at his feet and, as Jones tumbled over, his left arm collapsed under him. He was still down injured when the referee blew the final whistle. As Bremner accepted the trophy from the Queen, Jones was still receiving pitchside treatment for a dislocated elbow. Although Mick Bates advised Jones that he had already collected his medal, Jones, despite the pain, insisted on meeting the Queen. The sight of Jones agonisingly making his way to the Royal Box, with the help of Norman Hunter, was one of the defining images of the final.

In Scotland, although Hibernian hadn't won the Scottish Cup for 70 years, the feeling was that this could be their year. In goal they had the ever-reliable James Herriot. No, not that one. Well, not quite that one.

After writing his first book about his life as a vet, Alf Wight couldn't find a suitable pseudonym under which to publish his memoirs until one night, while watching football on the television, he was rather taken with the name of then Birmingham keeper, Jim Herriot. Wight/James Herriot went on to become a household name thanks to the 1975 film and subsequent television series, *All Creatures Great and Small*.

Hibs' colourful defensive line of Jim Black, John Blackley and John Brownlie was completed by Erich Schaedler, the son of a former German prisoner of war. Schaedler would be capped by Scotland, aptly against West Germany, and was a member of the squad for the 1974 World Cup in Germany.

His death aged just 36, in December 1985, continues to raise questions. His body was found in his car, in the countryside near his hometown in the Scottish Borders, with a single shotgun wound to the head. Schaedler's family still do not accept that he could have taken his own life. Before the game, Jock Stein announced to his players that it would be Jim Craig's last game. Craig was leaving to play for Hellenic in South Africa.

Stein was disbanding the Lisbon Lions to usher in the Quality Street Gang, the greatest set of youngsters to have ever developed at the same time in Scottish football. They included George Connelly, Kenny Dalglish, David Hay, Lou Macari and Danny McGrain.

In 1968, Scotland's national team boss, Bobby Brown, asked Jock Stein to supply him with some opposition for a warm-up match. Stein sent him the Quality Street Gang, which destroyed the Scottish team 5-2.

The Gang kept the trophies coming in for a while, but never reached the heights of their predecessors. Ironically, many of the players who were meant to take over from the Lisbon Lions left the club before Bobby Lennox, Jimmy Johnstone and Billy McNeill.

Celtic took the lead through McNeill after just two minutes. Hibernian's Alan Gordon scrambled an equaliser ten minutes later, but then the roof fell in. Just two weeks after his European nightmare, Dixie Deans grabbed a hat-trick, the first in a Scottish Cup Final since 1904. Jim Craig had one of his finest games, and it was from his surges down the right that Lou

Macari scored two late goals to complete the rout and give Celtic a record 19 goals for their Cup campaign.

In the second ever Women's Cup Final, Southampton Ladies beat Lee's Ladies of Kilmarnock 3-2, with a brace from Pat Judd and the other from Sue Lopez. Lee's were missing their leading scorer, the heavily pregnant Mrs Elsie Cook. As a bonus, the Southampton Ladies were now allowed to celebrate long into the night at one of the 500 Wimpey bars dominating the UK high streets. Until the end of 1971, women were banned from entering Wimpey Bars after midnight without a man, as it was assumed they were prostitutes.

Sue Lopez had returned from a year playing semi-professional football for Roma in the National Italian Women's League, just in time for the official lifting of the ban on women playing football. The Women's FA continued to run things themselves, as an affiliate of the FA, until 1993 when the FA realised it would make more sense for them to assume overall control of the women's game.

During the Women's European Championship in 2013, to the amusement of many, the FA celebrated '20 years of women's football', erasing the century of history that they'd previously tried so hard to suppress.

Lopez had made her debut for Southampton WFC in 1966 and was a regular in the side for almost 20 years, helping them win the Cup eight times between 1971 and 1983. Following her retirement in 1985, she became only the second woman to gain the FA Advanced Licence coaching qualification, and in 2000 she received an MBE for services to women's football. In 2004, she was the third woman to be inducted into the National Football Museum's Hall of Fame.

With the FA Cup won, the Leeds players left their wives to enjoy the post-match banquet and travelled by coach to Wolverhampton. They needed a draw there to become champions for the second time in four years and complete the Double.

If Leeds lost, a Liverpool victory at Arsenal on the same night would see the Reds win the title. Leaders Derby County could only be champions if Leeds lost and Liverpool failed to win. Standing between Leeds and immortality were a Wolves team in the middle of a two-legged UEFA Cup Final against Tottenham. To add further spice to the game, there was a whiff of corruption in the air. The day before the match, the *Sunday People* revealed that offers had been made to the Wolves players to throw the match.

A crowd of more than 50,000 packed behind gates that were closed long before kick-off. Not for the first time during the season, crush barriers gave way, injuring more than 70 people. Despite only needing a draw, Leeds tactics were all-out attack. Their appeals for an early penalty looked justified when Wolves' keeper Phil Parkes collided with Allan Clarke in the area. Their appeals were even louder in the 25th minute, when Bernard Shaw got both hands to a Clarke effort and, for a split second, was actually carrying the ball. A few minutes later, Peter Lorimer let fly with a powerful shot, which Parkes stopped with a full-length dive. Just before half-time and totally against the run of play, a Frank Munro drive found the net via a post to give Wolves the lead. As soon as the second half commenced, Leeds were back on the offensive.

Lorimer hammered a free kick in from 30 yards that Wolves somehow managed to scramble away, with another suspicion of handball by Shaw. In their chase for an equaliser, Leeds were leaving gaps in defence. In the 67th minute, John Richards' pass opened up their defence, allowing Derek Dougan to run through and slide the ball home.

In desperation, Revie replaced the struggling Clarke with Terry Yorath and pushed Jack Charlton into attack. The decision paid instant dividends when Bremner clawed a goal back. Lorimer headed on to the crossbar in the final minutes but, despite frantically pressing for an equaliser, the final whistle blew, leaving Leeds as runners-up for the fifth time in eight seasons.

Much has been made of Leeds playing their opening four home games away from Elland Road, but what lost Leeds the title was their away form. It was the losses at struggling Coventry, Huddersfield and Southampton that ultimately cost them. A point against any of them would have been enough to take the title.

With Leeds losing, Liverpool could win the title by beating an Arsenal side missing the injured Charlie George and Bob McNab. Emlyn Hughes hit the underside of the bar from 25 yards and there was a frantic final 20 minutes when, after hearing that Leeds were losing, Liverpool threw everything at Arsenal.

Two minutes from time, John Toshack diverted Kevin Keegan's mishit shot into the net, but the goal was disallowed by referee Roger Kirkpatrick for offside. Shankly sportingly congratulated Derby, saying they were worthy champions and the best team Liverpool had faced during the season.

On holiday in Majorca, Peter Taylor and the Derby team listened to the final minutes of the Leeds game on the radio. Brian Clough was in the Scilly Isles with his family. After he heard the news, he ordered champagne for everyone in the hotel.

Arsenal still had a derby to play against Tottenham at Highbury. In a match played in swirling wind and rain, Tottenham's Alan Mullery scored the opener after an hour. Ralph Coates waited until the last minute of the last league game to score one of the goals of the season. Collecting the ball ten yards outside his own penalty area, he set off on a 70-yard run. Using John Pratt as a decoy, Coates cut inside and squeezed his shot home. The goal was a worthy finish to the greatest League Championship in history.

At the end of the month, Derby County and Leeds United confirmed that they wouldn't play in the Charity Shield match at the start of the following season. To replace them,

Manchester City, who had finished fourth, would play Aston Villa, the Third Division champions. City won the match at Villa Park and would defend the trophy in the 1973 Charity Shield, despite finishing 11th and getting knocked out of the FA Cup in the fifth round. In 1974, FA secretary Ted Croker moved the match to Wembley and made the participation of the reigning League and FA Cup holders mandatory.

The following September, the *Daily Mirror* reported the suspicion of bribery before and during the Wolves-Leeds title decider. The *Mirror's* allegations were investigated by the police and the FA, but neither found a case to answer.

After Revie walked out on England in 1977, and gave the news exclusively to the *Daily Mail*, it was a signal for the rest of the press to declare an open season on him. The *Daily Mirror* printed their 'Revie File', alleging that he tried to fix games during his reign at Leeds. Amongst the allegations was the claim that Revie recruited Mike O'Grady, the former Leeds winger, who was on the Wolves books at the time, to offer his colleagues £1,000 per man to throw the final game of the 1971/72 season. The article was based on interviews with O'Grady and corroborated by Gary Sprake. The *Daily Mirror* further alleged that during the match, appeals were made by Leeds players to their opposite numbers to take it easy and to give away penalties.

After the *Mirror's* sister paper, the *Sunday People*, repeated the accusations, Revie and Bremner sued for libel. Although Revie decided not to pursue the matter, Bremner continued with his action. In 1982, his suit against the *Sunday People* and Danny Hegan was heard at the Royal Courts of Justice. Giving evidence for Bremner were Johnny Giles, Jack Charlton, Allan Clarke and Derek Dougan. Evidence was given on behalf of the defence by Danny Hegan, Frank Munro and Gary Sprake. Hegan told the jury that during the game Bremner had said to him, 'Give us a penalty, wee man, and I will give you a grand.'

Munro was discredited when he had to admit that the paper had paid £4,000 in airfares to bring him and his family to Britain on a visit from Australia, where he was now living. Mr Justice Bristow told the jury that at a criminal trial Bremner could be liable to two years' imprisonment and advised the jury, 'Think long and hard before you find Billy Bremner guilty of corruption.'

On 3 February 1982 the jury found in favour of Bremner, awarding damages of £100,000. The Leeds players were disgusted by Sprake's betrayal of Revie, who had stood by his goalkeeper despite his regular mistakes that had undoubtedly lost Leeds trophies. Sprake was ostracised by the close-knit Leeds players until his death in October 2016.

Birmingham travelled to London needing a draw at Orient to pip Millwall for promotion on goal average. Thousands of Millwall supporters boosted the crowd to Orient's highest of the season. Orient had their chances before Latchford bundled home future PFA chairman Gordon Taylor's curling centre in the 56th minute to settle Birmingham nerves.

In an attempt to get the game abandoned, an anonymous bomb warning led to an instruction to evacuate the stand, but the final whistle had already been blown. When the police eventually evacuated the stand, they found a firework, which went off harmlessly. As well as the bomb scare, Birmingham's moment of glory was spoilt by pitch invasions and fighting inside and outside the ground.

QPR finished a season that had promised so much with a comfortable 3-0 home win over Cardiff to finish two points behind Birmingham. The following evening, they won the *Evening Standard* five-a-side trophy, beating the current *Daily Express* champions, Southampton, in the Final.

Amateur Cup-holders, Hendon, pulled off the shock of the night by defeating Watford in the preliminary round. The non-league side were unlucky not to beat QPR in the next round. Phil Parkes rescued Rangers with three spectacular saves before Clement scored the decisive goal. In the semi-finals, QPR squeezed past West Ham on penalties after a goalless draw.

In the final, Gerry Francis equalised Brian O'Neill's opener. Mick Channon put Southampton ahead again, only for QPR's Mick McGovern to level. The player of the tournament, Dave Clement, grabbed QPR's winner in extra time.

In 1979, after 476 appearances and five England caps, Clement transferred to Bolton Wanderers for £170,000. Clement and his young family couldn't settle in the north, so after just one season he moved back to London to join Fulham. The following season he moved to Wimbledon where, in his ninth game, he broke his leg. Fearing the break might end his career, depression took hold, leading Clement to take his own life on 31 March 1982.[6]

Third Division Champions Aston Villa beat Chesterfield in front of a crowd of 45,567 to complete a memorable season. A brave performance from Chesterfield's amateur goalkeeper, Phil Tingay, kept them at bay until the 68th minute, when Ian Ross chipped in his first goal for the club. It was apt that Villa said goodbye to the Third Division against Chesterfield, who had been their opponents when their adventure began on a sunny August afternoon in 1970.

Brighton got the draw they needed to guarantee promotion at Notts County's expense. In just his second season in management, Brighton boss Pat Saward had shown he was one of the most talented young managers in football. The following season, he would be sacked shortly after Brighton's relegation and would never manage another league club.

Bournemouth couldn't get the two goals they needed to qualify for the following season's Watney Cup. Ted MacDougall, watched by Spurs and Leicester, misfired all evening as Tranmere picked up a vital away point in their quest to stay in Division Three. In their next game, it was Tranmere's old warhorse, Ron Yeats, who grabbed the winner against Notts County to earn his side the two points to save themselves.

Another veteran, 41-year-old Roy Sproson, made his only appearance of the season in his 761st and last game for Port Vale against Rotherham. Sproson was four years older than manager Gordon Lee. After Port Vale secured promotion in 1970, he had finally been allowed to drift out of the first-team picture, making just seven appearances last season.

More than 22,000 turned up to see goals from Matt Tees, Mike Hickman and Lew Chatterley against Exeter seal the Fourth Division title for Grimsby in the rearranged fixture.[7] The following evening, Southend clinched the runners-up spot with a 2-2 draw at home to Gillingham. Their celebrations were ruined by pitch invasions and fighting in the crowd.

Molineux hosted the first leg of an all-England UEFA Cup Final. Although Wolves had been pioneers at the birth of European football in the 1950s, it was their first and, to date, only European final. While there was a certain historical symbolism in having the UEFA Cup Final under the floodlights at Molineux, for the Tottenham players' wives it was a crushing disappointment. Earlier in the season, before their opponents were known, they had been promised an all-expenses-paid trip to the away leg.

The crowd of 38,362 was 15,000 less than would cram into the ground for the league match against Leeds. In the sixth minute, Martin Chivers hit the post with a fierce shot before Spurs had their own scare when Pat Jennings dashed out of the area and cleared the ball into the centre circle. Danny Hegan reacted quickly and let fly from 50 yards forcing his Irish team-mate to scramble back and tip his effort over the bar.

It took until the 57th minute for Spurs to draw first blood, Chivers rising to head in England's free kick after Phil Parkes hesitated. Spurs' lead lasted just 15 minutes, when a handball decision by Azerbaijan referee, Tofiq Bahramov,[8] allowed Danny Hegan's quick free kick to put Jim McCalliog clean through on goal. His shot hit Jennings' outstretched legs and deflected inside the near post.

John Pratt replaced Ralph Coates for the last 15 minutes as it appeared Spurs were happy to settle for a draw. Three minutes from time, Chivers was just inside the Wolves half when he took a pass from Alan Mullery. He weaved his way down the left before firing a glorious drive past Parkes from 30 yards. Commentator David Coleman advised the keeper to 'pick that one out'.

Two weeks later, the teams met in the second leg at White Hart Lane, the capacity crowd generating record receipts of £45,000. The match attracted minimal television coverage, ITV showing brief highlights on their midweek sports programme.

In the 29th minute, Martin Peters floated a free kick on to the head of an unmarked Alan Mullery. The Spurs skipper was knocked unconscious in the process of heading the ball home. After recovering, Mullery had a hand in Wolves' 41st-minute equaliser when the ball bounced off him to Ken Wagstaffe, who fired a curling left-foot shot into the net off a post.

Mike Bailey came on as a substitute for his first action in four months as Wolves put Spurs under tremendous pressure for the last 20 minutes to try to level the aggregate score, but the home side held firm, with Jennings again magnificent. At the final whistle, the home supporters invaded the pitch to celebrate Tottenham becoming the first English club to win two different European trophies. While his team-mates retreated to the safety of the dressing room, Mullery went for a solo lap of honour, escorted by 4,000 supporters.

Mullery rejoined Fulham in the summer where, despite dropping into the Second Division, he enjoyed an Indian summer. He scored *Match of the Day*'s goal of the season in January 1974 and earned the Footballer of the Year award as he captained Fulham to the 1975 FA Cup Final. His record of being the only player from outside the top division to win the award outright is unlikely to be equalled.

In the European Cup Winners' Cup Final, Rangers took on Dynamo Moscow in front of a three-quarters-empty Nou Camp stadium. It was an opportunity for the teams' managers to renew their own personal rivalry. The Rangers manager,

Willie Waddell, had played against Dynamo's manager, Konstantin Beskov, in the game at Ibrox during the Russian side's groundbreaking tour of Britain in 1945.

Although the Russians were the first team from the Soviet Union to compete in the final of a European competition, their support consisted of eight people from the Soviet Trade Company. The crowd was made up almost exclusively of Rangers supporters.

To add to Dynamo's problems, Vladimir Kozlov and Anatoli Kozhemyakin were both injured. The prodigiously talented Kozhemyakin was just 19, but had already won his first cap for the Soviet Union. Tragically, on 13 October 1974, Kozhemyakin was in an elevator with a friend when it got stuck between floors. His friend managed to climb out of a gap, but when Kozhemyakin followed, the elevator started moving, crushing him to death.

Dynamo's Yozhef Sabo, was due to finish his playing days at the Summer Olympics. In a professional career that began in 1959, Sabo had never missed a penalty, converting all 73 spot-kicks in more than 350 club matches and 40 internationals.

Although Dynamo's strength was in attack, they decided to sit back and contain Rangers. Their plan could hardly have failed more spectacularly as they conceded three goals inside 50 minutes. Colin Stein's opener in the 23rd minute led to the travelling fans undertaking the first of several pitch invasions, delaying the restart for several minutes. Five minutes before half-time Rangers doubled their lead when Willie Johnston headed home from eight yards. Just minutes into the second half, Johnston controlled a huge clearance by goalkeeper Peter McCloy before slotting home his second and Rangers' third.

On the hour, left-back Willie Mathieson was guilty of a lazy pass, which led to substitute Vladimir Eshtrekov pulling one back. From then on it was all Dynamo Moscow as Rangers began to wilt in the Barcelona heat. With three minutes to go, Dynamo got a second goal when Yevgeni Zhukov lifted the ball over McCloy. It hit the underside of the bar and went into the net. Had the game gone on for a few minutes longer, it's questionable as to whether Rangers could have held on, but the final whistle saw hordes of Scottish fans invade the pitch to celebrate.

The Rangers supporters had invaded the pitch five times during the game and would fight a pitched battle with the Spanish police at the end. Hundreds were arrested and thrown into jail. The pitch invasion prevented the trophy from being presented as usual. Instead, captain John Greig walked into a room where the UEFA committee handed him the trophy and curtly said: 'Rangers Football Club, winners.'

Due to the crowd trouble, UEFA considered replaying the Final, but contented themselves by banning Rangers from European competition for two years. The ban was reduced to one year after an appeal, but still left them unable to defend the trophy.

In the second game of the following season, Willie Johnston was sent off for throwing a punch at a Partick Thistle defender. The sending-off was the sixth of his career, earning him a 10-match ban. His disciplinary record had made his time in Scotland untenable which, together with dissatisfaction over his £60 per week wages, led to him moving to West Bromwich Albion for £138,000. The fee was a record for a Scottish League player and Johnston doubled his wages. He would revive his international career and become a legend at West Brom. By the time he retired in 1985, he had managed to accumulate 18 red cards.

The Cup Winners' Cup remained in Britain for the third successive year. With Tottenham becoming the fifth successive English team to win the UEFA/Fairs Cup, it seemed that Britain was finally getting the hang of European football. From 1973 until the ban in 1985, British teams contested a further 19 European finals, winning seven European Cups, two Cup Winners' Cups and four UEFA Cups.

In the European Cup Final, Ajax, playing Inter Milan at the home of their domestic rivals, Feyenoord, were the 7/4 favourites. The purists had wanted an Ajax-Mönchengladbach Final, instead they got a battle for the very soul of the game; the cynical defence of the veteran Inter side versus the youth and verve of Ajax's Total Football.

From the kick-off Ajax interchanged positions, passing the ball around as the Inter defence was twisted and turned by their movement. Somehow, the game remained goalless at half-time as the Italian's plan of soaking up pressure seemed to be working.

Two minutes into the second half, the Dutch scored a deserved goal after Ivano Bordon dropped Wim Suurbier's cross, allowing Johan Cruyff to stroke the ball home at the far post. Needing an equaliser, Inter pushed Sandro Mazzola forward and, midway through the half, Heinz Stuy did well to save at his feet.

Stuy holds the distinction of winning the most major trophies without ever winning an international cap. The only other Ajax player from that great side not to receive international recognition was Horst Blankenburg, the German libero's route to his national team being blocked by Franz Beckenbauer.[9]

Ajax made the game safe in the 77th minute after Cruyff rose to meet a Piet Keizer free kick, heading the ball beyond Bordon. Newspapers from all over Europe celebrated the triumph of Total Football over Catenaccio as the Inter tactics were exposed by the Ajax side. Ajax had completed the treble, a feat only previously completed by Celtic in 1967. In due course they would add the World Club Cup and the new European Super Cup to their trophy cabinet.

Sir Alf Ramsey named his squad for the return leg of the European Championship tie in West Berlin. The big shock was that Geoff Hurst had been dropped for the first time, replaced in the squad by Malcolm Macdonald. It was fitting that Hurst's last cap was against West Germany. He made his debut against them in February 1966, his greatest triumph came against them in the World Cup Final five months later, and his last great performance for England was against them in the 1970 World Cup.

England needed a two-goal victory to take the tie to a replay; an unlikely scenario given that Germany hadn't lost a home match since 1965. There was therefore a sense of dismay when Ramsey announced his team. Worried about the influence of Günter Netzer, Ramsey decided to nullify him by picking two midfield enforcers, Peter Storey and Norman Hunter.

As a bonus for armchair viewers, the match was shown live during Saturday's *World of Sport*.

In the first seven minutes, Martin Chivers had a shot hacked off the line by Horst-Dieter Höttges, and Rodney Marsh put a header over the bar. But that was pretty much the end of England's attacking intentions. The gamble of playing Marsh failed and he was withdrawn after an hour. Even though Malcolm Macdonald was on the bench, Ramsey played safe again, bringing on Mike Summerbee. Only in the last 20 minutes did Ramsey try to be positive, sacrificing Hunter for Martin Peters. The game petered out to a goalless draw, a result that saw England out of the European Championship.

The German coach, Helmut Schön, and Netzer were scathing about England's tactics. Netzer claimed that all the English team had autographed his leg, while Schön complained of England's 'brutal tackling aimed at the bones'. Ramsey countered by saying he was proud of his team's performance.

England did, however, come home to a warmer welcome than the Italians, who were pelted with tomatoes on their return from a 2-1 defeat to Belgium, West Germany's opponents for the semi-final.

England's youth team started their defence of the European Youth Tournament with a goalless draw against Belgium. With a little luck, Trevor Francis could have had a hat-trick, but had to content himself with the fourth in England's next game against

Eire. Steve Cammack's 50th-minute goal against Yugoslavia fired England to the semi-finals, where a Trevor Francis goal defeated Poland. In the Final against West Germany, at Barcelona's Nou Camp stadium, England took a ninth-minute lead through Phil Thompson from 30 yards, via the underside of the bar. Mick Buckley sealed the victory in the 57th minute, after good work from Alan Green, Francis and Cammack.

Gordon Milne's side had won the tournament without conceding a goal. The longer-term future also looked bright with the England Schoolboys' emphatic 4-0 win over West Germany at Wembley. England's scorers were John Trewick and Sunderland school friends Peter Stronach and Wilf Rostron. Rostron had recovered from gastroenteritis to score a brace. Disappointment was voiced in the press that the game was not broadcast live. The following season, the situation was rectified as England's match against Scotland was shown live on *World of Sport*. For the next ten years these schoolboy international games at Wembley held a special fascination, being one of the few live games televised.

Looking at the England line-up, Ray Wilkins is the first name that leaps out. Wilkins captained Chelsea at just 18 before going on to play for Manchester United, AC Milan, Paris Saint-Germain and Glasgow Rangers, among others, while winning 84 caps for England over ten years.

Trevor Ross, Wilf Rostron, John Sparrow and John Trewick should also ring bells. Ross, like Rostron, started his career at Arsenal, where he became a regular before transferring to Everton. He would win Under-21 honours for Scotland, highlighting the anomaly of the schoolboy system, that eligibility isn't based on birthplace but on where you went to school. The most famous example of this was, of course, Ryan Wilson – or Giggs, as he became better known.

Rostron played 17 games for Arsenal before moving on to Watford via Sunderland. He was Watford's player of the year in 1983, when they finished second in Division One. He was robbed of a Wembley return in 1984 when a sending-off against Luton meant he was suspended from captaining Watford in the FA Cup Final.

Despite making his debut at 16, John Sparrow never quite established himself at Chelsea, playing 74 games over six seasons, before drifting down the leagues and eventually into non-league football. Trewick started his professional career at West Brom, where he made 96 appearances[10] before transferring to Newcastle in 1980. Trewick would get a Wembley return in 1986 as part of Oxford's League Cup-winning side.

The third Chelsea player in the squad was substitute Clive Walker, who had a 17-year career with Chelsea, Sunderland, Fulham and Brighton, before enjoying a successful non-league career, most notably with Woking. Walker returned to Wembley with Sunderland in 1985, but missed a penalty as Sunderland lost in the League Cup Final to Norwich.

Joining Walker on the bench was Gordon Staniforth, who would go on to score more than 100 goals at Hull, York, Carlisle, Plymouth and Newport. As for the rest of the team, goalkeeper David Danson went to West Ham then Bournemouth and Cardiff. He wouldn't make a first-team appearance for any of them before dropping into non-league football. The captain, Terry Pashley, played 20-odd games for Burnley over six seasons before finally getting regular first-team football at Blackpool and Bury. Adrian Cooper made 14 appearances for Reading, Geoff Chalkin played three games for Swindon, and Keith Baker got one run-out for Grimsby. Rostron's old school pal, Peter Stronach, stayed in his home city and made three appearances for Sunderland before transferring to York, where he played 30 games. Of Michael Corcoran and Robert Atkins, who knows?

Perhaps the most typical example of an England Schoolboy's career trajectory was that of midfielder Frank Pimblett. As 14-year-olds, Frank Pimblett and Peter Reid had been the outstanding players in the Huyton Boys team that won the

English Schools Trophy in 1971. The team was coached by their English and PE teacher, Alan Bleasdale, who later gained national recognition as a television screenwriter.[11] Despite his subsequent success, Bleasdale is quoted as saying that coaching Huyton Boys to the English Schools Trophy was his proudest achievement.

Huyton Boys were called the greatest school football team ever and featured on a later television programme that covered the subsequent careers of the boys. Peter Reid would join Bolton on apprentice forms and there is little need to remind you of his subsequent career. Pimblett made an impressive debut for Aston Villa as a 17-year-old in 1975, but only played another eight matches, plus seven on loan at Newport, before being released. He went to Australia and spent a decade playing for Brisbane City before retiring in the same year as Peter Reid.

Although the 1972 Schoolboy side was an exceptionally strong one, it is fair to say that its players went on to have varying degrees of success. Realistically, you cannot expect every player who is an international at 15 to subsequently win full international honours as an adult, but for the majority to make little to no impact in a league of 92 clubs, across four divisions, never ceases to amaze. I wholeheartedly endorse Nick Hornby's contention that, while there is possibly a potential De Niro waiting tables in Hollywood, there isn't a George Best playing Sunday football. As Hornby points out, everyone gets watched. But from the England Schoolboy internationals of the 60s and 70s, only Clive Allen, Trevor Brooking, Mark Chamberlain, Steve Perryman, Kenny Sansom, Peter Shilton, Trevor Steven, Danny Thomas, Mark Walters, Steve Whitworth and Ray Wilkins went on to win senior caps.

In 20 years, just 11 of over 300 players capped at Schoolboy level won full international caps. Remember, these are the cream of 15-year-old players, the best of the best. For the most part, the majority couldn't get a game in the Fourth Division.

On the other side of the coin, the following internationals started in non-league football: Malcolm Macdonald, Cyril Regis, Stuart Pearce, Les Ferdinand, Chris Waddle, John Barnes, Ian Wright and Stan Collymore. Even with today's massive scouting budgets and bloated academies, recent England internationals Chris Smalling and Jamie Vardy were plucked from non-league football. It seems that, despite initiatives such as Lilleshall and club academies, developing talent still remains a lottery.

And so, to the Home Internationals , where club team-mates would become bitter international rivals for a week. George Best preferred to holiday in Marbella rather than meet up with the Northern Ireland squad. While there, he announced his retirement from football at the age of 26. 'My mind is made up about football. I'm sorry, but it's over. I won't change my mind.' To replace him, the Irish called up Brighton's Willie Irvine for the first time since 1969. When Best eventually returned to Old Trafford in July, he found his weight had increased by 25lb. No matter how hard he tried in his countless comebacks, his speed or fitness wouldn't return. Because of the Troubles, Northern Ireland's home fixture was moved to Hamden Park, granting the Scottish team three home games.

On the day that George Best announced his retirement from the game, Denis Law showed an undimmed enthusiasm for international football, some 14 years after his Scottish debut. Northern Ireland looked to have earned a draw in front of a two-thirds-empty Hampden Park when, four minutes from time, Lorimer intercepted a Pat Rice back pass. Law hooked his cross home for a record 30th goal for his country.[12] Law repaid the compliment with a pass to Lorimer to hammer home goal number two.

England dominated their opening game as Alf Ramsey's midfield enforcers, Hunter and Storey, didn't give the Welsh team time to settle at Ninian Park. Roy McFarland was superb against the triple aerial threats of Ron and Wyn

Davies and John Toshack, playing together for the first time since 1969.

England took a deserved lead midway through the first half when Emlyn Hughes burst forward from left-back and continued his run to tap in after Gary Sprake palmed Colin Bell's effort into his path. Rodney Marsh, thwarted earlier by an offside flag, wasn't to be denied his first international goal for long, doubling England's lead on the hour with a volley. Moments later it was 3-0 as Bell lobbed Sprake to give the score a more realistic look based on the balance of play.

For the next game against Northern Ireland, Ramsey decided it was time for experimentation. He was no doubt influenced by the fact that the Irish hadn't beaten England since 1957. First caps were awarded to Colin Todd and Tony Currie. Macdonald and Marsh retained their places up front while Larry Lloyd and Peter Shilton were drafted in to replace Roy McFarland and Gordon Banks. In midfield, Sir Alf loosened his grip a little, retaining Storey but drafting in Mike Summerbee to fill the gap vacated by moving Hunter into the back four to replace Moore. The starting line-up was the first not to contain a World Cup-winner since that July day six years before.

England started well enough, with Marsh at the heart of their best moves, but they couldn't breach the Irish defence, behind which Pat Jennings was superb. Then, totally against the run of play, Ireland scored in the 33rd minute. Danny Hegan's corner was fumbled by Shilton, allowing player-manager Terry Neill to stab the ball home.[13] Martin Peters replaced Currie, and Martin Chivers came on for Macdonald, to little avail. The 64,000 crowd slow-handclapped and whistled England off from their second consecutive home defeat.

The following night, Peter Lorimer's 72nd-minute goal was enough to beat Wales 1-0 at Hampden. As a result of England's loss against Ireland, Scotland would at least share the Home Internationals title. Northern Ireland's 0-0 draw against Wales left Wales without a goal in the tournament for the second successive year, a feat they would repeat in 1973.

With the 'Auld Enemy' meeting in the culmination of the Home Internationals , the domestic season was fittingly concluded with the 100th anniversary of the oldest international fixture in the world. As part of our meagre allowance of live football, both BBC and ITV broadcast the game.

England headed to Glasgow knowing that only a win would clinch the tournament, which made Ramsey's selection of the same line-up from Berlin mystifying. Ramsey, well known for his dislike of the Scots, picked Storey and Hunter in midfield. If his plan was to provoke the Scots, it worked. Scotland started well, but the game soon degenerated into a kicking match. Anyone trying to hold the ball in midfield was ruthlessly hacked down. Matters became so heated that the referee called the two captains together to ask them to calm down their players.

It took nearly 25 minutes for the Hampden crowd to see a break for some football when Storey kicked a deflected Asa Hartford shot off the line. Then, to almost complete silence, England scored against the run of play. Billy Bremner's wayward pass was intercepted by Alan Ball, who combined with Martin Chivers in the Scotland penalty area before his final prod sent the ball under Bobby Clark to roll slowly over the line.

After that short interlude for football, the violence continued. Much of the venom drained out of the game in the second half and play did improve, but Scotland generally pumped useless high balls into the England penalty area against Ramsey's more organised side. With ten minutes remaining, Ramsey replaced Marsh with Macdonald, who wasted a chance when a pass to Chivers would have presented the Spurs man with an open goal. The game ended as unhappily as it had begun, with Ball giving a two-fingered gesture to the Scottish fans as he walked off the pitch.

The fixture would mark the last international appearance of Gordon Banks. Just five months later, he would be involved in the car crash that ended his first-class career.

After 100 years, the 1984 Home Internationals would prove to be the last. Although the tournament gave Northern Ireland only their third title of the 88 completed tournaments, the trophy remains theirs as the most recent champions.

NOTES FROM ABROAD

Geoff Hurst and George Best scored for a European select in a star-studded testimonial for Uwe Seeler. The select – including Gordon Banks, Franz Beckenbauer, Bobby Moore, Bobby Charlton, Gianni Rivera, Gerd Müller, Eusébio and Dragan Džajić – beat Hamburg 7-3 in an entertaining game.

Jimmy Hagan's Benfica clinched the Portuguese title by beating Academica 3-1. The win was their third consecutive victory, a streak that would continue until April 1973. The record 29 consecutive domestic league wins helped Benfica to go through the following season unbeaten. Towards the end of a disappointing 1969/70 season, Benfica's directors felt that an English manager's discipline was needed at the club. They had already approached and been turned down by Ramsey when Charlie Mitten, who had connections in Portugal, recommended Hagan, who had been out of management for three years.

Hagan, recognising that a lack of stamina was a key issue, set a punishing physical schedule. The team's results immediately started to improve, and Benfica finished the season in second. The following season, Benfica won the title and reached the cup final, and in the 1971/72 season, they won the double and reached the European Cup semi-final, losing narrowly to Ajax. Hagan's success led to an extended tenure rarely achieved at the club, and when the end came it wasn't due to failure on the pitch, but down to a matter of principle.

In September 1973, Benfica awarded Eusébio a benefit match for which Hagan demanded the same level of preparation as he would for any other game. While Eusébio and others complied, Diamantino, Toni and Humberto Coelho did not.

Hagan dropped the three of them and refused club president Borges Coutinho's order to reinstate them. When Hagan walked out on to the pitch before the match, he saw the three players warming up. Recognising that the chairman had gone over his head, and remembering his earlier troubles when managing West Brom, he walked out of the stadium and quit.[14]

A tearful Eusébio arrived on Hagan's doorstep after the match to persuade the coach to at least attend his celebratory dinner later that evening. In 2001, Hagan's lifelong friend Eusébio visited Sheffield three years after his former manager's death, to unveil a bronze statue of Hagan at Bramall Lane.

Another British manager plying his trade abroad, Vic Buckingham, saw his Seville side lose to Real Madrid and confirm their relegation. Amancio and Santillana got two early goals, with Pirri adding two more in the second half to clinch Real's first domestic title in three years. When Francisco Gento retired following last season's Cup Winners' Cup final, Madrid carried out a major rebuild of the team. They ignored big names and invested in young homegrown talent. None of the new players were over the age of 22, so the new-look team was nicknamed the Baby Show. Unfortunately, the Baby Show's light flickered all too briefly, and the 1972 title would be their only major silverware.

Marseille retained their French title with a 4-2 win over Monaco, the prolific Yugoslavian, Josip Skoblar, scoring two to give him 32 goals in 35 games.

Johan Cruyff scored four when Ajax ended their domestic season with a 12-1 win over Vitesse. Eleven days earlier, Cruyff had scored one of the finest goals of his career after expertly controlling and knocking forward a 40-yard lofted pass before curling in a 25-yard shot in Ajax's cup final win over De Haag.

Italy's national goalkeeper, Dino Zoff, returned to the Napoli side for the game against Bologna, the first of an astonishing 332 consecutive league games over the next 11 years. The 30-year-old keeper's performances for Napoli would earn him a transfer in the summer to champions Juventus.[15]

Juventus were one of the European clubs who stated their desire for a 24-team 'super league' to include the continent's glamour clubs. Both the Football League and UEFA voiced their opposition to the plan.

On 7 May, Randy Horton scored two goals in the 3-3 draw against the St Louis Stars as the New York Cosmos kicked off their second season in the North American Soccer League (NASL). Both teams would reach the Soccer Bowl Final at the end of August. Clyde Best's old team-mate, Horton, would score his 22nd goal of the season in the Cosmos 2-1 win.

Horton and Best had formed a formidable front line for the Somerset Trojans in the late 60s in Bermuda. Although six years Best's senior, Horton had a longer wait to get his break before eventually moving to the Cosmos. He became their first superstar while also holding down a job at the Warner Bros. Jungle Habitat theme park. After the 1974 season, Horton was traded to the Washington Diplomats for whom he would play one season before returning to Bermuda.

In 1998, after a decade as a school principal followed by an equally long career in the Bermuda Department of Tourism, Randy Horton entered politics and was elected to the Bermuda Parliament, where he has remained ever since. In 2013, he was elected Speaker of the House of Assembly.

In a not unrelated event, on 26 June Nolan Bushnell and Ted Dabney co-founded Atari. Four years later, Bushnell would sell Atari to Warner Communications for an estimated $30m.[16] Under Warner, Atari would become the fastest-growing company in US history, accounting for a third of Warner's annual income. The money from Atari's games consoles bankrolled the New York Cosmos to become one of the most famous football clubs in the world.

The Cosmos had been founded in 1970 by Warner Communications president, Steve Ross. Even before they played their first game, their general manager, Clive Toye, visited Pelé on tour in Kingston, informing the Brazilian that he expected him 'to come and play for us one of these days'.

After retiring in 1974, Pelé discovered that, rather than having millions saved, he in fact owed millions due to a poor investment in the parts manufacturer, Fiolax. The Cosmos executives pounced, offering Pelé a contract of $1m for three years of playing, $1m for ten years of marketing rights, $1m for a 14-year PR contract, plus a $1m music contract. All that remained was for US Secretary of State and soccer fan, Henry Kissinger, to persuade the Brazilian government to release their national treasure.

On 8 June 1975, Pelé scored the equaliser on his Cosmos debut in the 2-2 draw with Dallas Tornado. The crowd was triple the normal as spectators came to watch Pelé and discover soccer. By 1976 soccer was one of the most-watched sports in America and the success of Pelé led the likes of Gordon Banks, Rodney Marsh, Eusébio, Gerd Müller and George Best to join the NASL.

In time the Cosmos added Lazio striker Giorgio Chinaglia, Franz Beckenbauer and Carlos Alberto to their roster. In Pelé's final season, the Cosmos won the 1977 Soccer Bowl and followed up with wins in 1978, 1980 and 1982.

Other clubs struggled to match the financial muscle of the Cosmos. They released Johan Cruyff from the exclusivity agreement he had signed with them, so that he could join the Los Angeles Aztecs and ensure some competition. The simple fact was that Cosmos had outgrown the North American Soccer League. While they could draw crowds of more than 70,000 at the Giants stadium, when they played away the crowds could be as low as a few thousand.

By the time they lost in the Soccer Bowl Final of 1979, to Vancouver, crowds were beginning to decline. Even before ABC ended their broadcasting deal, most clubs were making huge losses. Ultimately, even the Cosmos themselves could not survive. Warner's finances were running into difficulties. Atari, whose enormous profits had enabled Steve Ross to bankroll the team, had gone from a money-making machine to a financial millstone around the company's neck. The video game crash of 1983 brought losses exceeding $500m.

To fight off a hostile takeover bid from Rupert Murdoch, Warner Communications sold off several assets, including Global Soccer, the subsidiary that owned the Cosmos. The club was bought by a consortium led by their old striker, Giorgio Chinaglia, but they were unable to support the club's high wage bill and increasing debt. With the downfall of the Cosmos, the entire NASL was unviable and crashed. Seven years after Pelé had waved goodbye, the experiment was over, ultimately finished by *Donkey Kong* as Atari's rise and fall mirrored that of the Cosmos and the NASL.

POST-SEASON

'The camp was going crazy. There were
helicopters overhead, guards with guns.'

Nielsen

AT THE start of June, the Annual General Meeting of the
Football League was held at London's Café Royal. The main
topic was deciding who would be elected or re-elected into the
Football League.

Until 1986, clubs at the bottom of the Football League at
the conclusion of each season had to go, cap in hand, to endure
a vote by their League colleagues, who also considered the
applications of ambitious non-league clubs eager to take their
place. The non-leaguers regarded the election procedure as little
more than an old pals' act since, more often than not, the league
clubs seeking re-election retained their league status. Although
the bottom clubs faced re-election on an annual basis, since the
Fourth Division had been established in 1958, only two had
failed to gain re-election – Gateshead in 1960 and Bradford
Park Avenue in 1970.[1]

In danger this season were Northampton, Barrow, Stockport
and bottom club Crewe. Just four years earlier, Barrow had
been challenging for a place in the Second Division, but after
relegation to the Fourth Division in 1970 they went into a free
fall that saw them finish bottom of the League last season and
third from bottom this. Barrow's geographic isolation counted

against them, as did the decision by their board at the end of April to introduce a speedway track around the Holker Street pitch as a means of offsetting financial difficulties.

Hereford United, however, had a healthy balance sheet and average gates that were higher than most Third and Fourth Division clubs. They were also the media darlings after their FA Cup heroics, although they had only finished runners-up in the Southern League.

In the first ballot, Northampton, Crewe and Stockport comfortably received enough votes to retain their league status, but Barrow and Hereford tied on 26 votes for the fourth spot. The 11 other non-league sides, including future FA Cup winners, Wimbledon and Wigan, received one vote or less.[2]

In the second ballot, Hereford took Barrow's league place by 29 votes to 26. Wimbledon had to wait until 1977 to be voted into the League, and Wigan Athletic replaced Southport in 1978, even though Southport were seven points above bottom side Rochdale.

A more transparent direct promotion and relegation system was introduced from the 1986/87 season. Had it been in place in 1972, poor Barrow would have survived and Crewe would have been replaced, but not by Hereford. Hereford had only won the Southern League once, back in 1965, but the buzz that John Charles had created during his reign, together with their cup run, was enough to tip the balance in their favour.

In other business, a new 'points for punishment' plan would operate from the following season. Suspensions would now be measured in matches rather than weeks. It was also agreed that terrace admission prices would rise from 30p to 40p.

Items that failed to achieve the three-quarter majority were: Blackpool's three-up, three-down proposal[3]; Nottingham Forest's proposal to review the possibility of football on a Sunday[4]; Orient's request for loan transfers to stop after January and loans to be forbidden if the player involved had played more than 12 first-team games during the season[5]; and Everton's proposal to increase the half-time break from 10 to 15 minutes.[6]

On 15 June, at a Nottingham court, Tommy Lawton admitted obtaining cash and goods by deception. He pleaded guilty to seven charges of deception, totalling £314, and asked for 20 similar cases to be taken into consideration. Lawton had been the greatest centre-forward of his day, but had lost six years of his prime to the Second World War and played at a time when financial rewards, even for superstars, were in no way commensurate with their pulling power. While Lawton acknowledged that 'what we earned was a fortune compared to the man in the street', considering how much the clubs earned through the turnstiles, his wages were poor. After his playing career had finished, he took over at his former club, Notts County, but they were relegated from the Second Division at the end of his only season in charge.

Lawton then spent four years running a pub before joining Kettering for stints as manager and director. After losing his job as an insurance salesman in 1967, he opened a sporting goods shop, but was forced to close it after just two months due to poor sales. After a period of unemployment he found work at a betting company before returning to Notts County to work as a coach and chief scout. Lawton returned to the unemployment line at the end of 1969 when new manager, Jimmy Sirrel, appointed his own backroom staff.

By May 1970, he was forced to write to his friend, Richard Attenborough, asking for a loan of £250 and for possible employment. An interview about his fall from grace on ITV's *Today* programme led to a job as director of his own subsidiary furniture company, but the company went into liquidation the following year.

It was reported in court that, despite receiving £19.30 social security, he had been living beyond his means and continued to write cheques in the company's name. Lawton was sentenced to three years' probation and ordered to pay £240 compensation and £100 in costs.

In November 1972, a testimonial match was organised by Everton, one of Lawton's former clubs. Everton played a Great

Britain side containing Bobby Moore, Bobby Charlton and Peter Shilton. George Best withdrew at the last minute, donating £100 to make up for his absence. Despite the cash injection of around £6,000, Lawton's financial situation remained bleak. On two further occasions he narrowly avoided a prison sentence for failing to pay his rates. In August 1974, he was again found guilty of obtaining goods by deception after failing to repay a £10 debt to a publican, and he was sentenced to 200 hours of community service and ordered to pay £40 costs.

His fortunes improved a little in 1984, when he began writing a column for the *Nottingham Evening Post*. The following year, another former club, Brentford, organised a testimonial for him. Lawton died from pneumonia in 1996, aged 77. Seven years later he was inducted into the English Football Hall of Fame at the National Football Museum.

Although the domestic season was over, the FA Cup wasn't officially completed until a week before the 1972/73 season kicked off, when the third- and fourth-placed play-off took place. From 1954, the so-called eve of Cup Final match had been between England and England Youth, but according to an FA Cup committee meeting in 1969, the game had suffered a 'loss of appeal and decline in attendance'. The match at Stamford Bridge on the eve of the 1969 FA Cup Final had attracted a crowd of just 18,000.

The FA wanted a more competitive match, so decided an FA Cup third- and fourth-placed decider between the two losing semi-finalists fitted the bill, overlooking the fact that from the World Cup down, matches for third place are never popular. The first game in 1970, between Manchester United and Watford at Highbury, drew a crowd that was 3,000 less than the previous England versus England Youth fixture. A year later, the match between Stoke and Everton at Selhurst Park barely pulled in 5,000.

Because of their progress in both domestic cups Stoke had a fixture backlog and on the eve of the final played West Brom in a league game. They didn't get much of a summer break either, taking part in the Anglo-Italian Cup in June. Their four ties took them to 28 cup games for the season.

After a short rest, the new season began for Stoke – or, to be more precise, the previous one ended with their play-off FA Cup tie against Birmingham at St Andrew's. The match was played on the same day as the Charity Shield and the Watney Cup Final. Playing the match at the ground of one of the contestants did at least boost the crowd to a near respectable 24,000. The goalless draw marked the debut of Stoke's summer signing, Geoff Hurst.

Hurst was still only 30, but had been expected to join Third Division Bournemouth before Tony Waddington jumped in with a bid of £70,000. He had been keen on Bournemouth because he had recently gone into partnership in a clothing business that had its head offices in Hampshire.

Those who recall Hurst's hat-trick for West Ham against Hereford back in February will realise that, technically, he had played for two different clubs in the same FA Cup competition, a feat he shared with new team-mate, Jimmy Robertson, who had already played for Ipswich. Birmingham were in no position to protest as Bobby Hope and Tony Want had already played in the Cup for West Brom and Tottenham respectively. The match was decided by the first-ever FA Cup penalty shoot-out, won 4-3 by Birmingham.[7]

The matches hobbled on for another couple of years before being put out of their misery. The 1974 play-off between Leicester and Burnley attracted a crowd of 4,432, the lowest ever for a competitive game at Filbert Street. At that year's FA committee meeting, it was announced: 'Bearing in mind the lack of enthusiasm on the part of the clubs and public for this match, it was agreed that it should be discontinued.'

John Motson summed up the matches best: 'Much like the third-place play-offs in the World Cup, the matches were uniformly rubbish, with neither side in the slightest bit interested in prolonging the agony of failing to reach the Final.'

As his team hadn't qualified from the European Championship Final, early June saw Sir Alf Ramsey take an England Under-23 squad on tour to Eastern Europe. Much to his annoyance, Colin Todd and Alan Hudson withdrew from the squad, Todd because his wife was pregnant, and Hudson to do some painting and decorating on his home.[8] It was more likely that Hudson's absence was due to his irritation at not getting a game after being named in the Home International squad. Frank Worthington and Trevor Brooking were called up to replace them.

Worthington was on his way to Heathrow to jet out to Majorca when word came through that he was wanted for the Under-23 trip. Despite only scoring six goals for relegated Huddersfield, Frank Worthington had done enough during the season to catch Ramsey's eye. He certainly caught his eye when he turned up at Heathrow wearing leather trousers, high-heeled cowboy boots, a red silk shirt, a lime velvet jacket and black cowboy hat. Ramsey saw him and groaned, 'Oh Christ, what the fuck have I done?' 'I suppose I've always been a bit of a peacock,' Worthington later explained.[9]

Worthington's form on the tour was enough to persuade Bill Shankly to offer a club record £150,000 for him. Although Worthington failed the original medical because of high blood pressure, Liverpool were unconcerned, sending Worthington on a holiday to Majorca to relax. A threesome with a Swedish mother and daughter, and another romp with a Belgian lady while relaxing, did little to reduce Worthington's blood pressure. When he returned to Anfield his blood pressure had risen, forcing Liverpool to call the transfer off.

Whether his flamboyance would have added panache to the Liverpool side or slowed down their passing moves, as Marsh did at Manchester City, is a matter of conjecture. Instead, Worthington moved to Leicester for a reduced fee of £80,000 and, for the next five years, lit up Filbert Street while earning eight England caps.

England began the tour with a match against East Germany's Under-23s. They led 2-1 at half-time through goals by Jeff Blockley and Kevin Keegan, but the team struggled after Keegan was sent off in the 57th minute for retaliation. Jürgen Sparwasser scored East Germany's equaliser with six minutes to go.

Three days later England met the Polish Under-23s in Warsaw. Worthington, dressed in a more sober England kit, opened the scoring after 73 minutes. He controlled a cross on his thigh, turned, and, as the ball dropped, volleyed from 20 yards into the top corner. John Richards doubled the lead five minutes later, before Tony Currie added a last-minute third.

An unchanged England side had Peter Shilton to thank for their 0-0 draw against the Soviet Union Under-23s.

One of the delegates joining the tour for a free holiday was future FA chairman, Sir Harold Thompson. Known as a snob and bully, he treated pretty much everyone he had contact with poorly. He developed a particular animosity towards Ramsey, who complained, 'He always referred to me, even to my face, as Ramsey, which I found insulting.' Any chance of the men building a cordial relationship ended during a breakfast in the team's hotel one morning. The players found the smoke from Thompson's large cigar unpleasant and, on their behalf, Ramsey asked him to put it out. Thompson complied, but was infuriated to have been shown such disrespect. Sir Alf's fate was sealed from that moment on, as Thompson began an internal campaign to have him ousted. Ramsey's position had already been weakened by April's Wembley defeat to West Germany, who now met Belgium in the European Championship semi-final.[10]

NOTES FROM ABROAD

Although the Belgians were theoretically the home side for the match, so many German supporters travelled across the border that their numbers equalled their opposing counterparts. From the kick-off West Germany started strongly and got the opening goal in the 24th minute. Günter Netzer lifted the ball into the area for Gerd Müller to head home. Belgium had an equaliser chalked off for offside, but apart from that it was all Germany.

Things continued in the same vein after the interval when the Netzer-Müller combination struck again. Netzer's clever pass opened up the Belgian defence to allow Müller to slip the ball past Christian Piot. The Belgians were able to pull one back through Odilon Polleunis and both teams had chances to add to the score, but the game finished 2-1.

Given that Belgium's semi-final was televised live at the same time, it was no surprise that a tiny crowd of 1,659 turned out to see the other semi-final between the Soviet Union and Hungary. The tedious game was decided in the 53rd minute when Soviet midfielder Anatoliy Konkov's volley took a slight deflection on the way past István Géczi. The Hungarians spurned the chance of an equaliser when Sándor Zámbó missed a penalty. Antal Dunai and Miklós Páncsics had chances to equalise in the dying minutes, but the Soviets held on to reach their third European Championship Final in four tournaments.

Ten hours before the third-place play-off, five men were arrested for breaking into the Democratic National Committee headquarters at the Watergate Building Complex. Just over two years later, President Nixon would resign as a consequence of the burglary.

Belgium won the bronze in a match that turned out to be anything but historic. Raoul Lambert and Paul Van Himst gave Belgium a first-half lead, although there was some joy in the second half for the Hungarians when Lajos Kű converted a spot-kick for a consolation goal.

With no Soviet supporters making the journey west, West Germany's travelling fans made the Final as good as a home game. They expected a comfortable victory; it had only been a little over three weeks since Gerd Müller had scored all four in a win over the Soviets to inaugurate Munich's Olympic Stadium.

The West Germans started quickly as usual, with Uli Hoeness heading against the crossbar. Just as the Soviets started to find their feet, West Germany struck. Beckenbauer brought the ball out from the back and rolled a pass to Müller, whose lay-off bobbled up for Netzer. The midfielder's shot crashed off the bar and was half-cleared to Jupp Heynckes. He lashed an angled drive at goal, which Rudakov did well to save, but his parry found Müller, who chested the ball down and forced it home.

Although Germany dominated the half, they had a tendency to fade as matches wore on, while the Soviets' fitness usually told as a game went on. After the interval the Soviets began to push forward, but then, just as in the first half, West Germany scored. Netzer found Heynckes, who fed Herbert Wimmer for a weak shot that bobbled over Rudakov's outstretched arm into the corner. Five minutes later, Müller scored his second and Germany's third by lifting the ball over the keeper from close range. Although there was over half an hour left, the Germans took their foot off the gas, allowing the Soviets several opportunities to get back into the game, although they always looked capable of adding to the score if needed.

At full time the German supporters rushed on, surrounding the players, who retreated behind a protective cordon to receive the trophy. The pitch invasion led to UEFA decreeing that any major final must henceforth take place in front of stands that were either moated or fenced in. The Germans had proved themselves to be one of the great sides, easily the best to win the competition in its short history, with their 1972 side going on to be remembered with far more affection than their 1974 World Cup winners.

Although England looked to have been overtaken by West Germany, they were still confident of qualification for the 1974 tournament in West Germany. They had been drawn in what appeared to be an easy qualification group against Wales and Poland. Wales were already well known to England, and the upcoming Olympic tournament was an ideal opportunity to look at the Polish side.

Britain's Olympic team had been easily knocked out in the qualifying rounds by Bulgaria. The British team, managed by Charles Hughes, was manned from the Isthmian League, but the Eastern Bloc nations were technically amateur, so their Olympic squads were, by and large, their national sides. Starting with Hungary in 1952, the Olympic tournament had been dominated by Eastern Europe.

The West German hosts, coached by Jupp Derwall, won Group A with future Dortmund and Bayern Munich manager Ottmar Hitzfeld lining up alongside Uli Hoeness. The highlight of their first-round matches was the 7-0 drubbing of the United States. Despite the score, future New York Cosmos keeper, Shep Messing, had a great game to keep the score down to single figures.[11]

Group B was dominated by the Soviet Union, the bulk of the team from the recent European Championship Final joining the veteran Sabo and the prodigious Oleg Blokhin.

In Group C, future European footballer of the year, Allan Simonsen, scored a couple of goals to help Denmark finish runners-up to Hungary. Favourites for the group, Brazil, containing future Seleção stars Falcão, Dirceu and Roberto Dinamite, finished bottom after losing 1-0 to Iran.

As they now had an unexpected holiday for the rest of the tournament, a few of the Brazilian players decided to let their hair down. After enjoying a night out on 4 September, goalkeeper Nielsen and defender Fred returned to the Olympic village in the early hours of the morning to find it still locked up for the night. They noticed three bearded men and followed them in climbing a perimeter fence before the two groups went in separate directions ... Though the footballers heard some bangs later, they didn't think it was anything untoward. The night before, an Italian fencer had won her third Olympic medal and had celebrated with champagne and fireworks.[12] Fred joked, 'The Italians are still celebrating.'

The next morning the Brazilians discovered the truth behind the noises. The three men Nielsen and Fred had seen were part of an eight-strong faction of the Black September movement. Carrying handguns, rifles and grenades in duffel bags, they had broken into the apartment block housing the Israeli team. The terrorists would murder 11 members of the Israeli Olympic team and a German police officer, before the police killed five of them during a botched rescue attempt.

Although Steven Spielberg's 2005 film *Munich* does show two athletes jumping the fence with the terrorists, Nielsen and Fred's involvement remained unknown until a chance remark in a TV programme some 40 years after the event.

Poland dominated Group D, beating Columbia 5-1 and Ghana 4-0. Robert Gadocha grabbed five goals, Kazimierz Deyna hit three, and their captain Włodzimierz Lubański scored the other. Their blonde centre-half, Jerzy Gorgoń, scored both goals in their 2-1 win over East Germany to win the group.

Poland and Hungary won the second-round groups to contest the Final. East Germany and the Soviet Union shared the bronze medal after a 2-2 draw in their play-off. Six of the East German Olympic side, including Sparwasser, would play in the 1974 World Cup win over the West Germans.[13]

In the final, Deyna's brace gave the title to Poland and stopped the Hungarians winning a third consecutive gold. Not since the Hungarians in 1952 had a side so illuminated an Olympic tournament. Their star player, Lubański, had been overshadowed by Legia Warsaw's midfield pair of Deyna and Gadocha, who netted 15 times between them.

The following June, England lost to a Polish side containing six of their Olympic winners. In the return fixture at Wembley in October 1973, England laid siege to the Polish goal from the start but, with Jan Tomaszewski having the game of his life in goal, the visitors somehow got the required draw. Although England had 36 goal attempts to Poland's two, forced 26 corners, hit the woodwork twice and had four efforts cleared off the line, they were out. A little over six months later, Ramsey was sacked.

England didn't know at the time, but they had lost out to a team that – with a little good fortune – would have played in the 1974 World Cup Final. After winning all five of their games, Poland met hosts West Germany in the second group-stage decider to determine who met Holland in the Final. The waterlogged pitch hindered Poland's fast-paced, quick-passing football and they fell to a Gerd Müller goal with just 15 minutes remaining. The German full-back, Paul Breitner, certainly thought his team had been lucky. 'I can remember one game where I've always maintained we beat a team which was fundamentally better than us. In fact, it was definitely the best team in the competition and still didn't win the World Cup. I mean Poland in 1974.'

The winner of the Golden Boot, Grzegorz Lato, scored his seventh goal of the finals as Poland beat Brazil in the third-place play-off, sealing his place alongside Kazimierz Deyna in the World Cup select, chosen from all the players in the tournament.

Overlapping the European Championship finals was the Independence Cup in Brazil, starting on 11 June. To commemorate the 150th anniversary of the independence of Brazil, the President of the Brazilian FA, João Havelange, had organised a 'Little World Cup' in which 20 teams would take part. As the tournament went head to head with the more important European Championships, it is often overlooked. Given that it was a key step in assisting Havelange to take over FIFA, one could make a case for it being one of the most important ever held.

From 1961 to 2016, only Sir Stanley Rous, João Havelange and Sepp Blatter would hold the title of FIFA President. The three would oversee the transition of football from a Eurocentric colonial-inspired game, to the multi-billion-pound global industry it is today. It was Havelange's election in 1974 that pinpointed the moment that changed the direction of football, and the Independence Cup was pivotal to him winning the vote.

Havelange had competed as a swimmer in the 1936 Olympics in Berlin, aged 20, and would note the German penchant for organisation. Due to the Second World War, Havelange had to wait until the 1952 Helsinki Games to repeat his Olympic endeavours, this time competing in water polo. He earned his fortune building the transport business, Viação Cometa, but it was as a sports administrator that Havelange made his name, leading the Brazilian delegation at the Melbourne Olympics in 1956.[14]

He quickly rose through the ranks of the Confederação Brasileira de Desportos (CBD)[15], becoming president six months before the 1958 World Cup in Sweden. Under Havelange, the Brazilian squad that travelled to Sweden was perhaps the best prepared in its history, winning the 1958 and 1962 World Cups before meeting with failure in 1966.

In 1969, his appointment of João Saldanha to coach the Seleção infuriated the dictator Emílio Medici. Though he later sacked Saldanha, the damage had been done and Havelange was close to being unseated as the head of the CBD. Despite the distraction of the Saldanha appointment, Brazil triumphed in 1970 to win their third World Cup with Havelange at the helm.

After the World Cups of 1958 and 1962, and particularly due to the presence of Pelé, the Brazilian national team was often asked to play matches around the world – a diplomatic tool that both the government and Havelange took full advantage of. As part of his campaign to win the FIFA presidency, Havelange travelled to at least 86 countries that perhaps weren't great footballing nations, but whose votes carried equal weight to those of England, Germany and Italy. In the more remote footballing outposts, Havelange was not as well known as the

FIFA president, Rous, but Pelé, who accompanied him on many of his visits, certainly was.

In 1969, after a series of failed investments, Pelé was in debt to the sum of nearly quarter of a million dollars. Havelange arranged donations from the CBD, as well as helping the player to find commercial opportunities that aided his financial recovery. In return, Pelé canvassed for Havelange to win the FIFA presidency. Many delegates managed to secure either the Brazilian national team or Pelé's club, Santos, to play in their home country, as football matches were being converted into voting promises for Havelange.

FIFA[16] had been founded in 1904 and by the end of the Second World War, Europe represented more than half of FIFA's membership. The 1960s were a turning point for the composition of FIFA as more countries from Africa and the Caribbean joined. The Confederation of African Football (CAF) had been established in 1956 with only four members – Egypt, Ethiopia, Sudan and South Africa; at the time they were the only independent nations that weren't still under the influence of European colonialism. Despite their limited number of members, the CAF voted to expel South Africa for stating that they would only be sending either an all-white team or an all-black team to the first African Cup of Nations in 1957.

Sir Stanley Rous had been appointed FIFA president in 1961, after 32 years as the FA secretary. While a good administrator, Rous was a dedicated colonialist and his attitude to South Africa, together with not engaging with the non-European confederations, would lead to his eventual downfall.

Led by the Ethiopian, Yidnekatchew Tessema, the CAF were determined to be heard. A complaint in Africa and other smaller confederations was the lack of guaranteed spots in the World Cup finals. After the 1958 and 1962 world cups took place with only European and South American teams, the

CAF lobbied Rous and FIFA to be allowed one automatic place at the 1966 tournament. When this was denied, the Africans boycotted the qualifying tournament.

FIFA reacted to the African boycott by fining the African associations, but the boycott worked and the CAF was awarded a full place for the 1970 World Cup. Tessema's efforts in pushing African football's interests on the world stage saw him join FIFA's executive committee in 1966. It was clear to him that Rous needed to be replaced as president of FIFA if the CAF was going to continue increasing its number of places at the World Cup and growing its share of FIFA revenue, as well as opposing racial discrimination in sport.

Havelange promised to expand the number of teams in the World Cup and to offer these confederations more spaces in what was becoming an even bigger event than the Olympics. In return, Tessema promised Havelange that the African countries would vote for him. While Havelange organised the tournament ostensibly to commemorate Brazil's independence, he wanted to invite as many FIFA delegates as possible to have some face-time with. His plan was to have the World Cup-holders, Brazil, play at home against the strongest national teams in the world in an event similar to the World Cup.

The presence of England, Germany, Spain and Italy was taken for granted, but in early 1972 everything changed when their national federations began to cancel their participation. England were followed by Germany, Italy and Spain in withdrawing. To replace them, Havelange invited the Netherlands, Austria and Belgium, but they also declined. The Brazilians believed that the withdrawals were down to Havelange's campaign for the FIFA presidency. Havelange admitted, 'My candidacy is bothering a lot of people.'

The only European teams who would eventually travel to Brazil were France, Portugal, Ireland, Yugoslavia, Scotland, Czechoslovakia and the Soviet Union. The Soviets, having qualified for the European Championship finals, sent a second-string squad featuring none of the players who played in Belgium. Of the seven European entrants, Czechoslovakia and Scotland were seeded alongside the Soviet Union. Considering Yugoslavia had reached the European quarter-finals and Portugal finished above Scotland in their qualifying group, Scotland's seeding was hard to justify.

The field of 20 was completed by a strong South American presence and, with an eye on potential votes, Havelange invited an all-African selection, a North and Central American selection, and the Asian Cup winners, Iran.

The African squad was manned by players from Tunisia, Togo, Egypt, Morocco, Algeria, Ghana, Congo, Ivory Coast, Cameroon, Mali and Zaire. For many of the African countries, it was the first time they had been represented in an international football tournament outside their own continent.

The North and Central American (CONCACAF) side was represented by players from Honduras, Bermuda, Suriname, Jamaica, Trinidad and Tobago, Nicaragua and Haiti. The key for Havelange was that the African and Concacaf sides were populated by 18 different countries, which meant 18 potential votes. The CBD paid all the entrants' expenses, giving the delegates a free holiday. The only price was to listen to what Havelange was promising. To persuade Venezuela to attend, Havelange paid their football association $25,000, which all but guaranteed him their vote at the next FIFA Congress.

Fifteen of the countries had to play in three preliminary groups of five, after which the group winners would join the seeded Brazil, Scotland, Czechoslovakia, Uruguay and Soviet Union, in two groups of four. The winners of the second-round groups would contest the Final. Obviously, you could have had a seeded knockout and got away with 19 games, but – in a dress rehearsal for the bloated World Cup tournaments to follow – there were 44 games, including the always-popular third-place play-off.

Group A saw Argentina, France, the all-African selection, Colombia, and the Concacaf side compete. The pivotal game between Argentina and France finished goalless, but Argentina pipped France on goal difference after beating Concacaf 7-0 and Columbia 4-1. Argentina's Rodolfo Fischer, the San Lorenzo striker of German-Brazilian descent, helped himself to four goals in the thrashing of Concacaf. His form during the tournament would earn him a transfer to join Jairzinho at Botafogo.

Group B saw Portugal comfortably through with a 100 per cent record in a group that included Chile, Ecuador, Iran and the Republic of Ireland.[17] Ireland won their first two games against Iran and Ecuador, before losing to Chile by the odd goal in three.

Chile manager, Rudi Gutendorf, had arrived there by a circuitous route. After beginning his coaching career with FC Lucerne in Switzerland, he returned to his native Germany to coach MSV Duisburg, Stuttgart, Schalke and Kickers Offenbach. He had also travelled further afield to coach the St Louis Stars during the inaugural NASL season, as well as the Bermudian national team. In 1972, after leading the Peruvian side, Sporting Cristal, to win the National Cup, he was offered the Chile job.

In September 1973, while Gutendorf was preparing his team for the World Cup playoff against the Soviet Union, the Chilean army – led by Augusto Pinochet – seized control of the country. The wall Gutendorf had built in the national stadium for his players to practise shooting was used by Pinochet's firing squads to execute dissenters. In light of his close friendship with the deposed president, Salvador Allende, Gutendorf fled the country on the advice of the German ambassador.

He stayed in South America, managing the national teams of Bolivia and Venezuela. He remained busy over the next three years, managing 1860 Munich and Fortuna Köln, together with coaching Real Valladolid in Spain and the national sides of

Trinidad & Tobago, Grenada, Antigua and Botswana. While he was back in Germany, in 1977, he signed Kevin Keegan for Hamburg before player pressure forced him out after three months.

Upset, Gutendorf moved to the other side of the world to become the Australian national team manager before coaching New Caledonia, Fiji, Nepal, Tonga, Tanzania, Hertha Berlin, and Sao Tome & Principe. In 1984 he became the first foreign manager to win the Japanese league with Yomiuri SC, before taking charge of the national sides of Ghana, Nepal, Fiji again, and the Chinese Olympic team.

In 1988 he arrived in Iran just as the Iran-Iraq War was ending. Although he led the Iranian Under-23 team to the finals of the Asian Games, he was informed by the religious leaders of Iran that there was no room for an unbeliever on the Iranian bench. Gutendorf took three years out of the game before returning to take the reins as the first manager of the Chinese national team. Over the next six years, he also managed Mauritius twice, taking charge of Zimbabwe in between his two spells.

In 1999, aged 73, Gutendorf was approached by the German government to go to Rwanda on a diplomatic mission as much as a footballing one. He achieved credible wins against Uganda and the Congo and would describe the feeling of seeing Hutu and Tutsi supporters hugging one another when Rwanda scored as the greatest achievement of his lengthy career.

In 2003, after a four-year absence from the game, Gutendorf took his last official managerial post as manager of the Samoan national team. In a colourful coaching career spanning nearly half a century, the German managed clubs in Switzerland, Germany, Spain, America, Japan and Peru, as well as managing 18 national teams from China to Tanzania.

Ireland lost their chance of a top-two finish in their group when they lost 2-1 to Portugal, all three goals coming in a three-minute spell. An interesting footnote to the game was the substitute appearance of the reserve goalkeeper in the 84th minute. Jose Henrique was replaced by Felix Mourinho for his only cap.[18]

Yugoslavia overcame their all-South American opposition of Paraguay, Peru, Bolivia and Venezuela to win Group C. Their forward, Dušan Bajević, scored five against Venezuela and grabbed braces in the wins over Paraguay and Peru.

For the second group stage, Argentina and Portugal joined a desperately disappointing Uruguay and the Soviet Union side in one group. The seeded sides made little impression and the opening game between Portugal and Argentina would decide the eventual group winner. Miguel Brindisi opened the scoring, but Adolfo, Eusébio and Joaquim Dinis scored for Portugal in a 10-minute spell to give them the victory and eventually the group.

The other group saw hosts Brazil start their campaign with a dull 0-0 draw against Czechoslovakia at the Maracanã.

Whereas 115,000 watched Brazil's opening match, a crowd of just 4,000 witnessed Scotland's 2-2 draw against Yugoslavia the following day. Despite the withdrawal of players from Celtic, Rangers and Derby, Docherty could still name a strong squad.[19] Argentinian referee Ángel Coerezza, struggled to control the players during a bad-tempered affair played in a sweltering 80°F. After 63 minutes, Scotland were 2-1 up courtesy of Lou Macari's first goals for the national side. With ten minutes remaining, the tiring Scots had a gilt-edged chance to clinch victory, when Asa Hartford was bundled over for a penalty, but Willie Morgan's kick was saved. Scotland were punished in the 87th minute when Jovan Acimovic's shot was deflected in off Martin Buchan to give Yugoslavia a draw.

Billy Bremner was named man of the match and presented with a 'magnificent television set' as his prize. In the days when televisions were the size of what would now be a small family hatchback, transporting it back to Yorkshire must have proved a joy.

For their second fixture against Czechoslovakia, the Scottish party had to travel a thousand miles south to Porto Alegre. The Aberdeen goalkeeper, Bobby Clark, pulled off a string of outstanding saves to deny Jan Medvid, Vladimir Hagara and Jaroslav Pollák, as Scotland held on for a goalless draw that saw both teams booed off by the 6,000 crowd.

After two draws Scotland were still in with a chance of reaching the Final. Their next opponents, Brazil, had beaten Yugoslavia 3-0 in their second match, debutant Leivinha scoring two and Jairzinho adding the third.[20] Yugoslavia's win over the Czechs left Scotland needing to beat Brazil to make the Final, or a draw to progress on goal difference to the third-place play-off.

Brazil still had Brito, Clodoaldo, Gérson, Rivelino, Jairzinho and Tostão from their 1970 side, but despite pressure from Havelange, Pelé refused to come out of international retirement to play in the Independence Cup. Brazil's World Cup captain, Carlos Alberto, was out with the knee problems that would plague him for the next five years, so Gérson took over the captain's armband for the tournament. The other full-back from the World Cup, Everaldo, had been surprisingly omitted by manager Zagallo.[21] Leão replaced Felix in goal, which strengthened the side considerably. In fairness, Havelange in goal would have probably been an improvement.

Scotland put on an outstanding defensive performance in the first half and had their own chances to score. Lou Macari headed over the bar in the 32nd minute and Leão made fine saves from Willie Morgan and Alex Forsyth. After the interval, Bobby Clark saved from Dário before Gérson missed a glorious opportunity.

Dário was the man in form, having recently fired Atlético Mineiro to the first Brazilian national championship. He was a personal favourite of the Brazilian President, Medici, who suggested he should be included in the 1970 Brazilian team, to which manager Saldanha replied: 'I do not mess with his

Cabinet, he will not mess with my team.' Saldanha was soon replaced and Dário made the squad, although he wouldn't play. With Pelé now retired from international football, Dário had a chance to stake his claim.

Up until the age of 19, Dário had never played in an 11-a-side match. While in prison for the umpteenth time for burglary, a prison officer suggested he should use his prodigious leap, previously used to scale walls and escape chasing policemen, to outjump defenders on the football field. Dário vowed to turn his life around after one last crime, when he robbed two people for the money to buy a football. By the time he retired in 1986, he was second only to Hungarian legend Sándor Kocsis as the highest scorer of headed goals in football history.

With just ten minutes remaining, Rivelino collected the ball on the left wing and whipped in a cross that Jairzinho converted with a diving header to win the match. After the match, Docherty was scathing about the host's tactics: 'A good team does not use fouls to be able to win, and I was surprised that some Brazilian players used tactics for which they are not known.' The local papers supported Docherty's claim, criticising their own team's crude tackling while praising the Scots for their 'fair play and spirited defence'.

The third-place play-off between Yugoslavia and Argentina, and the Final between Brazil and Portugal, were played as a double header at the Maracanã. Yugoslavia took third place with a 4-2 win over Argentina. Dušan Bajević added another brace to finish as the tournament's top scorer with 13 goals. Miguel Brindisi scored both of Argentina's goals to crown a fine personal tournament.

It was apt that the Final of a tournament to celebrate Brazilian independence would be played between Brazil and Portugal – colony and home country reunited after 150 years and both ruled by right-wing dictatorships. That was as interesting as the Final got. The crowd was saved from extra time by Jairzinho's glancing header in the last minute.

The match was refereed by the Israeli, Abraham Klein, the finest referee of the era. Due to FIFA politics, Klein never got the opportunity to referee a World Cup Final, so had to content himself with this mini World Cup Final. For that alone, the tournament deserves more recognition.

The final marked Brito, Gérson and Tostão's last appearances for Brazil. Brito and Gérson would be 34 and 33 respectively by the time of the next Word Cup, but Tostão, who had only recently been transferred to Vasco Da Gama for £220,000, was only 25. Sadly, in August 1973 he was forced to retire after his eye problems resurfaced. Weary of football and fame, Tostão became a medical doctor, but 20 years later rejoined the football world to work as a respected journalist and television pundit.

The absence of the major European teams doomed the Independence Cup to commercial failure; it lost more than $10m. With ticket prices set too high, matches not involving the hosts were lucky to draw 15,000 spectators. The CBD had also paid for flight tickets and hotels for all the delegates, sending the tournament costs to over $21m. The CBD was funded by the Sports Lottery and its money was generally used by Havelange as his own private bank. In his book, *How They Stole the Game*, David Yallop accuses Havelange of plundering $6.5m of CBD funds to bribe national associations to vote for him rather than Rous.

Although the tournament wasn't a financial success, it did showcase Havelange's organisational skills and, more importantly, gave him the opportunity to meet football delegates from around the world. At the FIFA Congress in Paris later that summer, Rous cut himself further adrift from the non-Europeans by insisting the executive committee vote against plans to extend the World Cup from 16 to 24 teams for the 1978 tournament in Argentina.

Rous saw himself as the defender of European superiority at FIFA, but the African nations now had 37 votes to be won and saw Havelange as their ticket to gain influence with FIFA. With 60 per cent of the members from either Africa or Asia, the Europeans found themselves in a situation where an alliance between those two continents would end their power.

By 1974, Havelange knew he had the support of 12 Arab countries, ten countries from Central America, 12 African countries, plus France, Republic of Ireland, Greece, Cyprus, Turkey and Luxembourg from Europe – and that was without taking into account the ten South American countries that formed his power base.

Havelange promised to create more spaces for the lesser nations by changing the number of finalists in the next World Cups, from 16 to 20 in 1978, and then to 24 in 1982. He pledged to pour money into the less developed countries' national federations and promised to introduce World Cups at Under-20 and Under-17 levels – both tournaments that could be staged in the developing world.

The first round of voting on 11 June 1974 produced no winner; Havelange had won the vote but not the required two-thirds majority. A run-off was needed and this time a simple majority would suffice. Havalange's 68 votes to Rous's 52 ensured that FIFA was out of Europe's grasp for the first time since it was formed.

The African continent was recognised as the key factor in the election and, with Havelange in office, they reaped the benefits. The two big issues of the 1960s were soon resolved; the World Cup was expanded, and South Africa were expelled from FIFA by a vote of 78–9.

Now that Havelange had the presidency, he had to raise the money to make good on his promises. To bankroll his agenda, he commercialised the game as never before. To assist him, Adidas owner, Horst Dassler, established the Swiss sports marketing company, International Sport and Leisure (ISL). FIFA sold the rights to the World Cup for a fixed sum to ISL, which then went about making deals with individual sponsors.

The same was done for TV rights, which in time turned out to be even more lucrative.

Previously, soccer on TV had expanded slowly in continental Europe. Under Rous, FIFA had never taken advantage of soccer's commercial potential. Also, the spread of television itself was quite slow. In 1960 only 21 per cent of German households, 13 per cent of Italian households, 12 per cent of French households and two per cent of Spanish households possessed a television set. By 1970, the figures were 69 per cent, 54 per cent, 59 per cent, and 28 per cent respectively.

The total revenue of the 1986 World Cup in Mexico was estimated at nearly $100m, with one-third of the revenues coming from TV rights and one-third from sponsorship. Following Dassler's death in 1987 and the departure of key executives, ISL overpaid for sports rights in the 1990s, and was declared bankrupt in 2001. From 1989 to 2001, ISL had paid 185m Swiss francs in 'personal commissions' to sports officials and other people involved in the marketing of sports rights. In the 2008 fraud trial that arose from the collapse of ISL, a judge referred to the commissions as bribes.

FIFA's embrace of commercialism compromised its sporting integrity. While some of the money went into genuine development programmes, a lot went into the pockets of the delegates who secured Havelange's re-election. Although Havelange drew no salary as president of FIFA, his yearly expenses amounted to more than $1m. His expense account was enhanced by 'gifts' from ISL. Court documents released in 2012 show that Havelange and his son-in-law, Ricardo Teixeira, received £27m from ISL between 1992 and 2000.

No one can deny that Havalange grew world football during his reign. He set up tournaments such as the Under-20 and Under-17 world cups, the Women's World Cup and the Confederations Cup. All these tournaments were expenses rather than a source of income, but were paid for by the monetisation of FIFA. Football now generates money from TV rights and sponsorship deals that would have been unthinkable in 1974, because Havelange grew the global popularity of the game by taking the World Cup to Asia, Africa and the USA for the first time. By the time of the 2014 World Cup in Brazil, FIFA reportedly enjoyed revenues of $4.4bn, with profits of $2bn.

After his nominee, Sepp Blatter, took over in 1998, Havelange made himself honorary president for life.

POSTSCRIPT

*'They saw there was money to be made, and
looking back, I think they were quite right.'*
                                    Sandy Busby

*'Three cortisone injections in a lifetime
is about enough, whereas I was having
three every game.'*
                                    Kevin Beattie

THE 1971/72 season took place in a period of great change in Britain and around the world. Many of those changes continue to shape our society today. Football both reflected and was influenced by those changes.

The season was bookended by the Apollo 15 and 16 moon landings. NASA computers guided man across 356,000km of space from the Earth to the moon, returning them safely. The computers, costing $3.5m each, performed several hundred thousand operations per second and were the size of a car.

On 15 November 1971, Intel released the first microprocessor, which would revolutionise computing and eventually the world. Now, your near obsolete iPhone 6 is 32,600 times faster and can perform instructions 120,000,000 times faster than those NASA computers.

On the day Rangers won the Cup Winners' Cup, the Magnavox Odyssey video game console was first demoed, marking the dawn of the video game age. The next month, Atari was formed and would essentially fund the New York Cosmos into being the first financially doped football club.

The advent of video games now means that boys play FIFA instead of Subbuteo, undoubtedly a contributing factor in the epidemic of childhood obesity in Britain. Not that Subbuteo kept you fit, but trying to play on the green baize pitch – stretched out on the shagpile carpets of the day – meant that as long as there wasn't a monsoon, there was little excuse not to grab your Wembley Trophy Football and play outside.

For kids who feel FIFA is too energetic, they can entertain themselves with Football Manager, which even I will admit is a major improvement on Soccerama. Should you manage to crack the game and get unlimited funds, you will be able to mirror the business models of Manchester City and Paris Saint-Germain.

To be fair to those clubs, hasn't financial doping always occurred? Arsenal outspent other clubs in the 30s, Sunderland were known as the Bank of England club in the early 1950s, and Everton were known as the Mersey Millionaires in the 60s. During the 70s and 80s, the media fell over themselves to praise Liverpool's astute policy of buying young talent and seasoning them in the reserves, but let's not overlook the fact that the £300,000 paid to Chester for Ian Rush was a world record for a teenager and remained Chester City's record sale until they went bankrupt in March 2010. Liverpool were rich enough to pay big fees without the pressure of having to throw the player in at the deep end prematurely.

In the 1990s, Jack Walker's millions brought (or maybe bought) Blackburn the Premier League title before Abramovich's billions took spending to a new level. At the end of the 2016/17 season, the *Daily Telegraph* calculated the net spend on transfers by clubs over the previous three seasons. The top three clubs were Arsenal with £147m, Manchester United on £246m and Manchester City on £303m. On top of transfer fees, the top six – Tottenham, Liverpool, Arsenal, Chelsea, Manchester United and Manchester City – each spent between £120m and £220m on wages during the season.[1]

By 1972, the Summer of Love was long over and the lovable moptops had gone their separate ways. John Lennon was writing songs about The Attica State prison riots and Bloody Sunday, while Paul McCartney released 'Mary Had a Little Lamb'. As Britain was receiving the bills for the 60s, the hippies cut their hair to become skinheads. The 70s would become, for the great majority, what the previous decade had been for a privileged few.

The economy was in trouble, with unemployment hitting one million for the first time since the 1930s. Decimalisation was blamed for rising prices in the shops as inflation began to register in the national consciousness. On the positive side, the Prime Minister, Edward Heath, finally had agreement to allow the country to join the European Community, which apparently would solve all of its problems.

The pros and cons of Britain joining the European Community have been debated ever since, but it undoubtedly changed the face of British football for good. Back in 1971, there was barely a handful of foreign players. As well as Clyde Best, the Commonwealth supplied us with Canada and West Brom's Glenn Johnson, and South Africans, Colin Viljoen and Derek Smethhurst, played for Ipswich and Millwall respectively. The Treaty of Rome would bring an influx of foreign players to our shores, which has never abated. No one could argue against the fact that Ossie Ardiles, Eric Cantona, Thierry Henry, Dennis Bergkamp, Ruud Gullit and Gianfranco Zola added immeasurably to the domestic game, and to see them play in the flesh was a privilege. I defy anyone to say the same of Ahmed Fathy, Corrado Grabbi, Christian Negouai, Amaury Bischoff, Xisco, Per Kroldrup and Lee Dong-Gook.

In 2019/20, only seven Premier League sides had English keepers. Five of those sides had English managers, which is probably not a coincidence.[2] In 1971, even if you ignore Gordon Banks, Ray Clemence, Peter Shilton, Peter Bonetti and Pat

Jennings, there was still a huge depth of goalkeeping talent. Even when you dropped down to the Second Division, you had the likes of Phil Parkes, John Jackson, Kevin Keelan, Bryan King, Jim Montgomery and John Burridge.

The jingoistic view at the time was that continental keepers couldn't catch a cross, generally punching or flapping at them, so terrified were they of any physical presence. But nowadays football is essentially a non-contact sport and generally teams do not, thankfully, fire aimless crosses into the box. However, should the teachings of Charles Hughes make a comeback, modern keepers do seem to struggle to catch the modern ball, so the continental punching goalkeeper should remain in fashion. If he is 6ft 5in tall, then so much the better. The era of a 5ft 9in Ian McFaul or a 5ft 8in Laurie Sivell has long since passed.

Manchester City's new manager, Pep Guardiola, quickly moved on England keeper, Joe Hart, to enable him to sign sweeper-keeper, Claudio Bravo. As far as I could tell, as good as Bravo was with his feet, he wasn't terribly good at actually handling the ball. Maybe Dave Webb was ahead of his time? Guardiola replaced Bravo with the Brazilian, Ederson. A manager signing a foreign goalkeeper back in 1971 would have had his sanity questioned; signing a Brazilian keeper would have had him committed.[3]

On the subject of Brazilians, Santos and Brazil don't play friendlies around the world at the behest of João Havelange anymore.[4] The Brazilian national side now travels the world at the behest of Nike. As part of the contract between Nike and Brazil, Nike has the right to organise five international games a year featuring at least eight Brazilian first-team regulars. Since 2006, Brazil played Argentina in locations as far flung as England, Qatar, America, China and Australia.

Foreign players have been blamed for introducing diving into our previously unsullied game, although some of Francis Lee's tumbles might undermine that xenophobic theory somewhat.

Although we can now measure on Prozone whether our foreign imports are working hard for their inflated salaries, it isn't a new concept. Even back in the 50s, statisticians were breaking football down by numbers. Charles Reep could somehow spin numbers to prove that Hungary's win in 1953 was due to their superior long-ball game. After analysing the 1972 England-West Germany game at Wembley, Reep concluded that England had 'earned at least a 2-1 win'.

Once we joined the EU, we were an island no more; the ramifications of the Bosman ruling in the European Court of Justice would be felt just as keenly in the British game. Players could now move on a free transfer when their contract expired, and leagues were unable to enforce any quotas on foreign players from other EU countries. The subsequent wage inflation caused by Bosman means that many Premier League clubs are in all likelihood hurtling towards bankruptcy, according to a report titled 'We're so Rich it's Unbelievable' by financial analysts, Vysyble.

Tottenham made a record £223,000 profit for the 1971/72 season, double Liverpool's profit of £107,079. Manchester United announced a loss of £250,000, due mainly to the purchases of Ian Storey-Moore and Martin Buchan. The figures should seem laughable now, but many Premier League clubs now aspire to make such a profit, or any profit.

Back in 1972, the economics of football were simple. The average player's wage in the First Division was £85 a week, and the wage bill at a top club was around £200,000 a year. A club drawing a crowd of 45,000 would receive around £20,000 in gate receipts. Of that, the away team would take £4,000 and £800 went to the Football League pool. So, 21 home games at £15,200 netted a club £319,200. Add a couple of thousand pounds from the television deal, along with a tiny bit of merchandising income, and that was a top club's revenue. Their income comfortably covered the wage bill and left enough money for a couple of transfer buys. The current wage bills of

£200m a year are more than even the most successful club's inflated match-day and broadcasting revenue.

The Vysyble report, based on the accounts of all Premier League clubs between 2008/09 and 2015/16, claimed Premier League clubs had lost £2 billion in those eight years. One of the report's co-authors, Roger Bell, warned: 'Our analysis shows clubs are losing a record £876,700 every single day. Despite TV bringing in huge amounts of cash every year, it does not meet the many millions spent on players' wages.' In 1991/92, the last season before the Premier League was formed, the wage bill for Division One was £44m. The Premier League wage bill for 2017/18 topped £2bn.

Chelsea and Manchester City accounted for more than half of the league's losses over the report's eight-year period. But unless their owners get bored with owning a football club or run into personal financial problems, the clubs will continue to thrive. As for the other clubs, as long as the 70 per cent increases in domestic TV rights continue every three years, they should continue to just about keep their heads above water. But in 2018 that bubble seemed to have burst. Sky paid £3.579bn for the 2019–22 rights, a significant reduction on the £4.1b the broadcaster paid for the 2016–19 seasons. From August 2019, BT began to show 52 live games a season at a cost of £975m over three years.

Amazon entered the market by striking an undisclosed deal to live-stream exclusive coverage of 20 matches a season to UK Prime Video members at no extra cost to their existing subscription.

The ferocity of competition between Sky and BT Sport, which boosted the Premier League clubs' coffers for the 2016–19 cycle, has calmed a little after the two companies signed a deal in December 2017 enabling each to offer the other's channels.

The average viewing for live football on Sky is beginning to fall. Sky argue that the total number of people watching the Premier League is at its highest based on people watching

Premier League coverage across all of its platforms for a *minimum of 15 minutes*. The problem is that the internet, social media and video games are affecting the way that younger fans in particular interact with the game. How long before the *minimum of 15 minutes* becomes the maximum?

People are too busy playing with their smartphones to concentrate on anything on which there is no obligation to focus. The social media spectator can now escape the 90-minute commitment and watch the game in fragments, on demand, anytime, anywhere. Watching a full match is often tedious; why not absorb it via the social media channels? On average, the ball is only in play for a little over an hour, so why watch a game with your undivided attention for an hour and a half? Maybe televised football could be repackaged? Take two games, chop out the half-hour where the ball is out of play and edit out the boring bits to get the best 25 minutes of action from both games. Maybe call it *Match of the Day*?

Back in 1972, a live game was a treat to be savoured, but now the oversupply means Sky promotes a Monday night clash between Brighton and Huddersfield as if it were a World Cup final. The spreading of kick-off times across the whole weekend only undermines dramatic tension. The big kick-off to a season was just that; everyone kicked off their season at exactly the same time. Now the Premier League kicks off with a solitary game on a Friday night.

Match-day income and the television revenue is swallowed up by players' wages, but luckily the clubs can fall back on merchandising, the other big growth in football. Or can they? Looking back, it seems naïve how poorly clubs used to exploit their brand. As we saw in February's chapter, it was Leeds, together with Admiral, who had the brainwave of copyrighting their kit. So you can blame Leeds for having to buy your child a new kit every other season.

The fact that you have to buy at least two other kits you can probably lay at Manchester United's door. They brought out a third kit in 1971, wearing it against Southampton, Stoke, Sheffield United, Forest and Arsenal. Given all those teams wore red, United obviously couldn't wear their normal kit, but what was wrong with their all-white kit?

It is hard to claim, however, that Leeds or Manchester United were at the cutting edge of branding and merchandising. In 1972, Jack Charlton and his wife owned the merchandising stall outside Elland Road, and Matt Busby owned the club shop at Old Trafford. In 1969, in lieu of a testimonial, the club gave Busby a 21-year lease on a wooden hut in the Old Trafford car park, for which he paid £5 a week rent. Busby turned the hut into a souvenir shop, which was run by his son, Sandy. Eventually they outgrew the hut and the souvenir shop was incorporated into the back of the stand facing Warwick Road. It took the club until 1987 to take the shop back when, with two years left on the lease, Sandy Busby sold it to the club for £200,000. 'They saw there was money to be made, and looking back, I think they were quite right,' said Sandy, with not a little understatement.

As great an appointment as Martin Edwards made in Alex Ferguson, the appointment of Edward Freedman was just as important. Freedman had an instinctive feel for the game's commercial potential and, with the Spurs Chairman Irving Scholar, had initiated a merchandising revolution at Tottenham. After being head-hunted by Edwards, Freedman was appalled by what he found at Old Trafford. The club shop was primitive, with too few tills to serve the relatively small number of customers it attracted. Freedman doubled the number of tills in the shop and expanded the premises, initiating a mail-order business before moving on to the merchandising. United, like most clubs, just looked at merchandising as a small bonus revenue stream. If someone came to them wanting to make a pen featuring the club badge, they would sell them a licence for a small sum. Freedman bought back as many licences as he could, moving production to a small number of trusted suppliers. Manchester United's revenue on merchandising, apparel and product licensing now tops £100m. As most club shops now have a special section for pets, that worry of what to buy your dog for Christmas is now over.

In February, it was the German match-fixing scandal in 1971 that ultimately led to Eintracht Braunschweig introducing shirt sponsorship into the game. This allows Manchester United to coin another £53m per season. Unfortunately, just as the money from match-day receipts and TV revenue goes into players' wages, the windfall from merchandising and shirt sponsorship disappears into transfer fees and agents' fees. During the 2018/19 season, Premier League clubs paid £260m to agents. More alarmingly, England's second tier, the Championship, parted with over £50m. We have come a long way since questions were asked in Parliament in 1972 over the £4m spent on transfers during the 1971/72 season. In the summer of 2019, £1.4bn was spent on transfers.

Unfortunately, most of that transfer money goes abroad. What little stays in the English game doesn't often trickle below the Premier League. In 1971, clubs paid four per cent of net gate receipts into a central Football League pool, and the television and pools money was also shared equally throughout the league.

The transfer market arguably acted as another important mechanism for redistributing income. Up to May 1972, five of the highest 11 transfer fees between English clubs were paid to clubs outside the First Division. The lower leagues were also where many players gained their early experience. Of the 24 players capped by England during the 1971/72 season, 13 started their career outside the First Division. Nowadays Premier League clubs actively poach talented players from the smaller clubs' academies before they even hit puberty.

In 1985 the Manchester United chairman, Martin Edwards, said, 'The smaller clubs are bleeding the game dry. For the sake of the game, they should be put to sleep.' How long before the euthanasia plans come to fruition?

On the positive side, due to the huge cost of players, there is more evidence of clubs looking after their welfare. The clubs protect the investment they make, sparing no expense when it comes to looking after an injured player. Squad rotation means that generally no player plays with an injury.

The wonder drug of 70s football was cortisone, a steroid that reduced inflammation and allowed players to return quickly from injury. Injections of cortisone were given liberally, with little thought given to the potential side effects. Trainers were treating groin strains with two injections a week to keep their key players going through the season. As well as turning players' bones into Swiss cheese and setting them up for a lifetime of arthritis, cortisone in large amounts can also cause sterility. Southampton's Jim Steele regularly had two injections a week in his groin. A specialist later explained that the injections were the reason he was unable to father children. Footballers are now advised to avoid cortisone completely, or limit intake to one injection per year.

Many retired players say their clubs put pressure on them to play when not fully fit and gave them poor medical treatment. Before the Premier League, few clubs had a full-time club doctor and most physiotherapists were former players, who, while not wanting to go into management, wanted to stay in the game. At best, they completed a week-long first-aid course. Injured players were often treated with a rubdown in the dressing room after the match or a cold sponge on the pitch.

Tommy Smith, who retired in 1980, was declared 40 per cent disabled by rheumatoid and osteoarthritis, and underwent a series of operations resulting in new knees, hips and elbows. Smith said: 'The truth was that in those days footballers were not treated that well. The club doctor would only turn up on match days. The physio was usually an old player who didn't fancy coaching. It really was primitive compared with today.'

Bobby Robson called Kevin Beattie the best English-born player he'd ever seen. But after his 23rd birthday, Beattie could barely complete half a season. The specialist who advised him to retire at 27 otherwise he would be on crutches in ten years, also told him that if he had gone to see him first, he could have played on until he was 40. At 50 Beattie was unable to walk more than half a mile on his arthritic knees. 'My knees were knackered. According to modern medical science, three cortisone injections in a lifetime is about enough, whereas I was having three every game – two before the kick-off and one at half-time. I certainly don't blame anyone; the injections were given in all good faith.'

Players' wages were structured around three components: a low basic salary, appearance money and a win bonus. Hence the PFA has struggled to get the FA to admit that the clubs are liable, because in many cases players themselves asked for cortisone to speed their return from injury, while others agreed to play when not fully fit, so that they could earn appearance money. A player out injured saw a thinner pay packet than one playing in a winning team. Squad rotation was unheard of. Managers rarely changed the team if everyone was fit, so the players feared not getting their place back in the side after a long lay-off. Tommy Smith again: 'In those days, if you didn't play you didn't get appearance money and that could affect how much you took home at the end of the week. You couldn't afford to stay out of the team for too long. There were times when I shouldn't have played and the club knew this. There were matches when they needed me or sometimes, I needed the money.'

I admit to finding squad rotation infuriating. Paying £50 to watch a bunch of teenagers I have not heard of play in a League Cup tie always hurts, but seeing the heroes of my youth hobbling around on crutches hurts more.

Even sadder are the heroes who gave me so many memories and who now struggle to remember their glory days themselves. The following all played their part in the story of the 1971/72 season:

Jeff Astle:
Peter Bonetti,
Stan Bowles,
John Charles,
Bobby Charlton,
Jackie Charlton,
Tony Dunne,
Tony Hateley,
Jimmy Hill,
Dave Mackay,
Billy McNeill,
Joe Mercer,
Gerd Müller,
Chris Nicholl,
Bob Paisley,
Martin Peters,
Sir Alf Ramsey,
Ron Saunders,
Dave Sexton,
Tommy Smith,
Nobby Stiles
Matt Tees,
John Tudor,
Dave Watson,
Ray Wilson,
Alf Wood,
Frank Worthington.
All suffered – or continue to suffer – from dementia.

The match ball used for the FA Cup Final in 1972 was pretty much the same as the one used in the first Cup Final 100 years earlier. Thanks to leather's natural properties, the balls lost their shape and absorbed water, so gained weight in rainy conditions. Jeff Astle described heading the ball on a wet day as like 'heading a bag of bricks'. By the late 80s, match balls consisted of a latex bladder with 32 synthetic leather panels stitched around it. The result was a football that kept its shape and did not absorb water. Time will tell if the new ball has decreased the high incidence of Alzheimer's in former players, but the signs don't look positive.

In 2017, former Republic of Ireland international, Kevin Doyle, retired from professional football on medical advice after suffering persistent headaches. Doyle, a renowned header of the ball, said in a statement: 'This year it has been clear to me that heading the ball was becoming problematic, and causing me to have repeated headaches.' Dr Michael Grey, a neuroscience expert at Birmingham University, believes the modern football poses just as much risk as the one used in the 60s and 70s. 'It doesn't matter if the balls are lighter. If the balls are more aerodynamic and the players are bigger and are kicking the ball harder, the velocity increases and the force of the impact stays the same or is even greater.'

Back in 1972, if you won the European Cup you could proudly proclaim yourselves the best team in Europe. Nowadays, if you win the Champions League it generally proves you are the biggest spenders in Europe. The Champions League is a wonderful competition. My family loved it when Tottenham qualified for the first time in 2010. They played the Dutch Champions, holders Inter Milan and Italian champions AC Milan, before being knocked out by Real Madrid after a draw that made a Scottish World Cup group look easy.

My main gripe is that it isn't really the Champions League. Since 1997/98, when the tournament was expanded to allow the runners-up in domestic leagues to enter, only half the tournaments have been won by the reigning domestic champions of their countries. I struggle with a Champions League where Liverpool can win after qualifying for it by finishing fourth, 30 points behind their domestic champions. When Liverpool won it in 2005, they came fifth in the league, 37 points behind the champions. Were Liverpool the best team in Europe in

2005 when they hadn't won their domestic league for 15 years? Definitely not, but I would say they almost certainly were in 1976, when they won the lesser UEFA Cup.

The only other European trophy now is the Europa League, but after the Champions League has hoovered up all the glamour clubs, your team will find itself playing Finnish postmen until the knockout phase. By the time you get to the last 16, it is at the business end of the domestic season and most supporters are praying their team is knocked out so they can concentrate on the vital job of clinching fourth place in the Premier League.

Back in 1971/72, we had the European Cup, the UEFA Cup, and the Cup Winners' Cup. The UEFA Cup, though a lesser tournament, often had the form-teams competing in it. Liverpool won it in 1973, and the First Division title, a feat they repeated in 1976, the year before they won the European Cup. Ajax in 1992, Juventus in 1993 and Bayern Munich in 1996, were as good as any side in Europe at the time. The 1971/72 UEFA Cup had Real Madrid, Juventus, AC Milan and Leeds taking part, so it was pretty competitive. The Cup Winners' Cup could admittedly be a bit more of a mixed bag, but in 71/72 it boasted the likes of Liverpool, Bayern Munich and Barcelona.

People look at the routes taken to win the European Cup in the 70s and 80s and denigrate the low quality of the opposition, but that is to judge them by present-day standards rather than in their own time. Many of the now unknown Eastern European teams of the era were very good sides. The biggest question for many is whether the present-day crop of players are better. Modern football watchers, who believe football started in 1992, certainly believe so. They insist that the players are quicker, fitter and better athletes.

Back in 1971, Colin Bell was widely acknowledged as one of the fittest and hardest-working players in English football. He had been monitored covering an astonishing eight kilometres in a 1960s match, a distance that would have him perceived as lazy now. Premier League footballers cover around 12 to 14 kilometres per match, and a great percentage of that is run at top speed. Even goalkeepers have been recorded as covering five kilometres. The days of players turning up with a hangover and eating a pre-match meal of steak and chips, with two cortisone injections in their knee before the match starts, are over. They couldn't get away with it now.

For a direct comparison, let us look at two former Manchester United number sevens, George Best and Cristiano Ronaldo. Best's self-destructive instincts might have been accelerated by the riches on offer today, but I struggle to think of any skill Ronaldo has that Best didn't. Both fast, balanced, two-footed, could dribble, shoot, superb in the air and could tackle. My mistake, Best was the only one who could actually tackle.

Best also had to be tougher. Today the players are protected far more than they were in his day. More protection allows them to show their skills without the worry of being consistently fouled. Were Ronaldo to play against Revie's Leeds, he would have been subjected to at least eight fouls before the referee even felt inclined to talk to a Leeds player. It is also doubtful Ronaldo would have been walking out on to the quagmire of a pitch if he wasn't always 100 per cent fit.

Also, the talent pool was more evenly spread in the 70s. When Manchester United play against an average Premier League team, you can guarantee that the players on United's bench will be better than the opposition's star player. Were that not the case, then United would be buying him post-haste, to sit on their bench for the return game.

I am certain a peak George Best would be a revelation in today's game, but as great a player as I think Ronaldo is, I would fear for his safety against the Leeds or Southampton sides of Best's era.

Ronaldo's main rival for the title of the greatest player in the world is Lionel Messi. The Argentinian is Barcelona's star player and possibly their greatest of all time. In comparison, his countryman Diego Maradona's time at Barcelona is viewed as a failure. Maradona only scored 38 goals in his two seasons at Barca; Messi has scored more than that in each of his last ten seasons. But we have to remember that Barcelona were not a great side when Maradona was there, and they scored fewer goals than they do now. They only scored an average of 1.79 goals per game in La Liga, compared with their average of 2.8 during the Messi era. So yes, Messi has scored a lot more goals than Maradona, but then so has the team. The changes to offside and the back-pass rule have made the game faster and the players need to be fitter, but they have also undoubtedly made it easier to score. I have my doubts that Messi could have scored the same number of goals in the defensive 70s and 80s.

Also, Barcelona were one of the best sides in Europe even before Messi was a regular. He has certainly enhanced them, but he has never carried a team, as Maradona did at Napoli, or lifted an average team to win a World Cup, as Maradona did in 1986. If football is all about athleticism and speed, how did another Argentinian, Juan Román Riquelme, dominate games in the modern era playing at little above walking pace?

As I said earlier in the book, I have little doubt that some legendary wingers survived their career with one trick. No doubt slow-motion replays from ten angles would reveal enough of the magic to show a defender how to nullify them. But let's not forget that the same replays have also shown present-day players the Ferenc Puskàs drag-back, the Johan Cruyff turn and countless George Best dummies. Is it such a leap of imagination to think that Cruyff or Best might learn a few new skills if playing today?

Another myth is that present-day tactics are more sophisticated. Don Revie would be surprised to learn that Mourinho's dossiers are revolutionary. If false nines are such an innovation, what was Nándor Hidegkuti doing back in the 1950s? The development of Barcelona's tiki-taka was influenced by Cruyff, but surely no one can doubt that if his 1972 Ajax team felt inclined to play tiki-taka, they had the wit and players to carry it out.

Staying with that Ajax team, would pressing be a total mystery to Johan Neeskens and his team-mates? How vastly different was the Claude Makélélé role to what John McGovern did for Brian Clough for many years? All that has changed is the jargon. Tackling has been all but outlawed and what little remains has been rebranded as turnovers. You might question whether Ron Harris would be as effective in the present-day game. He would certainly need to refine his game to stay on the pitch for long, but Bobby Moore or Franz Beckenbauer, whose games didn't revolve around tackling, would thrive today. I'm not saying that the players of the past were better than current players, but the argument that players today are better because some science has evolved is complete nonsense. Skill is timeless.

While we are on the subject of skill, let's have a look at our 70s mavericks. In light of Günter Netzer's performance at Wembley, there was a recurring question throughout the rest of the decade; if the German side could revolve around a maverick such as Netzer, why couldn't England find a long-term place for at least one of Rodney Marsh, Peter Osgood, Alan Hudson, Charlie George, Tony Currie, Frank Worthington or Stan Bowles? The first question is, did Germany accommodate Netzer or just tolerate him? While Netzer enjoyed a 10-year international career, a third of his caps were earned during the 1971/72 season while Wolfgang Overath was struggling with injuries. After the 1972 European Championship, Netzer would only play another six full internationals and make a 20-minute cameo in the 1974 World Cup. Except for one glorious season, to say he was a regular – or that Germany built their team around him – would be a gross exaggeration. That said, his 37 caps compare favourably with the 46 caps that our seven mavericks earned between them.

Before we speculate as to what might have happened for our mavericks on the international stage, we can't overlook how little they achieved in club football. Netzer won as many club medals as all of our seven mavericks combined. Our mavericks won one title, three FA Cups, one League Cup and two Cup Winners' Cups between them.

By the summer of 1972, our mavericks should have had their peak years ahead of them. Charlie George and Alan Hudson were just 21, and the oldest, Marsh, was a month younger than Netzer at 27. But by then most of our mavericks had won everything they were going to win. Netzer inspired his clubs to success; our mavericks, for the most part, gave us memories. You could argue that Worthington never played for a top-class side, but he did blow his chance to go to Liverpool. Osgood, Hudson, George, Marsh and Currie played for Chelsea, Arsenal, Manchester City and Leeds, which were all top teams of the day. Remember, it was an era where the talent was spread around; it was only from 1976 that Liverpool began to dominate.

We would never find out whether these players were good enough for the world stage, because Alf Ramsey and his successors favoured men they could trust. Ramsey preferred a system to off-the-cuff anarchy. In 1966, all of our world-class players, bar Greaves, played because Ramsey *believed* in them. Our mavericks could barely get a game because he didn't. Francis Lee felt, 'If you get four or five caps for your country, you've had a chance, and it's up to you to take it.'

Five caps does not sound much of an opportunity, but there were fewer international games in the 1970s. To persist with a player through 10 to 15 games would have kept him in the side for nearly two years – through to the finals of a tournament, when it was too late to find out that the player was not international class or that you couldn't fit him into your side.

Geoff Hurst believed: 'The flair players in the 70s weren't in the same class, and so he couldn't trust them with a free role in the way he could Bobby Charlton. Bowles or Worthington were entertainers, would try things at inappropriate moments, blow hot and cold. If a genuine genius like Greaves couldn't find a place in the team, Ramsey certainly couldn't accommodate Frank Worthington, who wasn't in that class.'

So, were the mavericks given a fair chance for the national team? Osgood, Hudson and George were certainly ill-served, but Frank Worthington played in eight successive internationals, Marsh played in seven successive internationals, and Currie played in five out of Ramsey's last six matches, only missing Ramsey's last game in charge due to injury. I would say Worthington, Currie and Marsh had a good opportunity to stake a claim for England, and even Bowles got a chance, but none of them shone. Maybe it was the result of overly defensive tactics. Or maybe, just maybe, they simply weren't as good as Netzer. But before you make up your mind, watch West Germany's 1972 win at Wembley. Notice that when Franz Beckenbauer moves forward, Netzer drops back into defence to fill the gap. Compare that with Osgood, who would run 100 yards to join in a fight, but not ten yards for a pass.

On the subject of Bobby Charlton, with the new money flowing into the game, players can now afford hair transplants The comb-overs sported by the likes of Charlton and Ralph Coates have sadly died out. Now tattoos are all the fashion. Back in 1972, they were generally only sported by members of motorcycle gangs and merchant seamen.

Much of what grates about modern football was around back in 71/72; it was just at an embryonic stage or in moderation. We had coloured boots, for a start. Alan Ball wore white and Charlie George red in the 1972 Cup Final. In the 2013 FA Cup Final, 20 players were in non-black football boots. The book begins six months after the Ibrox disaster, and I deliberately included some incidents throughout the season that made it clear that grounds were unsafe. Nearly all the factors were already in place for a Hillsborough.

The fight on the pitch between hooligans before Spurs played Chelsea in 1975 was one of many incidents throughout the 1970s and 80s. Ten years later, Chelsea chairman Ken Bates installed a 12-foot-high electric fence all around the Stamford Bridge pitch before the fixture between Chelsea and Tottenham. Only the threat of legal action from the GLC stopped it from being switched on. With hindsight the idea seems insane, but many supported the innovation at the time.

As crowds dwindled, the hooligans were emboldened, finding that they formed an ever-increasing proportion of those attending. By the end of the 70s, hooliganism had reached its adolescence; in the 80s it reached a brutal maturity.

Following the Hillsborough disaster, The Taylor Report finally brought in all-seater stadiums and hooliganism pretty much died out. At £50 a ticket, who can afford to be thrown out? The downside to the high cost of tickets is that it isn't just stopping hooligans attending matches. So it's a trade-off. You are paying a fortune to sit in an all-seater stadium with little atmosphere, but at least you are safe.

You may complain about the ludicrous wages paid to the players, but I wonder what happened to all that money when clubs pulled in crowds of 70,000 and paid their players £12 a week? It certainly wasn't spent on the facilities. The Taylor Report pointed out: 'The safety and comfort of those on the terraces has not been regarded as a priority.' Another quote from Taylor is worth repeating. 'It is a depressing and chastening fact that mine is the ninth official report covering crowd safety and control at football grounds. After eight previous reports and three editions of the Green Guide, it seems astounding that 95 people could die from overcrowding before the very eyes of those controlling the event.'

Hillsborough already had a history of injuring its customers. In 1914 a wall collapsed, injuring 75, and in 1934 a man was crushed to death inside the ground. The history at Ibrox was even worse. The tragedy of 1971 was the third time people had died there. In 1902, 25 spectators were killed when a section of the wooden terracing collapsed. In 1961, two people died and 44 were injured on a stairway exit. In 1967, 11 people were injured on the same stairway, and in 1969 another 30 were seriously injured – on the same stairway. Sadly, I'm sure you can guess on which stairway the 66 people were crushed to death in 1971.

Hillsborough was caused, in part, by football's contempt for their customers, and to quote from Rob Smyth and Georgina Turner's *Jumpers for Goalposts*: 'If clubs didn't always treat their supporters well when they were still making the bulk of their money out of them, the impact of the increasingly obscene broadcast deals has been to turn casual disregard into barely concealed contempt.'

It was sad to write of the post-retirement struggles of Tommy Lawton and how our World Cup winners had to sell their precious medals. But, for the time, the players were well paid. With the riches now on offer, surely it's impossible that the present players will struggle when they retire?

According to XPro, a charity for ex-professional footballers, two out of every five players are made bankrupt within five years of retiring from professional football. With the increased coverage of the game, there are far more opportunities for ex-players to earn money from punditry work. Gary Lineker earns around £1.8m per year, which is more than he earned as an extremely well-paid player. But for every Lineker there are the likes of Lee Hendrie, John Arne Riise, Keith Gillespie, Eric Djemba Djemba, Carl Cort and Celestine Babayaro. All earned millions from Premier League football only to end up in financial distress.

Former England goalkeeper David James' football memorabilia was auctioned off after his bankruptcy in November 2014. James was estimated to have earned more than £20m during his playing career. Admittedly, he paid his ex-wife, Tanya, £3m when they split, but that was in 2005. He played in the World Cup in 2010, so had at least another five years at the top to regroup financially. Now that clubs have improved their care of their players' physical health, maybe they will start to help them look after their financial health?

And so to the big question; is football better now? You can now go to a game without the worry that you might end up in casualty later that day. Stadiums that were tired and run-down are now clean, modern and safe, although a seat in them can only be afforded by the above-average earners. The likes of Maine Road, Highbury, The Baseball Ground, Filbert Street and Upton Park have all been consigned to history. Sadly, I used to be able to name all 92 grounds, but would now struggle to name just the Premier League ones.

Skilful players are no longer kicked out of games or permanently injured, as football is virtually a non-contact sport. The Champions League lets us regularly watch the likes of Messi and Ronaldo, but the financial rewards for success perpetuate the domination of football by a select handful. Imagine giving the winners of the Olympic 100 metres semi-finals a 10-metre start in the final? Because that is our Premier League. Despite the Sky hype, the air of the unexpected has been largely removed from the game.

In the 20 seasons from 1995/96 to 2014/15, only four different teams won the Premier League. In the same 20 seasons, only seven different teams won the FA Cup. In 1972, Derby became the seventh different team to win the title in seven seasons, and Leeds were the tenth different Cup winner in ten seasons. If anything, the FA Cup was the glamour prize in domestic football back in 1972. Forget the best team over a 42-game season; the winners of a random six-game knockout often took the lion's share of the glory. Now, most Premier League teams would swap that glory for fourth place.

Manchester United pulled out of defending the FA Cup in 2000. Roy Keane has since said: 'The Premiership and the Champions Cup were the only trophies we were concerned about.' Compare his comments to Billy Bremner's on the eve of the 1972 Final. 'I've won a Championship medal, a European medal and countless Scotland caps, but sometimes I think I'd swap the lot for an FA Cup winner's medal.'

Although the big clubs treat the FA Cup as an afterthought, they still dominate it. In the 25 finals from 1996 to 2020, only two teams other than Arsenal, Chelsea, Manchester City, Manchester United and Liverpool have won it. In that period Arsenal and Chelsea won it 15 times between them.

Today's game is faster, less brutal, has more goals and you can see foreign superstars playing in our safer grounds. Should you not wish to leave your armchair, you have access to an abundance of live football and need never miss a goal scored anywhere. What is missing from the modern game is an old-fashioned word – charm. Watching the full-time results painfully print up on the Teleprinter, or queuing to pick up the Saturday evening paper if you missed them. Watching a sea of scarves swaying on the terraces instead of portly middle-aged men in replica shirts slumped in their seats texting. Actually wondering at the start of the season who will win the silverware. Knowing a drawn FA Cup Final will give you a bonus live game to watch. Seeing the centre-forward replace an injured keeper. Wondering what your local garage will be giving away this season or whether you will ever open a packet of football cards that doesn't contain John Aston.

It's still a great game, but when you look back at a season like 1971/72, it does leave you wondering, what happened to the romance, the characters, the unexpected and the charm?

STOP PRESS

AS I was finishing the book I was delighted to see Barrow back in the Football League. After 48 years and 40 different managers, including David Johnson, Brian Kidd, Ron Yeats and Vic Halom, they are back.

Since being relegated in 1972, Barrow have spent their time in the top-two levels of non-league football, with five relegations and promotions. Along with winning the FA Trophy at both the old and new Wembley, they have survived a compulsory winding-up order, being thrown out of the Conference, and battling to win back the ownership of their ground.

To illustrate their luck, on the first occasion in the programme's history that *Match of the Day* decided to feature one of their games, the FA Cup first-round tie against Bristol Rovers, the cameras managed to catch James Cotterill's punch at Bristol Rovers' Sean Rigg. The referee missed the incident, so without the presence of the cameras it is doubtful whether Cotterill would have received his subsequent four-month sentence for assault.

They were voted out of the League in somewhat controversial circumstances, but this time around, in 2020, the situation was straightforward – they simply needed to get promoted back into the League. But Barrow never seem to do anything in a straightforward manner. With nine games to play they were top of the National League table and four points clear of second-placed Harrogate Town. Then the Covid-19 pandemic struck and the season was suspended as the country went into lockdown. In June 2020, National League clubs voted to decide final standings on an unweighted points-per-game basis. Barrow were confirmed as champions of the National League and were back.

ACKNOWLEDGEMENTS/
BIBLIOGRAPHY

Material for the book has been derived from a wide range of sources such as the archives of the *Daily Mirror* and *Daily Express*, magazines such as *The Blizzard, FourFourTwo* and *BackPass*, and Rothmans Football Yearbooks. The yearbooks have been called Sky Sports Football Yearbooks for the last 15 years.
The following books were referred to:

Anderson, C. S. D., *The Numbers Game: Why Everything You Know About Football is Wrong* (Penguin Books Ltd, 2014)

Bagchi, R., *The Unforgiven: The Story of Don Revie's Leeds United* (Aurum Press, 2002)

Baker, D., Kelly, D., *Classic Football Debates Settled Once and For All, Vol.1* (Ebury Press, 2009)

Ball, P., *Morbo: The Story of Spanish Football* (WSC Books Ltd, 2001)

Batty, C., *Kings of the King's Road: The Great Chelsea Team of the 60s and 70s* (Vision Sports Publishing Ltd, 2004)

Bellos, A., *Futebol* (Bloomsbury Publishing PLC, 2002)

Belton, B., *East End Heroes, Stateside Kings: The Amazing True Story of Three Football Players Who Changed the World* (John Blake Publishing Ltd, 2008)

Bose, M., *The Spirit of the Game: How Sport Made the Modern World* (Constable, 2012)

Bowler, D., *Winning Isn't Everything: A Biography of Sir Alf Ramsey* (Orion Books, 1999)

Brodie, J., *Sheffield Wednesday The Complete Record: Matches to Remember* (DB Publishing, 2011)

Bushby, A., *Falling for Football: The teams that shaped our obsession* (Ockley Books, 2014)

Campomar, A., *Golazo!: A History of Latin American Football* (Riverrun, 2014)

Chapman, P., *The Goalkeeper's History of Britain* (Fourth Estate, 2008)

Clarke, G., *Newcastle United: Fifty Years of Hurt* (Mainstream Publishing, 2006)

Cloake, M., *Taking Our Ball Back: English Football's Culture Wars* (Martin Cloake, 2014)

Davies, H., *The Glory Game* (Mainstream Publishing, 1972)

Dawson, J., *Back Home: England and the 1970 World Cup* (Orion Books, 2001)

Fielder, R., *The Complete History of the European Championship* (Robert Fielder, 2016)

Fisher, J., *Aston Villa Greatest Games* (Pitch Publishing, 2015)

Freddi, C., *The Complete Book of the World Cup* (Willow, 1998)

Giles, E., *Derby County: Champions of England 1971/72 & 1974/75* (Desert Island Books, 2005)

Glanville, B., *The Story of the World Cup* (Faber & Faber, 2001)

Goldblatt, D., *Futebol Nation: A Footballing History of Brazil* (Penguin, 2014)

Goldblatt, D., *The Game of Our Lives: The Meaning and Making of English Football* (Viking, 2014)

Gordon, A., *Denis Law: King and Country* (Arena Sport, 2013)

Greaves, J., *The Heart of the Game* (Sphere, 2005)

Hamilton, D., *The Footballer Who Could Fly* (Cornerstone, 2012)

Hamilton, D., *George Best, Immortal* (Windmill Books, 2014)

Harris, T., *Sport: Almost Everything You Ever Wanted to Know* (Yellow Jersey, 2007)

Hartrick, David., *50 Teams That Mattered* (Ockley Books Ltd, 2012)

Healey, Tim., *That's Right You're Fired* (Ballpoint Press, 2017)

Hermiston, Roger., *Clough and Revie: The Rivals Who Changed the Face of English Football* (Mainstream Publishing, 2011)

Hesse, U., *Tor!: The Story of German Football* (WSC Books Ltd, 2002)

Hesse, U., *Bayern* (Yellow Jersey, 2017)

Hornby, N., *Fever Pitch* (No Imprint, 1993)

Horton, S., *Liverpool FC: Ending the Seven-Year Itch: The Story of Liverpool's 1972/73 League Championship and UEFA Cup Winning Season* (Vertical Editions, 2012)

Jennings, A., *The Dirty Game: Uncovering the Scandal at FIFA* (Arrow, 2016)

Jovanovic, R., *Moving The Goalposts: A Sideways Look at What Really Matters in Football* (Pitch Publishing Ltd, 2012)

Kelly, C., *Johan Cruyff: The Total Voetballer* (JMD Media, 2012)

Kelner, M., *Sit Down and Cheer: A History of Sport on TV* (John Wisden & Co Ltd, 2012)

Lawton, J., *Forever Boys: The Days of Citizens and Heroes* (Wisden, 2015)

Lovejoy, J., *Bestie: A Portrait of a Legend* (Sidgwick & Jackson, 1998)

Ludden, J., *From The Stars: Sir Matt Busby and the Decline of Manchester United 1968–1974* (Empire Publications, 2014)

Matthews, T., *Football Oddities* (The History Press, 2005)

McCartney, I., *Manchester United: Busby's Legacy* (Amberley Publishing, 2014)

McLintock, F., *True Grit* (Headline, 2005)

Mingle, S., *When England Ruled the World: 1966–1970: Four Years Which Shaped the Modern Game* (Pitch Publishing Ltd, 2016)

Mitten, A., *The Rough Guide to Cult Football* (Rough Guides, 2010)

Moore, D., *Derby County Champions at Last: A Diary of the Rams' Triumphant 1971/72 Season* (DB Publishing, 2012)

Onuora, E., *Pitch Black: The Story of Black British Footballers* (Biteback Publishing, 2015)

Pelé, *Pelé: The Autobiography* (Simon & Shuster UK Ltd, 2006)

Plenderleith, I., *Rock 'n' Roll Soccer: The Short Life and Fast Times of the North American Soccer League* (Thomas Dunne Books, 2015)

Powell, J., *Bobby Moore: The Definitive Biography* (The Robson Press, 2014)

Reade, B., *44 Years With The Same Bird: A Liverpudlian Love Affair* (Pan Books, 2009)

Roberts, J., *Sod This, I'm off to Marbella* (Trinity Mirror Sports Media, 2010)

Rolls, Tim, *Stamford Bridge is Falling Down* (Tim Rolls, 2019)

Ronay, B., *The Manager: The absurd ascent of the most important man in football* (Hachette Digital, 2010)

Shindler, C., *Four Lions: The Lives and Times of Four Captains of England* (Head of Zeus, 2016)

Shindler, C., *The Worst of Friends: The Betrayal of Joe Mercer* (Mainstream Publishing, 2010)

Smart, A., *Best, Pelé and a Half-Time Bovril: A Nostalgic Look at the 1970s – Football's Last Great Decade* (John Blake, 2014)

Smyth, R; Turner, G., *Jumpers for Goalposts: How Football Sold Its Soul* (Elliott & Thompson, 2011)

Stark, M., *Glam Soccer!: A Story of the Colourful Years of English Football League Clubs –1976* (Dog Ear Publishing, 2014)

Stead, P., *The Red Dragons: The Story of Welsh Football* (Y Lolfa, 2012)

Sutcliffe, R., *REVIE ... Revered and Reviled* (Great Northern Books Ltd, 2010)

Szymanski, S., *Money and Football: A Soccernomics Guide* (Bold Type Books, 2015)

Taylor, M., *The Association Game: A History of British Football* (Routledge, 2007)

Tomkins, P., *Dynasty: Fifty Years of Shankly's Liverpool* (GPRF Publishing, 2008)

Tossell, D., *Big Mal: The High Life and Hard Times of Malcolm Allison, Football Legend* (Mainstream Publishing Ltd, 2008)

Tossell, D., *In Sunshine or In Shadow: A Journey Through the Life of Derek Dougan* (Pitch Publishing Ltd, 2012)

Tossell, D., *Playing for Uncle Sam: The Brits' Story of the North American Soccer League* (Mainstream Publishing Ltd, 2003)

Tossell, D., *Tommy Doc: The Controversial and Colourful Life of One of Football's Most Dominant Personalities* (Mainstream Publishing Ltd, 2013)

Walvin, J., *The People's Game: The History of Football Revisited* (Mainstream Publishing Ltd, 1994)

Ward, A., *Football Nation: Sixty Years of the Beautiful Game* (Bloomsbury Publishing PLC, 2009)

When Saturday Comes. *When Saturday Comes: The Half Decent Football Book* (Penguin, 2005)

Wilson, J., *Angels With Dirty Faces: The Footballing History of Argentina* (Orion Books, 2016)

Wilson, J., *Behind the Curtain: Football in Eastern Europe* (Orion Books, 2006)

Wilson, J., *Brian Clough: Nobody Ever Says Thank You: The Biography* (Orion Books, 2011)

Wilson, J., *Inverting the Pyramid: The History of Football Tactics* (Orion Books, 2008)

Wilson, J., *The Anatomy of England: A History in Ten Matches* (Orion Books, 2010)

Wilson, J., *The Outsider: A History of the Goalkeeper* (Orion Books, 2012)

Winner, D., *Brilliant Orange* (Bloomsbury Publishing PLC, 2000)

Yallop, D., *How They Stole the Game* (Constable, 2011)

NOTES

Introduction

1 Soccer had hoped that Stuart Hall was its only connection to the seventies' child abuse scandals but even then Chelsea's youth coach, Eddie Heath was abusing young players.

2 In 1972 there were 1.6 millon colour televisions in people's homes, around one in ten. Colour sets wouldn't outnumber black-and-white sets until 1976.

Pre-Season

1 As he would prove as a key member of QPR's tilt at the title in 1976.

2 He had returned to England to become player-coach at Coventry that summer.

3 Despite finishing fourth, Derby were banned from playing in Europe after being found guilty of 'gross administrative negligence.' Derby's crimes included paying Dave Mackay to write articles in the club programme at £20 a time.

4 He had taken over as player-manager of Second Division Swindon.

5 Bobby Robson, Joe Harvey and Bertie Mee would rack up their ten-plus years in the future.

6 As of August 2020, David Moyes is their 18th permanent manager in the 28 years of the Premier League.

August

1 For Halifax it was the first leg of a unique Manchester treble. In 1980 they knocked out Manchester City 1-0 in the third round of the FA Cup and in 2011 they did the double over FC United of Manchester in the Evo-Stik League Premier, the seventh tier of English football.

2 Leeds next visited Colchester's Layer Road in 2007 for a league game. Colchester were the favourites as they were mid-table in the second tier and faced bottom club Leeds.

3 The uncle of athlete Steve Cram.

4 Kenny Dalglish once said, 'George is part of the history and tradition of this club and it would be more relevant if he left than if I left.'

5 Keegan would play alongside Callaghan in the 1977 European Cup Final.

6 Fifteen years later it would cost QPR £400,000 to rectify their lack of foresight.

7 Birchenall and Currie would become famous for the 'kiss' at Bramall Lane in 1975. Currie recalled the incident, 'As I remember, I was tracking him back towards the Bramall Lane end and we ended up tumbling over and sat up facing the goal. He just turned to me and said: 'give us a kiss TC' and that's what happened.' When Birchenall was asked what his worst moment in football was, he said 'Kissing Tony Currie … Every year we have to re-enact the kiss and he gets uglier by the year.'

8 It was Currie who conceded the penalty from which Glenn Hoddle scored the only goal for Spurs.

9 Until 1983 gate receipts for league games were shared. The away side got 20 per cent of gate revenue.

NOTES

10 The sacrifice of the 'eight saviours of the club' is marked by a plaque outside of the stadium funded by the Bristol City Supporters Club and Trust. The Ashton Gate Eight incident led to the introduction of the Football Creditors' Act, which means players and other clubs are paid before external creditors. So now the player will get his £100,000 a week for the length of his contract, but the St John Ambulance service often get nothing.

September
1 Native Qataris make up just 15 per cent of a population of two million.
2 Rofe wouldn't sign for Leicester until August 1972 by which time the fee had risen to £112,000.
3 The Liverpool defeat at White Hart Lane would be their last in a league game in London until losing at Highbury on 1 February 1975.
4 Father of Gary and Kevin Mabbutt.
5 John McAlle would play for Wolves for another ten years but would never score another goal. He would finish his career with two seasons at Derby. While there, he scored on 27 December 1983 against Cardiff, 12 years after his last goal. He netted again 11 days later away to Cambridge in the FA Cup. Five games later he retired.
6 Father of future Liverpool keeper Pepe.

October
1 The next international played in Northern Ireland would be in March 1975 against Yugoslavia.
2 It was only in February 1972 that it was announced that Scotland, Wales and Northern Ireland, would finally be guaranteed the release of their players for international matches. This, together with the parentage rule, was a huge help to them in qualifying for major tournaments.
3 Mick Lambert's place in the history books is for being a substitute. He is the only player to appear as a substitute in both a Test match and an FA Cup final. As a member of the Middlesex ground staff, he appeared as a substitute fielder for England against Australia in June 1968 at Lords. Nearly 10 years later Lambert sealed the second half of his unique double when he came on as substitute for Ipswich Town against Arsenal in 1978. Lambert was also an outstanding tennis player and some believe he could have turned professional at that sport.
4 In September 2017, after commentating on around 2,000 games, Motty announced that he would retire at the end of the season.
5 To keep the connection with the Primrose family alive it was given to Bob as a middle name.
6 The exotically named Ryszard 'Dick' Krzywicki of Huddersfield was the son of a Polish soldier who had served near Wrexham. The wartime Polish community had already supplied Ray Mielczarek, who earned a Welsh cap in 1971, and would provide Eddie Niedzwiecki in the 1980s.
7 Holton would transfer to Gregg's old club, Manchester United, halfway through the following season where he would gain everlasting cult status and represent Scotland in the 1974 World Cup.
8 Sydney Yates, the Shrewsbury chairman, had served in the RAF during World War Two where he had been the navigator for Captain James Thaine, the pilot of the ill-fated Munich disaster aeroplane.
9 Neil Rioch was the first Englishman to touch the ball in the 1966 World Cup Final. Uwe Seeler had kicked the match off for West Germany and Wolfgang Overath misplaced a pass out to the right wing. As it went out of play, Neil was the ball boy who picked the ball up and threw it to Martin Peters.
10 Both McDermott and Mortimer would go on to win European Cup winners medals.
11 Football Preview would be renamed Football Focus in 1974.
12 Yes, it was the origin of the phrase in current parlance for a team which plays a more direct style from front to back.

13 Maybe he felt 'The Good Old Days' had ended for Wednesday.
14 OK I made that bit up.

November

1 In 1971 penalty shootouts were still in their infancy.
2 I say hat-trick, technically the keeper saved the third penalty, but Johnston knocked in the rebound.
3 They would prove themselves to be amongst the best forwards in the world during the 1974 World Cup.
4 Remarkably Müller missed three consecutive spot-kicks for Bayern earlier in the season after which the penalty duties were passed onto Franz Roth. Although lethal in the penalty box Gerd Müller still holds the Bundesliga record for missed penalties with 12.
5 October's Chapter should hopefully explain all.
6 Hartford was named after his father's favourite singer, Al Jolson, whose real name was Asa Yolson.
7 Despite his superb conversion rate for City, Lee missed both the penalties he took for the national team in 1969. He nearly hit the corner flag against Portugal and hit the crossbar against Wales. After the Wales game Ramsey said to Lee, 'Francis, I don't think that taking penalties for England is your vocation.'
8 Daines would be the hero the following November when Spurs won *The Daily Express* crown by beating Ipswich in the final on penalties.
9 The goal against Forest didn't kick-start a goal rush for Astle. He got one more goal before the end of the season to give him just two in 22 games. In his last two injury ravaged seasons for West Brom he would only manage a further six goals.
10 This might have given Alvechurch the advantage. Their manager Rhys Davies understood endurance having run the marathon for Wales at the 1956 Commonwealth Games.
11 The attendance was a record for a West Ham testimonial and wouldn't be bettered until Mark Noble's match in 2016.
12 Former West Brom player Tony Brown has Chopper beat by being awarded three testimonials: in 1974, in 1981 when the match was held at new club Torquay against Manchester United, and another back at the Hawthorns in 1999 when the Jamaican World Cup team played West Brom.
13 ITV neglected to show his winning goal in their highlights of the game. They were screening the first half while still editing the second half and managed to leave the bit of film with Fritsch's winner on the floor.

December

1 Under today's three-points-for-a-win system, Manchester United would have held a seven-point lead over Leeds United.
2 He would not play again for Liverpool before moving to Cardiff in 1974.
3 Sunderland would only get 15 minutes of football from 'Yogi' before injury brought a premature end to his career.
4 Celtic paid notoriously low wages, when David Hay went on strike in 1973 he was on a basic £65 a week.
5 The incident was later famously recreated in a football sketch in the 1990's *Fantasy Football League* programme in which Gemmell kicked comedian Frank Skinner.
6 Clark was a month older than Gemmell.
7 He would come out of retirement after three years to play 17 games for Tranmere.
8 The figure is even more impressive, given that Arsenal, Liverpool and Manchester City, were all playing away.
9 Ian Moore was generally known as Ian Storey-Moore during his career.
10 The original theme tune, used from August 1964 to August 1970 was Drum Majorette by Arnold Stock.
11 Before he moved to *Match of The Day* in 1973.
12 See October's chapter.

13 He would only grow to 5ft 9in.

14 Bowles had been signed in October.

15 Scunthorpe would slump and didn't win any of their last six games but had done enough to snatch the last promotion place.

16 The final Varsity game at Wembley took place in 1987. Since then over half the Varsity games have been played at Craven Cottage where, in 1993, Chris Hollins, son of ex-Chelsea player John and future *Strictly Come Dancing* winner, scored in Oxford's 5-0 win.

January

1 They wouldn't move their base to Headingley until 1903.

2 Or ninth if you count Danny Blanchflower's aborted appearance.

3 Steve is the younger brother of Olympic bronze medal hurdler John.

4 Carlin wouldn't be able to push Notts County over the line this season but would play a major role in their promotion to the Second the following season.

5 In a season where the historical view is that Leeds dominated the league until just falling at the last, this would be the only week that they actually headed the table.

6 Unfortunately, this would prove to be a temporary remission for Morgan. He would make a further ten appearances in the season before being forced to retire. His twin brother Ian would undergo a cartilage operation later in the month and would also retire early.

7 Unusually for a centre-half he would score in both his last two appearances.

8 A seventh member of the side, Larry Lloyd, would win two European Cup winners' medals with Nottingham Forest.

9 It is fair to say Catterick never was the same again. Coming so soon after the Ball transfer this ended Everton's glory days until the mid-eighties.

10 Had away goals counted double West Ham would have booked their Wembley place after the second game.

11 In 1978 Boston, the Northern Premier League winners, would miss out on league status because their ground wasn't up to standard. Wigan would take their place.

12 In the end Brazil didn't invite a Great Britain side as it wouldn't contain any of Sir Alf Ramsey's squad and simply invited Scotland instead.

13 At the age of 32 Harland would finally achieve his ambition of playing in the top tier but sadly only for half a season before injuries forced his retirement.

14 Phillips never broke into Birmingham's senior side but would be a prolific goalscorer for Brentford, Northampton and Southend, amongst others.

February

1 On 19 February, after much negotiation, an agreement was reached between the National Union of Miners and the Government and the miners returned to work on 28 February.

2 Generally, teams received £87.50 for regional games or £250 for nationally networked matches.

3 Eleven years and 121 days after his first.

4 It was later discovered that Griffiths had played for 70 minutes with a broken leg after a collision with Fred Potter during the first half.

5 George would later be a member of a consortium whose horse, Earth Summit, won the 1998 Grand National.

6 The subject of his son Gary's 2005 *William Hill's Sports Book of the Year*, *My Father and Other Working Class Football Heroes*.

7 He transferred to Northampton Town in November 1977 for whom he would play 68 games before retiring. He stayed in the area to become a policeman, rising to the rank of detective inspector.

8 Despite the Ibrox disaster, little had been done to make the grounds safer.

9 His luck deserted him the day of the record's release when he missed City's FA Cup semi-final clash against rivals West Bromwich Albion at Villa Park due to an ankle injury.

10 Pelé estimated that Santos banked well over $20m from their tours.

11 Betting against your own team was not uncommon among professional players at the time, generally as insurance against the loss of their win bonus.

12 As recounted in the September chapter.

13 Kay had since been transferred to Everton.

14 It was one of the first times that such evidence was used in court. Kay would be 'invited' to visit the Kray twins to explain the new procedure with taped evidence.

15 Tony Kay had to wait until August 1974 before his life ban was lifted. The FA seemed harsher on Kay than the other two, but he had led something of a roguish life since his ban.

16 The last time he played before being banned substitutes weren't allowed.

17 Equivalent to about £33 in 2021.

18 The side lost another star player, Lutz Eigendorf, to a car accident in 1983 but it was revealed in 2000 that Eigendorf had been a casualty of the Cold War rather than a motoring tragedy. The Dynamo Berlin player had defected from East Germany in 1979 to play for Kaiserslautern. Shortly after his transfer to Braunschweig in 1983, his 'accident' was arranged by the Stasi, East Germany's secret police.

19 Equivalent to roughly £72,000 at the exchange rate of the time.

March

1 See December's chapter.

2 Coincidentally in the team's third round replay last season, Huddersfield had their keeper Terry Poole stretchered off with a broken leg after a collision with Latchford.

3 City were top of the First Division, four points ahead of Leeds.

4 Corrigan would miss seven games but would return for the last game of the season; the 2-0 win over Derby.

5 Lorimer was legendary for his right-footed shot which could exceed 90mph. One penalty was recorded at 107mph.

6 It is quite likely that Forest had contacted Frank O'Farrell and informed him that he still had an opportunity to sign the player.

7 If you have one of the Bobby Moore OBE coins they are quite rare.

8 As we saw with West Ham's attempt to sign Mordechai Spiegler, signing players from abroad was near impossible for English clubs.

9 Babington's move back to Huracan in 1978 would pave the way for the transfer of the club's midfielder and star of the recent World Cup, Ossie Ardiles, to Tottenham Hotspur.

10 As Manchester City were known at the time.

11 He would leave the club for Oldham in the summer.

12 It would prove to be his only League goal in over 150 appearances for Lincoln.

13 David Herd not only quit Lincoln City, but football too. He never took another job in the game.

14 George senior had played for England against Holland in 1935.

15 When he made his England debut against Brazil at Wembley in 1963, he became the first son of a former player to be also capped by England.

16 He had originally made his debut in goal for West Brom in 1969

17 Only Grabowski would be fit in time to play England.

18 Banks the greatest goalkeeper in the world never earned more than £100 a week throughout his career.

April

1 Connaughton would replace Stepney for three games in eight days and then never play for United again.

2 Manchester City would not win a league game at Ipswich until December 1994.

3 Stoke would be cleared in the summer, much to the anger of Leeds and Liverpool who had been fined £12,500 between them for fielding weakened sides in the two previous seasons.

4 Milne was also the part-time manager of the England Youth team who would win the European Youth Championship at the end of the season.

5 Manchester United would sign him from Portsmouth in November 1974, but he was long past his best.

6 The case would be settled out of court with a payment of £1,400 to Coleman.

7 When Jimmy Greenhoff scored for Manchester United in the 1979 FA Cup semi-final, it gave him the unique feat of scoring in two semi-finals for two different teams on the same ground.

8 Knox was the first substitute to score in a football league game and on 27 December 1965 he was the first substitute to take over in goal and save a penalty.

9 Moore's propensity for playing his way out of trouble would be exploited by Łubański the following year when Poland beat England in a World Cup qualifier in Katowice.

10 Muller would score a similar goal two years later to win the World Cup.

11 Netzer would only win two more caps.

May

1 A record he held for 30 years.

2 His company once employed comedian Peter Kay, who mentions his time there in his autobiography: *The Sound of Laughter*

3 Charlie George swears he counted them all and there were only 3,900.

4 In the 48 subsequent finals we have only had five new winners; Southampton, Ipswich, Coventry, Wimbledon and Wigan. You could of course say that Crewe or Hartlepool would have had little to no chance of winning the cup, but I would counter with the fact that Wigan and Wimbledon weren't even in the league in 1972.

5 The words of *Abide with Me* were written by Henry Francis Lyte in 1847 while on his death bed.

6 Clement's family had suffered another tragedy in 1979, when his 24-year-old brother Trevor was killed with a knife by a jealous mistress. In 2006 his brother Lee was murdered but his body was not found until the killer confessed five years later.

7 The original fixture in March had been abandoned after 18 minutes due to fog.

8 For those for whom the name of the referee rings a bell, yes it is our old friend Tofik Bakhmarov the incorrectly called Russian linesman from 1966.

9 The closest Blankenburg got to international football was when selected for a star studded XI in the Six versus the Three match at Wembley in 1973 to celebrate the entry of the United Kingdom, Ireland and Denmark into the EEC. The half-full Wembley might have been an indicator of how polarising the EEC would become.

10 When on West Brom's groundbreaking tour to China in 1978 Trewick declined a visit to the Great Wall of China with the wonderful comment 'once you've seen one wall, you've seen them all'.

11 Yes, the writer of *The Boys from The Blackstuff*, among other things.

12 Law shares the record as the highest goalscorer for Scotland with Kenny Dalglish. However, it would take Dalglish 102 games to achieve the same total.

13 Player-manager Terry Neill had only turned 30 a fortnight before but had always been precocious. He captained Bangor at the age of 17 and both Arsenal and Northern Ireland at 21. He was chairman of the PFA at 24, became player-manager of Hull City at 28, player-manager of Northern Ireland at 29, managed Spurs at 33 and Arsenal at 36 before quitting the game at 41.

14 Future disciplinarian, Don Howe, led a strike in 1964 because manager Jimmy Hagan wouldn't let the players wear tracksuit trousers in the cold weather.

15 Napoli would only account for the first two of his 332 consecutive games.

16 Dabney had left the company in late 1973. Apparently, he felt uncomfortable with the drinking and drug culture pervading the company at the time. He did, however, retain enough shares to become extremely wealthy.

Post Season

1 Elected in their place were Peterborough and Cambridge United respectively.

2 Yeovil were the only other non-league team to receive a vote.

3 Which would be introduced for the 1973/74 season.

4 This would also occur during the 1973/74 season.

5 Alan Mullery's loan to Fulham had caused enormous resentment.

6 This wouldn't change until 1988 by which time live football was being shown on the television. It was driven by the need for the television companies to get more adverts in than any thought of giving the players a longer rest time or supporters more time to use the facilities.

7 A penalty shoot-out would not be seen again in the FA Cup for another 20 years.

8 Both subsequently received two-year international bans from the FA. Todd would return to the full England side in April 1974. Hudson would return to the Under-23 fold in March 1974 before winning two caps in 1975.

9 Worthington boasted in his autobiography *One Hump or Two?* that he was the first man in Britain to own a tank top.

10 Or The European Nations Cup as it was known then.

11 Before Pelé joined, Messing was the player who had got the Cosmos the most media exposure by posing naked in the December 1974 issue of *Viva* magazine.

12 Antonella Ragno-Lonzi, having won bronze in 1960 and 1964, took gold in the women's foil.

13 Uli Hoeness would have the unlucky double of playing in both the 1972 Olympic and 1974 World Cup defeats to East Germany.

14 He would become a member of the International Olympic Committee (IOC) in 1963.

15 The Brazilian Football Association.

16 Fédération Internationale de Football Association.

17 Ireland had suffered a pre-tournament blow when their star player Johnny Giles was forced out with a back injury.

18 Father of José. Felix Mourinho's other claim to fame is saving a penalty from Eusébio on the striker's debut for Benfica.

19 The Scottish FA had only been persuaded to allow Docherty to take a team when they received a guarantee of £10,000 for each match played.

20 Leivinha's nephew Lucas Leiva would later play for Liverpool.

21 Everaldo won the last of his 24 caps in April 1972 despite only appearing on the losing side once and having an outstanding 1970 World Cup. He would die in a car crash with his wife and daughter in 1974.

Postscript

1 My prediction for the top 6 for this season and every subsequent season. Unless a billionaire buys a different club of course.

2 British managers are also becoming as rare as unicorns. Back in 1971/72, Ronnie Allen, Jimmy Hagan, Vic Buckingham, Alan Ashman, Joe Mallett and Brian Birch were all coaching big sides abroad. Somewhere along the way football decided British managers couldn't manage.

3 Felix from Brazil's 1970 side looked as if he had won a newspaper competition to play in the World's greatest side.

4 Since Pelé retired no one has much interest in seeing Santos anymore.